Specialized dementia care
units

# Specialized Dementia Care Units

# The Johns Hopkins Series in Contemporary Medicine and Public Health

CONSULTING EDITORS:

Martin D. Abeloff, M.D.
Samuel H. Boyer IV, M.D.
Richard T. Johnson, M.D.
Paul R. McHugh, M.D.
Edmond A. Murphy, M.D.
Edyth H. Schoenrich, M.D., M.P.H.
Jerry L. Spivak, M.D.
Barbara H. Starfield, M.D., M.P.H.

# Specialized Dementia Care Units

*EDITED BY*
Dorothy H. Coons

*Associate Professor Emeritus*
*and Associate Research Scientist*
*The University of Michigan, Ann Arbor*

formerly

*Director, Alzheimer's Disease Project*
*on Subjective Experiences of Families*
*and Director, Alzheimer's Disease Project*
*on Environmental Interventions*

The Johns Hopkins University Press
Baltimore and London

Second printing, 1992

The Johns Hopkins University Press
701 West 40th Street
Baltimore, Maryland 21211-2190
The Johns Hopkins Press Ltd., London

The paper used in this book meets the minimum requirements
of American National Standard for Information Sciences—Permanence
of Paper for Printed Library Materials, ANSI Z39.48-1984.

**Library of Congress Cataloging-in-Publication Data**

Specialized dementia care units / edited by Dorothy H. Coons.
        p.   cm.—(The Johns Hopkins series in contemporary medicine
and public health)
    Includes index.
    ISBN 0-8018-4076-7 (alk. paper)
    1. Dementia—Patients—Long term care.   2. Dementia—Patients—
Long term care—Psychological aspects.   3. Long-term care
facilities—Administration.   I. Coons, Dorothy H.   II. Series.
    [DNLM:   1. Alzheimer's Disease.   2. Dementia.   3. Nursing Homes—
organization & administration.   4. Progressive Patient Care—
organization & administration.   WM 220 S741]
RC521.S65   1990
362.2'6—dc20
DNLM/DLC
for Library of Congress          90-4743
                                                  CIP

*To my husband George,*
*with loving memories*

# Contents

# Foreword

First described by Alois Alzheimer in 1907, Alzheimer's disease is a progressive, degenerative disease that attacks the brain and results in impaired memory, thinking, and behavior. Symptoms include a gradual loss of memory, decline in the ability to perform routine tasks, disorientation in time and space, difficulty in learning, and loss of language and communication skills. The disease gradually strips away mental and physical abilities, eventually rendering sufferers incapable of caring for themselves. The life span of a patient with Alzheimer's disease can range from three to more than twenty years after the onset of symptoms.

Alzheimer's disease is the most common form of dementing illness, affecting approximately 4 million Americans today. It is the fourth leading cause of death among adults, taking more than 100,000 lives annually. Approximately 10 percent of the population over sixty-five years of age is afflicted with the disease. The proportion rises to 47.2 percent in those over the age of eighty-five, which is one of the fastest growing segments of the U.S. population. It is estimated that, unless a cure or a means of prevention is found, 12–14 million Americans could be affected by the year 2040.

The impact of Alzheimer's disease or a related dementing disorder extends beyond the patient. The caregiver—usually a spouse or other family member—becomes the second victim of the disease. Those afflicted with dementia often require twenty-four-hour care and supervision. Families provide approximately 70–80 percent of the care required by Alzheimer patients, including assistance with mobility, personal care, and behavioral problems. In addition to the tremendous stress of providing care, families also bear most of the financial burdens of the disease. The cost to a family caring for the patient at home currently averages $18,000 a year. The cost can, and often does, bankrupt the family.

At some point in the course of the disease, the family's caregiving efforts must be supplemented by outside services, such as respite care, in-home services, and adult day care. Families are the primary providers of care during the early and middle stages of the disease, but most must eventually turn to nursing homes to provide care and supervision in the later stages. More than 50 percent of all nursing home patients are victims of Alzheimer's disease or a related disorder.

There are few resources, programs, or services available to help families cope with this tragedy. The cost of care for people with Alzheimer's disease and related disorders—including diagnosis, treatment, nursing home care, home care, and lost wages (for both patient and caregiver)—is estimated at $80–90 billion annually, and most of it is borne by families. The annual cost of nursing home care ranges between $24,000 and $36,000.

Medical research offers the hope for understanding and eventually eliminating Alzheimer's disease. During the past ten years, scientists have made significant advances in understanding the disease. Researchers are investigating several theories about the causative factors, but their efforts are complicated by indications that there may be more than one form of the disease. Suspected causes include, but are not limited to, a genetic predisposition, a slow virus or other infectious agents, environmental toxicants, and immunological changes.

While finding the cause is the principle focus of research, scientists are also seeking better diagnostic procedures, more effective treatments, and better ways to cope with the effects of the disease. As medical and allied health professionals advance sophisticated research and case management, the options for caring for the person with Alzheimer's disease have increased. Assistance provided at adult day care centers, at home, at retirement homes, and at nursing homes offers the person with Alzheimer's disease different living arrangements. Special care units in nursing homes have developed in response to a variety of factors, as Nancy Mace reports in Chapter 4 of this book: (1) the rising number of people with dementia in nursing facilities, (2) the perceived risk to a physically vulnerable resident if a resident with dementia becomes combative, (3) the market response to an increasing public awareness of and demand for specialized care, and (4) a humanitarian desire to improve the quality of life for people with dementia.

In *Specialized Dementia Care Units*, Dorothy Coons has enlisted significant authors from several disciplines. Together they present a valuable commentary on the form and function of dementia care units, focusing on the complex issues involved in their creation and operation. This well-organized guide will assist professional caregivers who are planning and/or implementing compassionate, high-quality care for persons with dementia. For families, it provides insightful suggestions for increasing the benefits of their interactive role with the facility and with their family member.

This book emphasizes the individuality of people with dementia. The authors propose changing the stereotypical image of the person with Alzheimer's disease as a "patient" whose difficult behavior must be controlled to that of a "person" whose needs as a unique human being fight for recognition and validation. An environment that can be responsive to the person's changing capabilities will allow that individual to enjoy a sense of contribution and importance by performing the daily activities of living congruent with his or her fluctuating abilities.

Through concise, clear descriptions, the authors present numerous examples of the underlying philosophy of an individualized, "wellness-fostering" environment, a milieu that emphasizes the person's existing capabilities. Dorothy Coons states, "The criteria for defining the therapeutic milieu present a philosophy of humanism that attests to the dignity and worth of human beings and the right of the individual to achieve a sense of self-realization and of being accepted and valued."

The therapeutic milieu is a living environment that is as positive and supportive as is possible for people with Alzheimer's disease. It recognizes that all elements of the immediate environment may have some effect upon the patient. The elements of the environment are here evaluated and thoughtfully planned to assure that Alzheimer patients can enjoy social and even productive roles in keeping with their changing needs. Potential benefits of dementia-specific care affect not only the resident and his or her family but also other residents of the facility, the staff, and/or the facility owners or stockholders. The authors relate research findings about the development of specialized dementia care units, as well as data about measuring the impact of this environment on the resident with dementia.

The authors prepare the reader for understanding the need for change in caring for patients with dementia, starting with Coons's examination of the roadblocks and building blocks for championing quality-of-care issues. Succeeding chapters provide detailed information about residential living models and a comparative study of special dementia units in nursing facilities, including sites in the United States, England, Canada, and Australia.

Experts review the architectural planning and design elements specific to the special care unit. Governmental issues are surveyed and analyzed for their effect on the implementation of dementia-specific units. The book emphasizes concrete examples of principles, guidelines, and assumptions to serve as the foundation for creating prosthetic environments for the fluctuating abilities of this impaired population. The text concentrates on critical personnel issues: training imperatives; the integral role of the staff in creating the therapeutic environment; the impact of staff approaches and activities on patients' behaviors.

Assessment and intervention are key components in discussing the management of the effects of Alzheimer's disease. The final chapter explores at length the physician's role within the interdisciplinary team and his or her key position in diagnosis and multidimensional assessment.

For the family, this book provides insight into the harmony and partnership that can be created between staff and family members when each person's role is defined and shaped by the needs of the patient. Adversarial barriers can be lowered when there is a balanced understanding of the effects of adaptive approaches in assisting the person with Alzheimer's disease, be it the use of humor or reminiscence to create a sense of joy, belonging, and being social.

*Specialized Dementia Care Units* offers the health care professional and the family member alike concrete guidelines for maximizing the effectiveness of the special care environment for the person with Alzheimer's disease. This book offers supportive evidence and information regarding the advances, benefits, and challenges in fostering an individualized plan of care.

EDWARD F. TRUSCHKE
President, Alzheimer's Association

# Contributors

URIEL COHEN, D.Arch., Associate Professor, Department of Architecture, School of Architecture and Urban Planning, University of Wisconsin–Milwaukee

KRISTEN DAY, B.Arch., Program in Architecture, School of Architecture and Urban Planning, University of Wisconsin–Milwaukee

JOSEPH J. GALLO, M.D., Director, Division of Long-term Care, Levindale Hebrew Geriatric Center and Hospital, Baltimore, Md.

LILA GREEN, Humor Educator; Faculty Leader, National Seminar Program, American College of Health Care Administrators; Member, National Speakers Association; Visiting Professor, University of Michigan

NANCY L. MACE, M.A., Consultant, Office of Technology Assessment, U.S. Congress; Coordinator, Sir James McCuster Training Programs, Perth, Australia; formerly Assistant in Psychiatry, Johns Hopkins University School of Medicine

KATIE MASLOW, M.S.W., Project Director and Senior Analyst, Office of Technology Assessment, U.S. Congress

KEYA RAY, M.Arch., School of Architecture and Urban Planning, University of Wisconsin–Milwaukee

WILLIAM REICHEL, M.D., Director, Department of Geriatrics and Aging Services, Boston Evening Medical Center; Clinical Professor of Community Health, Division of Family Medicine, Tufts University School of Medicine; Adjunct Professor of Family Medicine, Brown University

ANNE ROBINSON, M.A., Director, Dementia Project, Eastern Michigan University, Ypsilanti, Mich.

BETH SPENCER, M.A., M.S.W., Geriatric Social Worker; Lecturer in Gerontology and Social Work, Eastern Michigan University; Co-director, Caregiver Connections: Help for Families of Older Adults, Ann Arbor, Mich.

SHELLY E. WEAVERDYCK, Ph.D., Lecturer, Department of Pschology, The University of Michigan; Consultant in Geriatrics and Cognition; Cognitive Intervention Specialist, Glacier Hills Nursing Center, Ann Arbor, Mich.

GERALD D. WEISMAN, M.Arch., Ph.D., Associate Professor, Department of Architecture, School of Architecture and Urban Planning, University of Wisconsin—Milwaukee

Dorothy H. Coons, Anne Robinson, Beth Spencer, and Shelly E. Weaverdyck were members of the staff of the Institute of Gerontology, the University of Michigan, at the time of the Wesley Hall project. They were responsible for the planning and implementation of that project.

# Preface and Acknowledgments

The health care system for the past decade has been facing the formidable challenge of how to care for persons in varying stages of Alzheimer's disease. A major movement in response to the challenge has been the development of special dementia units. This book examines the many components that must be considered in the establishment of this new and largely untested model of care.

The book reflects the complexities involved in the creation of dementia care units. The authors, therefore, come from diverse backgrounds and fields. They were selected because each, in his or her own way, has had extensive experience and possesses important knowledge relative to the treatment of cognitively impaired persons or the development of units especially designed for their care.

To provide readers with the most recent information available, the authors have freely called upon knowledgeable people to share their expertise and experience. As a result, many persons have been helpful in the preparation of this book. I especially want to thank the residents, the staff, and the family members who participated in the project described in Chapter 3. A number of people shared with me the experiences they have had with relatives or with impaired persons they have known or with whom they have worked. Their stories appear throughout the book. For some of these warm and touching vignettes I wish to thank Dana Berry-Richardson, R.N., Betty Harrison, Betty and Robert Little, and Terry Whyte, Administrator, and Tannis Booth, Secretary, Department of Programming, from Fir Park Village, Port Alberni, British Columbia.

The staff members of a number of facilities that have established dementia care units shared their experiences and findings with us in lengthy questionnaires and related materials. Nancy L. Mace and I wish to thank the following people for the information they provided:

Bonnie Barthman, Coordinator of Special Unit, and B. L. Donaldson, Administrator, Methodist Manor, Storm Lake, Iowa

Marsha Bowsher, Coordinator of Special Unit, and Kathy Boling, Administrator, Green Hills Center, West Liberty, Ohio

Kathleen Bullock, Program Coordinator, Special Care Unit, and Chris Bowman, Administrator, Eastern State Hospital, Williamsburg, Virginia

Barbara Calamita, Coordinator of Special Unit, Dolly Bheemaswarroop, Director of Health Services, and Steven Raichilson, Administrator, Menorah Park Center for the Aging, Beachwood, Ohio

Susan Gilster, Executive Director, The Alois Alzheimer Center, Cincinnati, Ohio

Ann James, Head Nurse, Special Care Demonstration Project, Baycrest Center for Geriatric Care, Toronto, Ontario

Lorna K. Miner, Coordinator of Special Unit, and Gretchen Cluff, Administrator, Americana Healthcare Center, Davenport, Iowa

Helen Morning Star, Coordinator of Special Unit, and David Douma, Administrator, Porter Hills Presbyterian Village, Grand Rapids, Michigan

Gail Nugent, Social Worker, and John E. Kern, Administrator, Algona Good Samaritan Center, Algona, Iowa

Evelyn O'Connor, Coordinator of Special Unit, and Connie Amick, Assistant Aministrator, Chelsea Methodist Retirement Home, Chelsea, Michigan

Carol Pratt, Alzheimer's Unit Nurse Manager, Gloria B. Raphael, Director of Social Work Services, Dorothy Varholak, Vice-President in Charge of Nursing, and Irving Kronenberg, Administrator, Hebrew Home and Hospital, Hartford, Connecticut

Beverly Simkins, Coordinator of Special Unit, and Irene McCulla, Administrator, Iowa Masonic Nursing Home, Bettendorf, Iowa

Carolyn Sorensen, Nurse Administrator, Morningside Manor, San Antonio, Texas

Deannie Strickland, Coordinator of Special Unit, and Jacob O. Strickland, Administrator, Shady Oaks Nursing Center, Monroe, Louisiana

Jan Tapprich, Coordinator of Special Unit, and Todd Jacobsen, Administrator, Davenport Good Samaritan Center, Davenport, Iowa

Peggy Tribble, Director, Alzheimer's Program, and Elaine Burge, Administrator, Wesley Woods Center–Budd Terrace, Atlanta, Georgia

Bengt Winblad, Professor and Chief Physician, Department of Geriatric Medicine, Huddinge University Hospital, Huddinge, Sweden

Mary Zolly, Coordinator of Special Unit, and Michael Weinfield, Executive Vice-President, Hebrew Home of Greater Washington, Rockville, Maryland

We are grateful to all of them for their willingness to give us the information we needed so that we could compare their methods, problems, and outcomes. We wish to thank both Geri Hall, Gerontology Clinical Nursing Specialist, Department of Nursing, The University of Iowa, and Christopher Johnson, Executive Director, Institute of Gerontology and Alzheimer's Resource Center, Northeast Louisiana University, for their support and assistance.

I am especially grateful to Fran A. Gruda for her careful preparation of the manuscript, and to Lena Metzelaar for her work in the compilation of the index. I wish to thank Wilma Donahue and Beth Spencer for their interest, ideas, and willingness to read and react to various chapters. I extend my special thanks to Wendy Harris, acquisitions editor, Carol Zimmerman, production editor, Mary Yates, copy editor, and to others at the Johns Hopkins University Press for their support and guidance throughout the preparation of this book.

# Introduction

# A Concept in Search of Standards

DOROTHY H. COONS

Probably few developments in the health care arena have moved with the speed and unstructured abandon of the proliferation of new Alzheimer's or dementia care units around the country. Alzheimer's disease was essentially unknown to the general public even as recently as the early 1980s, but it is now a term with which many people are familiar. It has become a household word, and any evidence of forgetfulness may trigger the fear of being a victim of the disease.

Alzheimer's disease is usually considered a disease of old age, affecting people in their 70s and 80s, but it may occur as early as age 40. Loss of memory and failure of judgment are early symptoms. Personality and mood changes may also be present, but the beginnings are insidious and difficult to diagnose. Irreversible brain changes occur, and the illness progresses through various phases of deterioration. The phases vary in length, and people may live for several to ten or more years. They may become increasingly difficult to communicate with and, in the later stages, unable to recognize family members or caregivers (Rao 1986). Because the disease is irreversible, a major focus in designing programs of care for Alzheimer's victims is on quality of life and giving them the supports they need to function as well as possible.

Families have reported that in the mid-1980s, when the term was beginning to surface, their relatives who had the diagnosis of Alzheimer's disease were unpopular candidates for nursing homes because of their potential behavioral problems. With the prediction that the numbers of persons with Alzheimer's disease or related dementias would increase to epidemic proportions in the very near future has come the development of a new type of treatment unit—the special dementia care unit.

1

The term *special dementia care unit* would seem to imply that it is distinctly different and that it is designed to meet the needs that are uniquely characteristic of the persons it is to serve. Unfortunately, the units have taken many forms, some of which fall far short of providing the special care and the milieu that will enable people with dementia to function maximally, to get satisfaction from life, and to live with dignity. In many cases the units can make no claims to being special except that they are segregating persons who are bothersome to other residents and staff. Some facilities merely relabel units that have been segregated in the past. If health care specialists accept the belief that persons with dementia differ greatly in their needs and capacities from persons who are intact but physically impaired, then the facilities designed for dementia should be appropriately different with reference to goals, staff approaches, and the activities that are made available for resident involvement.

Admittedly there is need for much more research to determine the impact of the various components of the environment on the well-being and quality of life of persons with dementia. But much is known currently about the characteristics of a therapeutic milieu and their effects upon elderly people. The special adaptations needed to respond to victims of dementia have been well demonstrated in some of the dementia care units already established.

This book has been written for professionals who are involved in the treatment of persons with dementia and for state and federal personnel responsible for the development of regulations that influence the care of dementia victims. It provides comprehensive guidelines for the planning and implementation of dementia care units, including the need for physician involvement, design issues, the training of the staff, the creation of an engaging and supportive milieu, and the process by which change can occur even with the inevitable roadblocks. Parts of the book will be of use to family members and other direct caregivers, and for the teaching of physicians, nurses, and architects preparing to work with or respond to the needs of elderly persons with dementia.

Difficult behaviors have become a major focus in describing the effects of dementia. This has predominated to the extent that the victim may no longer be viewed as a person with needs and emotions to which staff members can respond. This book acknowledges that the disease can lessen the impaired person's ability to maintain control and can cause some of the difficult behaviors. It also presents the point of view that many factors in the environment itself can cause stress and consequently increase the frequency and the intensity of the behaviors. Throughout the book, the authors have consistently emphasized a philosophy of care that enhances individuality.

Some questionable practices have emerged as a standard part of long-term care in the name of safety and protection against falls. Throughout the book there are references to the overuse of physical restraints and excessive medication and the harm they can cause. These dehumanizing practices, which strip the elderly person of all sense of freedom and dignity, have become so much a part of our system of care that in many situations alternatives are not considered and the practices are difficult to change.

Some of the unique characteristics of persons with dementia would indicate directions for designing appropriate treatment environments. Many in the early and middle stages of the disease are physically active and not in need of extensive medical care. Alzheimer's victims are frequently lucid and at least occasionally aware that they are losing the capacity to function even though they may have difficulty expressing their worries and fears. Persons with dementia will frequently respond to humor and lightheartedness. Even though they may no longer be able to learn new tasks and information, in the early and middle stages they may be able to continue to do tasks that were a part of their everyday life when they were well. They may not remember the names or relationships of relatives, but they are often responsive to them and benefit from their presence. All of these characteristics need to be considered in designing dementia care units.

The literature is rampant with ambiguities about what is the appropriate and therapeutic milieu for victims of dementia. Chapter 1 of this book attempts to define the characteristics of a wellness-fostering environment. It cites some of the differences in the theories about environmental design for dementia as delineated by experts in the field. In many instances the theories, when operationalized, are remarkably similar. Chapter 1 also contrasts the immediate and long-range goals and treatment techniques for dementia units as opposed to those designed for mentally ill elderly persons. Chapter 13, on interventions, discusses some of the problems that arise when treatment modalities designed for persons with other types of illnesses are applied to those with dementia.

Because many in the early or middle stages of the disease are not in need of medical care, a psychosocial model of treatment would logically be more appropriate than a medical model. This shift in focus, techniques, and methodology requires that many changes be made in the traditional care setting. But innovation and change will not occur without a degree of risk. The strategies for bringing about change need to be carefully analyzed and implemented, and the roadblocks examined and dealt with if possible. Over time, the innovations themselves will have to be evaluated and amended as needed. This process is discussed in Chapter 2.

Chapter 3 describes the characteristics and needs of a specific group of elderly persons selected for a special dementia unit and the changes made in the unit design and operation to accommodate those needs. The unit was established in a retirement home and therefore was not bound by many of the restrictions applied to nursing homes.

Chapter 4 describes the characteristics of some of the dementia care units established in nursing facilities. The author discusses many of the differences that exist among the units surveyed and identifies ways in which state and federal policies have affected their development.

Architectural design, like all factors shaping dementia care units, has been the target of much experimentation and conflict. The authors of Chapter 5 present criteria for designing units that will help create a physical environment that is warm, manageable, and homelike. Prototypes are suggested for freestanding units and for the remodeling of the traditional nursing home to reduce the institutional and medical image.

There are barriers to innovation, and to the development of creative treatment programs, that support mediocrity. State and federal regulations are frequently cited by administrators as reasons for maintaining the status quo. In many instances the regulations prevent the worst abuses but do nothing to ensure good care. Chapter 6 presents a thorough examination of state and federal policies and their impact on the treatment of elderly persons with dementia. The authors present a strong case against the development of federal guidelines for the implementation of special dementia units, arguing that such an action is premature and may, in fact, inhibit innovation.

The direct service staff play a major role in creating the milieu in dementia care units. Because persons with dementia are often sensitive to what is occurring around them, it becomes exceedingly important that staff members be aware of any problems they may be creating and learn to adapt accordingly. Much of what is suggested in this book regarding staff involvement and interaction with residents requires training that focuses on communication skills and the development of an understanding of the dementia victim. Chapter 7 gives a detailed description of training topics and teaching methodology that have been designed for the staff who will be working in special dementia units. Because the work is often stressful and demanding, the staff need strong administrative support and understanding. Chapter 8 presents methods by which the supervisory staff can help the direct service staff avoid burnout and acquire the skills they need to solve problems.

The ambience of a dementia care unit is contingent upon many things, but especially upon the relationships between residents and staff members and upon the opportunities the residents have to be involved in stimulating, appropriate, and pleasurable activities. Families too play a major role in helping a relative maintain ties and continuity with the past and feelings of being valued and loved. Chapter 9 discusses the importance of activities that are familiar and manageable and suggests a variety of staff approaches that can ease tension and help reduce the frequency of difficult behaviors. Chapter 10 emphasizes the value of humor and lighthearted activities and illustrates in vignettes the capacities of cognitively impaired persons to respond to, and even initiate, humor. The importance of viewing family members as partners in the care of their relative is discussed in Chapter 11. The author also suggests a number of training sessions that can be offered to families to help them feel more comfortable in the unit and become better able to respond to a relative's needs.

Chapter 12 focuses specifically on methods of assessment that can help the staff recognize both the capacities and the problems the resident may be having. Chapter 13 demonstrates how careful assessment can lead to more appropriate and effective intervention.

A major problem in the development of dementia care units has been the absence of physicians who are trained to work with people with dementia and who gain satisfaction in treating the elderly. Chapter 14 discusses the role of the physician in dementia care units and presents detailed information on diagnosis, medications, and the role of the physician on the treatment team.

The book emphasizes throughout the uniqueness of people with dementia and the possibility that they may be the most reactive of all elderly persons in need of treatment to the failures in our system of care. The authors have attempted to erase the stereotypical image of the person with Alzheimer's disease as being a "patient" whose "problem behaviors" must be managed and controlled. Instead, each person is presented in many true vignettes as an individual with feelings and sensitivity.[1] The book stresses the need for the creation of an environment that is fluctuating and responsive to changing capacities—an environment that will help even the very impaired maintain a sense of person and continue to function as well as he or she is able.

Large sums of money are now being invested throughout the

country to support research on the cause and treatment of Alzheimer's disease. Until these answers are found, our health care system will be faced with the need to provide care for huge numbers of persons who are now, or will become, victims of dementia. The authors of this book hope that the information offered here will provide present and future guidelines to health specialists who are responsible for the care of those with Alzheimer's disease or other irreversible dementias.

The capacities, behaviors, and needs of people with dementia vary tremendously among those in various stages of the illness. An environment appropriate for those in the early stages would be too demanding and would lack the supports and care needed by persons in the latter stages. A challenge for the future will be the study and determination of changes that need to be made in the physical environment, in staff approaches, and in the opportunities for involvement as people become more impaired and less able to manage. The establishment of a series of graded units designed for specific groups that are fairly homogeneous as to capacities and needs would offer a refinement in our system of care that is now largely lacking. The diagnosis of Alzheimer's disease alone is not sufficient as a basis for admitting people to, or for the designing of, dementia care units.

## Note

1. The names of residents that appear in vignettes throughout this book have been changed.

## Reference

Rao, D. G. 1986. Dementia. In *A better life: Helping family members, volunteers, and staff improve the quality of life of nursing home residents suffering from Alzheimer's disease and related disorders*, edited by D. H. Coons, L. Metzelaar, A. Robinson, and B. Spencer, 159–172. Columbus, Ohio: Source for Nursing Home Literature.

# Chapter 1

# The Therapeutic Milieu: Concepts and Criteria

DOROTHY H. COONS

It is estimated that 1.5 million persons in the United States suffer from severe and irreversible dementia, and this number is expected to increase by 60 percent by the turn of the century (U.S. Congress, Office of Technology Assessment 1987). The cause of Alzheimer's disease and its possible prevention or cure confound researchers at present, and it is estimated that it will be well into the next century before answers will be found. With this increase of dementia to epidemic proportions, Americans will be faced with the challenge of providing humane and therapeutic care for the millions of victims whose families will no longer be able to care for them at home.

The provision of dementia care has been in a period of transition. One study, completed in 1983 (Chenoweth and Spencer 1986; Coons et al. 1983), found that many Alzheimer's victims were refused admission to nursing homes on the basis of diagnosis alone. Many facilities apparently considered them to present management problems and burdens beyond the staff's ability to cope with. Since the completion of that study, however, health care providers have become well aware of the need to provide care for this group of elderly persons. The result has been the development of a new designation of care—the dementia care unit.

The term *dementia care unit* is used here to identify a living area that is largely self-contained and self-sufficient in terms of services, staffing, and congregate space. Meals are served in the area or unit, and activities are offered there. In the context of this book, the "units" house and are designed for a specific group of people with Alzheimer's disease or related dementias who are segregated from those with differing needs and capacities. In some instances units will be parts of extended complexes such as nursing or retirement homes; or they may be freestanding and operating apart from any larger facility.

In recent years the number of dementia care units in this country has increased rapidly. One survey by Sloan and Mathew (1988) found that Ohio, California, and New York State alone had a total of 107 such units, with many more in the planning stages. While the numbers vary greatly from state to state, partly because of state regulations, there is an obvious movement toward the establishment of such units.

Health care providers have disagreed strongly over the issue of whether the cognitively impaired should be integrated with more competent persons or segregated in areas specially designated for their care. Lawton (1981) pointed to the need for impaired persons to have available the role models of mentally alert residents who are engaging in social interactions and other activities. He reported, however, that in a consumer's survey staff members and relatives of dementia residents strongly favored their separation from more intact persons. Nursing personnel were especially concerned about the anxiety and frustration felt by nonimpaired residents when they were forced to be in frequent contact with confused persons.

Those favoring segregation argue that the needs of cognitively impaired persons differ greatly from the needs of those who are mentally alert and that a single environment cannot be designed to accommodate persons with a wide range of needs and capacities. An environment appropriate for intact persons will be too demanding and will lack the protection essential for those with dementia, while the milieu specially designed for impaired persons will be too confining and limiting for alert residents.

Pynoos and Stacey (1986), in examining policy issues related to specialized facilities, warned against the establishment of special units that may develop the stigma of the back wards of mental hospitals and create problems of accountability, isolation, and low staff morale. They characterized the therapeutic and prosthetic environment as one that fosters improvement where possible and compensates for individual deficits. It maintains the resident at the highest level of functioning, offers appropriate environmental and social stimulation, creates a personal milieu that encourages autonomy and promotes individuality, and provides a reasonable balance between privacy and safety. These represent characteristics of a number of units that have been established by persons seeking to improve the quality of life for dementia victims.

Those creating dementia care units are faced with many difficulties. They are attempting to design therapeutic environments for a group of persons who differ greatly from the physically impaired elderly in nursing homes. Little research has been done to determine the impact of environmental factors on persons with dementia. Under the best of conditions, it is difficult to bring about change in institutional settings. Efforts to introduce a totally new model of care can seem to present insurmountable problems.

In a critique of existing special Alzheimer's units, Ohta and Ohta (1988) illustrated the wide diversity in concepts and methods used in designing such units in this country. By categorizing them according to philosophy, environmental design, and therapeutic approach, the authors described three types of units. *Type 1* offers only custodial care. Changes in the physical environment may be limited to the addition of locks on exit doors to prevent wandering from the unit. The staff members focus on attending to the physical needs of residents, and other activities are almost nonexistent. As a means of controlling behaviors both physical restraints and psychotropic drugs are used routinely. The staff see the beneficiaries of such a unit to be the patients and the staff in other parts of the facility who no longer have to cope with the behaviors of the impaired persons. *Type 2* emphasizes the need to help residents function as independently as possible. Treatment is individualized, and activities offer opportunities for persons to use their physical, social, and cognitive abilities to the extent possible. The physical environment is also individualized by furnishing residents' rooms with their own furniture and mementos. A variety of interventions are tested to keep the use of physical restraints and drugs to a minimum. *Type 3*, like type 2, uses individualized care plans, and offers a variety of activities to help each individual remain involved and functioning at the highest level. This type of unit places strong emphasis upon quality of life and affirmation of the individual's right to personal dignity, privacy, self-esteem, and affection. Physical restraints are seldom, if ever, used, and drugs are prescribed only occasionally and are carefully monitored. These units, usually small and staffed with well-trained and consistent personnel, have what Ohta and Ohta called "an elusive quality" that sets them apart even from type 2 facilities. The beneficiaries of both types 2 and 3 are the impaired residents, the staff, and family members.

This chapter discusses the concepts and practices that have affected the design of some of the special units that have already been established and will identify the criteria defining a therapeutic milieu. Chapter 3 will describe the process by which the therapeutic concepts were applied in the designing of a residential living unit for persons in the middle stages of Alzheimer's disease or related dementias.

## Issues in Designing Dementia Care Units

Only a few dementia care units can be cited here to illustrate the
efforts that have been made in the United States and other countries
to design therapeutic settings for persons with dementia. Many units
have been able to bring about positive changes in residents' behaviors,
awareness, and quality of life. A few units throughout the world
have produced dramatic changes. The various units illustrate a
number of differences and similarities in concepts and practices.
There seem to be fairly consistent references, however, to the belief
that the environment becomes increasingly important as individual
competence decreases, and that it is essential that the physical, social,
and psychological environment compensate for or counteract deficits.
It is of primary importance that the facility adapt to the behaviors
and changing capacities of residents at this crucial period when they
are becoming increasingly impaired and are ill equipped to adjust to
a hostile or unaccepting environment (Pynoos and Stacey 1986;
Lawton 1981).

Many issues must be considered in the establishment of dementia
care units. The variations in policies and practices in units already
functioning in the United States and other countries reflect the
difficulties involved, the differences in philosophy, and the impact
of cost factors and state (or provincial) and federal regulations (see
Chap. 6).

### Size

The potential benefits of units that house a small number of
impaired persons (from 6 to 15 persons) are discussed in Chapter 3.
Renovation costs and the difficulties of implementing structural
changes in traditional nursing homes, however, sometimes prohibit
the establishment of small, homelike settings. Some large units with
well-trained, accepting, and caring staff members have demonstrated
that it is possible to create a calm and involving environment even
with populations of 40 or more persons (Sorenson 1988). From
financial and staffing perspectives, some nursing homes have chosen
to establish units housing 25 to 30 persons, believing that they can
be staffed more effectively and efficiently than small units (Orr
1987). Those who have the opportunity to build new facilities have
the advantage of being able to establish small, manageable units and
to test out innovative designs (Boling 1988).

## Physical Design and Furnishings

Issues related to architectural design, colors, and furnishings in special units are some of the most controversial and varied in application. Much more research is needed to determine the characteristics of the environment that are essential in providing individuality, security, safety, and an appropriate level of stimulation.

In treatment settings, congregate areas, such as dayrooms, dining rooms, and activities areas, have traditionally been large and open to accommodate many residents. The establishment of small rooms, however, each distinctive in design, color, and furniture, can be much more inviting, far less overwhelming and stressful, and easier to identify (Calkins 1988).

The dearth of private sleeping rooms in many long-term care facilities reflects cost and regulatory factors, and the fact that some states limit the number of private rooms because of third-party payment regulations. Serious consideration needs to be given to the building of units that provide private sleeping rooms for persons with dementia to accommodate their need for privacy and to enable families to create a familiar environment by furnishing their relatives' rooms with personal furniture and memorabilia. Some people claim, however, that a person with Alzheimer's disease is more content with a roommate and that the two can be a stabilizing influence on each other (Greene et al. 1985). Koncelik (1976), however, believed that in double-occupancy rooms one resident may have a negative impact on the health status of the other. He stated that "aside from the marginal chance that two patient-residents will be compatible, the combination of patient-residents in two-bed rooms must be regarded as generally detrimental to rehabilitation, general physiological and mental health, and, of course, the concept of residency."

Colors are very much a matter of personal preference, and they affect people in different ways. Older people perceive colors differently because of changes in the lens of the eye, and they have difficulty differentiating colors of the same intensity (Hiatt 1981). These are complex issues that need to be considered in dementia care units. Primary colors used tastefully may enable persons with visual impairment to differentiate areas or items. Lawton (1981) recommended a richness and diversity of color, decor, and graphics. To the extent possible, residents should have opportunities to make decisions about colors to be used in their personal space (Calkins 1988).

Noxious noise, such as intercoms, buzzers, and loud telephone bells, can be disturbing and stressful for anyone, and especially for persons with dementia. The question to be considered is whether a particular sound is pleasant or appropriately stimulating or whether it causes agitation. One study of 99 dementia care units in 34 states reported that more than half of the units used acoustic or sound-absorbent ceilings to reduce noise. A lesser number applied sound-absorbent wall surfaces, and about one-third used carpeting on floors (Kwon and White 1988). Some special units play soft, familiar background music as a soothing agent (Greene et al. 1985) and use selected television programs of interest to residents to stimulate and trigger discussions (Boling 1988).

Units that follow the model of the lowered stress threshold reduce noise and stimulation by eliminating ringing telephones, public address systems, television, and radios (Hall and Buckwalter 1987; Hall et al. 1985). This model is based on the fact that as Alzheimer's victims become more impaired they are less able to receive and process stimuli. It is a principle of the model that agitated behaviors can be a sign of an inappropriate level of activities and stimuli, and that the level should be modified accordingly to reduce stress.

### The Use of Drugs and Physical Restraints

The literature reporting on the care of the cognitively impaired has consistently recommended that the use of pharmacologic interventions and physical restraints, including geri-chairs, be limited, and that if they are applied they be monitored closely and eliminated as soon as possible. Alternatives should be considered and tested in efforts to avoid the use of restraints (Teno and Silliman 1988). Robbins and colleagues (1987) recommended as alternatives more frequent monitoring by the staff, transfer to a private room if a person is potentially harmful to others, and therapies that foster human dignity. Several unit coordinators have reported that they have never used physical restraints or have gradually eliminated their use completely (O'Connor 1988; Morning Star 1988; Nugent 1988; Tribble 1988).

Beers and colleagues (1988) reported on the dangers of using high levels of sedative/hypnotic and antipsychotic drugs and warned against the use of drugs with strong anticholinergic properties that can cause confusion, constipation, urinary retention, and worsening of dementia (see Chap. 14).

### Avoiding Staff Burnout

The problem of staff burnout can be a constant worry to coordinators of dementia care units. Some facilities have developed a policy of staff rotation (Boling 1988; Cleary et al. 1988; Hall et al. 1985). This requires that all staff members receive training to prepare them to work in the unit. There are inherent problems in both the policies of staff rotation and of maintaining a permanent shift assignment. Permanent assignments may lead to feelings of unequal workloads, but frequent rotation makes it almost impossible to carry out consistent programing activities and individualized care plans. Staff members also are usually unable to develop close relationships with residents and co-workers when they spend only short periods of time in units (Edelson and Lyons 1985; Mace and Gwyther 1989). The additional problem with the practice of staff rotation is its implication that some residents, especially the cognitively impaired, are difficult to care for and that no staff member can cope with the work situation for more than short periods of time.

In a number of dementia care units, aides are responsible for the various activities that occur daily in addition to resident care (Boling 1988; Cluff 1988; Nugent 1988; Raphael 1988). This practice places additional demands on aides' time, but it can also create a far more interesting job that enables them to use their various talents and acquire new skills.

It is generally recognized that dementia care staff members need strong support and positive reinforcement from the administrative staff, that ongoing training is essential, and that there needs to be time set aside for the staff to discuss their frustrations and get help with problem solving. All of these interventions can help reduce the possibilities of staff burnout (see Chap. 8).

### The Philosophy of Care

Even though the interpretation of and strategies for designing and implementing dementia care units differ markedly, a number of principles seem to be accepted as essential to therapeutic programs. It is generally recognized that there is a need to match the environment to individual competencies and to ensure that the demands of the setting are not beyond the resident's capacities to function. This requires an individualized approach and training that teaches the staff how to identify and build upon the resident's strengths. The importance of staff selection is reflected in the frequency with which it is mentioned that staff members need to be caring, affectionate, and accepting. The goal is to help them create a milieu that is supportive and safe, yet warm, enjoyable, and stimulating.

Some units maintain consistent schedules of activities to provide stability; others favor flexible schedules that will respond to the changing moods and needs of residents. Either system can be compatible with the belief that residents should have freedom to move about and to make choices about how, when, and where they will be involved. Some health specialists emphasize that the therapeutic milieu should offer positive environmental stimulation, while others stress the importance of reducing stimuli. Even with these differences in emphasis, there is agreement about the need to provide activities that enable residents to function maximally, to enjoy life, and to continue to be aware of and involved with their surroundings.

Despite differences in methods of implementation, the criteria listed below describe in essence the characteristics of many of the units that have succeeded in developing environments that have had a positive impact on the care of persons with dementia.

## The Therapeutic Milieu

The criteria defining the therapeutic milieu present a philosophy of humanism that attests to the dignity and worth of human beings and the right of the individual to self-realization and a sense of being accepted and valued. The application of this philosophy to the care of persons with dementia is particularly challenging. While the treatment modality recognizes the devastation wrought by the disease and the inevitable deterioration and diminishing of capacities over time, it provides a milieu that helps the person achieve, to the extent possible, feelings of being a significant and respected part of the world in which he or she lives (Coons and Reichel 1988).

The concepts presented here have been tested and refined for several decades by the staff of the Institute of Gerontology of the University of Michigan in a variety of housing and treatment settings for the elderly (Donahue et al. 1960; Gottesman et al. 1966; Coons and Spencer 1983; Coons 1989). Their most recent application was in the experimental project for persons with dementia described in Chapter 3. Adaptations and modifications were made in each project to accommodate the specific population for which the milieu was being designed. There has emerged from these research and demonstration projects, and from the works of others, a basic philosophy and set of criteria critical to the establishment of a therapeutic milieu that will enable elderly people, even the severely impaired, to live with dignity (Burnside 1976; Boling et al. 1983; Lawton 1980). Following are the criteria that define the therapeutic milieu:

1. The environment has the potential for being the most thera-

peutic when it is designed for a population that is homogeneous as to needs and degrees of impairment.

2. The organization of the environment encourages maximal autonomy and freedom.

3. The therapeutic environment offers sensory and social stimulation.

4. The therapeutic environment encourages and recognizes individuality.

5. The therapeutic environment provides a program of activities that enables residents to maintain continuity with the past and to continue in normal social roles appropriate to adults.

6. The therapeutic environment fosters human dignity.

### The Homogeneity of the Population

The selection of a homogeneous population is crucial in the designing of dementia care units. The diagnosis of Alzheimer's disease or of other irreversible dementias is not sufficiently discrete as a basis for grouping. Those in the early and middle stages of dementia have capacities and needs far different from those in the latter stages, and the environmental factors of the unit must respond to those differences.

Some health specialists recommend that if a facility is attempting to serve a large number of persons with dementia, several small, self-contained graded units be established to care for persons with varying degrees of impairment. The graded units can be designed so that floor plans, colors and furnishings, and the styles and methods of the staff are similar throughout. The types of activities, certain features of the physical environment, and staff approaches, however, will require modification to respond to the changing needs of residents. As they become more impaired, residents can be moved to the graded unit that is most appropriate for them. This design may provide a means of avoiding the trauma that many elderly persons experience when they are transferred from one facility to another when they require more care.

### Autonomy and Freedom

Enabling residents to maintain maximal control over their own lives, a major goal in the therapeutic milieu, is not easy to achieve in congregate settings. Strict rules and rigid routines become the mode in many facilities to the extent that few options remain open to residents. Freedom, as defined here, includes the right of residents to choose whether they will participate in activities, where they will spend time, and, to the extent possible, when they will bathe, take a nap, or get up in the morning. The capacities of severely cognitively impaired elderly persons to make choices may be limited, but staff members can help residents maintain at least some control by reducing the range of choices. A resident, for example, may be overwhelmed if she is asked to choose what dress she would like to wear for the day from a closet full of clothes. If a staff member holds two dresses before her, however, she may be able to select one.

Total loss of control over one's life can be devastating to any elderly person living in an institutional setting and can cause agitation and aggressive behaviors (Cohen-Mansfield and Billing 1986). These behaviors, in turn, can lead to the use of physical restraints, one of the most drastic methods of depriving persons of their freedom. Health specialists now recognize that the use of restraints may result in severe emotional and physical problems and even strangulation (Young et al. 1988; Di Maio et al. 1986). Electronic equipment is being developed and tested that will provide protection and yet allow for freedom of movement (Widder 1985). One device, for example, sends signals to the staff when a person is attempting to get out of bed. Close and prompt staff surveillance is required if the device is to be effective.

Equally dangerous and manipulative is the excessive use of psychotropic drugs (see Chap. 14). Prescribed as a means of controlling behavior, they essentially strip individuals of all personality, all capacity to function, and all ability to maintain control over any part of their lives (U.S. Congress, Office of Technology Assessment 1987).

### A Stimulating Sensory and Social Environment

The physical environment in some facilities follows the design of the acute care setting. The institutionalized monotony of colors and furnishings and the long double-loaded corridors lack stimulation and create a maze that is both disorienting and impersonal. In contrast, the stimulating sensory environment provides visual cues to assist with orientation, colors that are easily visible and interesting, and art and other accessories that are appealing and serve as foci for conversations and interactions.

In settings that are understaffed or in which the staff are poorly trained, social interactions may be at a minimum. Emphasis is upon getting routine tasks completed on schedule, often with little or no exchange of words between the staff and the residents, and activities are often trivial and monotonous, with little change from day to day and with little happening that is exciting and involving.

The richness of a milieu is illustrated in the abundance of opportunities offered from which residents may choose, the extent of needed sensory stimulation, and the quality of social interactions. Stimulation, as defined here, is not synonymous with stress. Both over- and understimulation can cause stress. When properly selected and controlled, stimulation can help persons continue to be involved with and alert to their surroundings.

### Maintaining Individuality

In efforts to devise regulations that will ensure safe and financially feasible care, our system has essentially erased the possibilities for impaired persons to maintain a degree of individuality. As mentioned earlier, regulations and cost factors often restrict the number of private rooms available in nursing homes. This, as well as the limitations on the amount of personal furniture and possessions residents may bring with them, makes it impossible to provide rooms that express the individuality and special past interests of the residents. The presence of personal possessions not only helps residents maintain identity, but also helps the staff develop a sense of each person as an individual with a unique history.

The Centre for Policy on Ageing (1980) of the Nuffield Lodge of London made these somewhat whimsical recommendations for care homes in their Home Advice Broadsheets: "As much as possible of the resident's former environment should be brought with her. This includes the physical environment—at least some familiar furniture, photographs, ornaments and pictures and if possible a favourite chair. . . . Do not be deterred by protests from domestics about dusting. Dusting cherished possessions is in itself excellent mental and physical therapy, and, in any case, no-one ever died of household dust."

In a study in Denmark (Andersen 1987) on the differences between excellent and ordinary nursing homes, it was found that staff members in the excellent homes knew more about residents' interests and about their capacities before coming to the home than did staff members in ordinary homes. Knowing each person as an individual caused the staff to assess residents as being less dependent than did the staff in ordinary homes when rating residents with similar degrees of impairment. At the same time this knowledge enabled the staff to help residents maintain a sense of continuity with the past.

The activities and opportunities for involvement at times lack individualization and may become routinized and generalized under the label of therapy. There has developed a situation in which normal activities of everyday life are acceptable only when they are labeled as therapies (Kane 1987). Pet therapy is acceptable; having one's own pet is not. Reminiscence therapy is considered supportive; fragmented conversations about one's earlier life may be construed as dwelling on the past.

The policy of some facilities is one of dispossession; the resident, on admission, may be expected to remove street clothes and change into the "uniform" furnished by the institution (Boling et al. 1983). Such practices are humiliating and essentially deny the resident opportunities to maintain a sense of personal being. Being well-groomed according to one's own standards and wearing personal clothes, hair style, and makeup are essential in maintaining individuality. These practices can increase self-esteem and help persons maintain a sense of identity.

### Activities That Provide Continuity with the Past

When opportunities for involvement are limited to the basic routines of receiving medications, bathing, dressing, eating, and sleeping, residents face long hours of inactivity with few diversions. They are forced to abandon the cherished lifestyles and interests that gave meaning to their lives. Many of the difficult behaviors attributed to persons with Alzheimer's disease may be a result of boredom. For example, the restless wandering that occurs may represent one of the few activities that mentally impaired persons can initiate, and it may subside when meaningful and interesting opportunities for involvement are introduced by the staff (Mace 1990).

Much has been written about the reversal of roles of the adult caregiver and the impaired older person. Admittedly, the adult assumes responsibility for the care and protection of the elderly. The description of the person with dementia as childlike and infantile, however, creates an attitude that leads to many of the indignities that occur in dementia units, and the use of such inappropriate activities as children's coloring books or paper dolls. It is often assumed that persons with dementia are no longer aware of or sensitive to their surroundings and that they have lost all capacity to function. Neither of these assumptions is true for many persons, even those who are severely impaired, and if activities or practices seem childish they should be avoided.

Spouses who are caring for a wife or husband with dementia may also find themselves assuming many of the responsibilities originally managed by the impaired person. Roles too may change. The husband as caretaker may find himself in the role of homemaker, and the wife who is caring for her husband may become the money manager for the first time in their married life (Mace and Rabins 1981). It becomes a challenge to determine what tasks or parts of tasks impaired persons may continue to be involved in to help them maintain as long as possible a sense of role continuity.

The therapeutic milieu enables residents to participate in activities that parallel those of everyday life. Most noninstitutionalized people are involved each day in dressing, eating, and sleeping, but they also perform routine household tasks, socialize, and pursue special interests or work. In a nurturing milieu, residents have opportunities to share in tasks that are familiar and satisfying and that can help them maintain a continuity with the past, feelings of normalcy, and a sense of achievement. The assumption in such a program is that residents, even the severely impaired, are still able to manage certain tasks or parts of tasks (Mace 1987; Zgola 1987). To ensure success, staff members need to be skilled in evaluating residents' remaining capacities and in selecting tasks at which they can succeed. The availability of opportunities for residents to continue in normal social roles and familiar activities minimizes the role of "patient," with its focus on sickness, and emphasizes the wellness in each individual.

### Fostering Human Dignity

In a discussion of the need to preserve the dignity of elderly persons, Verwoerdt (1976) noted that dignity, like its counterpart, shame, is possible only when one is seen or heard by another. Dignity is lost not in private but in public. Verwoerdt maintained that to protect the dignity of an older person, the individual must have access to privacy and space to call his or her own.

The procedures, routines, and environmental factors in many treatment settings have insidious ways of destroying the personal dignity of residents. For example, multiple-occupancy rooms often offer no provision for the privacy that is essential to maintaining a sense of dignity and worth. The use of divider curtains between beds is an effort to provide at least visual privacy, but this is a meager gesture toward helping each individual maintain feelings of having his or her own space and territory.

The staff can easily fall into the habit of discussing residents in their hearing as if they were inanimate objects or totally unaware of what is happening. At times staff members may refuse to listen to the problems or concerns of residents, especially if they are no longer able to communicate clearly. This gives the message to residents that they are unworthy of the staff's time.

There are even more blatant practices that are ego destroying and devastating. In some facilities caring for the severely impaired and incontinent, residents sit in dayrooms nude from the waist down for ease of mopping (Mace 1985), and toilets are without doors to simplify staff surveillance. Residents who are overweight or difficult to manage are lifted into the tub totally nude, sometimes by members of the opposite sex. Staff members need to be taught alternatives that will help the individual retain self-respect and a sense of dignity (Edelson and Lyons 1985).

An assumption in the therapeutic milieu is that each individual, regardless of the degree of impairment, has a right to live with dignity. At times only the behavior of cognitively impaired persons can give an indication of when they are embarrassed or ashamed. To foster human dignity, staff members need to be sensitive to the potential feelings of residents and to recognize when situations may be alien to their standards of decency and privacy. It is important that the staff working with all elderly persons have an understanding of and empathy with them and a belief that each individual is worthy of respect.

## The Application of the Concepts of the Therapeutic Milieu to Persons with Dementia

As mentioned earlier, any treatment modality needs to be carefully analyzed and applied appropriately to the population for which it is being utilized. In the context of the rehabilitation of the *mentally ill*, as applied in earlier Institute of Gerontology projects, the therapeutic milieu was designed to offer security but a the same time create the expectation that the residents would respond and function at their levels of ability at the moment. Rehabilitation occurred as demands were systematically increased until residents reached their maximal levels of performance. These expectations and demands were expressed through the creation of a physical environment, a social environment, and a program of daily activities that attempted to prepare the mental patient to return to the community. Through a structured series of meaningful expectations, the mentally ill person was helped to regain a sense of personal worth and to learn to cope, to the extent possible, with the realities and expectations of the out-of-hospital world (Gottesman et al. 1966).

In the therapeutic milieu for persons with Alzheimer's disease, the structure, the interventions, and the ultimate goals differ greatly from those in a program of rehabilitation. The therapeutic milieu for dementia victims is designed to help individuals continue to function maximally, to remain aware of and enjoy their surroundings, possibly to retard deterioration, and to live with dignity. The interventions provide a program of opportunities in a relaxed and accepting style that does not create, and may actually reduce, stress. The structure follows a pattern of reducing expectations for involvement and functioning as the person becomes more impaired. Adjustments must be made in staff approaches, in the physical environment, and in the program of activities to accommodate the gradual but inevitable decrease in abilities. The changes are made in ways that will give the necessary support and still enable the individual to maintain personal identity and a sense of dignity.

The static environment is stifling for the staff, and devastating and sickness fostering for the impaired elderly. The therapeutic milieu is a living environment that, by using humane and ego-supporting methods, grows in its capacity to respond to the constantly changing needs of residents.

## References

Andersen, B. R. 1987. What makes excellent nursing homes different from ordinary nursing homes? *Danish Medical Bulletin, Journal of the Health Sciences*, Special Supplement Series, no. 5, 7–11.

Beers, M., J. Avorn, S. B. Soumerai, D. E. Everitt, D. S. Sherman, and S. Salem. 1988. Psychoactive medication use in intermediate-care facility residents. *Journal of the American Medical Association*, 260(20):3016–3020.

Boling, K. 1988. Response to questionnaire. Green Hills Center, West Liberty, Ohio.

Boling, T. E., D. M. Vrooman, and K. M. Sommers. 1983. *Nursing home management: A humanistic approach*. Springfield, Ill.: Charles C. Thomas.

Burnside, I. M. 1976. One-to-one relationship therapy with the aged. In *Nursing and the aged*, edited by I. M. Burnside. New York: McGraw-Hill.

Calkins, M. P. 1988. *Design for dementia: Planning environments for the elderly and the confused*. Owings Mills, Md.: National Health Publishing.

Centre for Policy on Ageing. 1980. *Mental health and illness in old people's homes*. London: Nuffield Lodge.

Chenoweth, B., and B. Spencer. 1986. Dementia: The experience of family caregivers. *Gerontologist*, 26(3):267–272.

Cleary, T. A., C. Clamon, M. Price, and G. Shullaw. 1988. A reduced stimulation unit: Effects on patients with Alzheimer's disease and related disorders. *Gerontologist*, 28(4):511–514.

Cluff, G. 1988. Response to questionnaire. Americana Healthcare Center, Davenport, Iowa.

Cohen-Mansfield, J., and N. Billing. 1986. Agitated behaviors in the elderly. *Journal of the American Geriatrics Society*, 34(10):711–721.

Coons, D. H. 1989. The therapeutic milieu: Social-psychological aspects of treatment. In *Clinical aspects of aging*, 3rd ed., edited by W. Reichel, 154–162. Baltimore: Williams and Wilkins.

Coons, D. H., B. Chenoweth, C. Hollenshead, and B. Spencer. 1983. *Final report of the project on Alzheimer's disease: Subjective experiences of families.* Ann Arbor: Institute of Gerontology, University of Michigan.

Coons, D. H., and W. Reichel. 1988. Improving the quality of life in nursing homes. *American Family Physician*, 37(2):241–248.

Coons, D. H., and B. Spencer. 1983. The older person's response to therapy, the in-hospital therapeutic community. *Psychiatric Quarterly*, 55(2/3):156–172.

Di Maio, V. J. M., S. E. Daas, and R. C. Bux. 1986. Letter to the editor. *Journal of the American Medical Association*, 255(7):905.

Donahue, W., W. W. Hunter, D. H. Coons, and H. Maurice. 1960. Rehabilitation of geriatric patients in county hospitals. *Geriatrics*, 15(4):263–274.

Edelson, J. S., and W. H. Lyons. 1985. *Institutional care of the mentally impaired elderly.* New York: Van Nostrand Reinhold.

Gottesman, L. E., D. H. Coons, and W. Donahue. 1966. *Milieu therapy and the long-term geriatric patient.* Ann Arbor: Institute of Gerontology, University of Michigan.

Greene, J. A., J. Asp, and N. Crane. 1985. Specialized management of the Alzheimer's disease patient: Does it make a difference? *Journal of the Tennessee Medical Association*, Sept., 559–563.

Hall, G. R., and K. C. Buckwalter. 1987. Progressively lowered stress threshold: A conceptual model for care of adults with Alzheimer's disease. *Archives of Psychiatric Nursing*, 1(6):399–406.

Hall, G. R., M. V. Kirschling, and S. Todd. 1985. *Sheltered freedom: The creation of an Alzheimer's unit in an intermediate care facility.* Iowa City: University of Iowa Hospitals and Clinics.

Hiatt, L. G. 1981. The color and use of color in environments for older people. *Nursing Homes*, May/June, 18–22.

Kane, R. A. 1987. Quality of life in long-term institutions: Is a regulatory strategy feasible? *Danish Medical Bulletin, Journal of the Health Sciences*, Special Supplement Series, no. 5, 73–81.

Koncelik, J. A. 1976. *Designing the open nursing home.* Stroudsburg, Pa.: Dowden, Hutchinson, and Ross.

Kwon, O. J., and B. J. White. 1988. Physical aspects of specialized units for Alzheimer's patients in long-term care facilities. Refereed paper for American Association of Housing Educators, Oct.

Lawton, M. P. 1980. Psychological and environmental approaches to the care of senile dementia patients. In *Psychopathology in the aged*, edited by J. O. Cole and J. E. Barrett, 265–278. New York: Raven Press.

Lawton, M. P. 1981. Sensory deprivation and the effect of the environment on management of the patient with senile dementia. In *Clinical aspects of Alzheimer's disease and senile dementia*, edited by N. E. Miller and J. D. Cohen, 227–249. New York: Raven Press.

Mace, N. L. 1985. Testimony at hearing before the Select Committee on Aging, House of Representatives, Ninety-ninth Congress, Washington, D.C.

Mace, N. L. 1987. Principles of activities for persons with dementia. *Physical and Occupational Therapy in Geriatrics*, 5(3):13–27.

Mace, N. L. 1990. The management of problem behaviors. In *Dementia care: Patient, family, and community*, edited by N. L. Mace. Baltimore: Johns Hopkins University Press.

Mace, N. L., and L. P. Gwyther. 1989. *Selecting a nursing home with a dedicated dementia care unit.* Chicago: Alzheimer's Disease and Related Disorders Association.

Mace, N. L., and P. V. Rabins. 1981. *The thirty-six-hour day.* Baltimore: Johns Hopkins University Press.

Morning Star, H. 1988. Response to questionnaire. Porter Hills Presbyterian Village, Grand Rapids, Mich.

Nugent, G. 1988. Response to questionnaire. Algona Good Samaritan Center, Algona, Iowa.

O'Connor, E. W. 1988. Response to questionnaire. Chelsea United Methodist Retirement Home, Chelsea, Mich.

Ohta, R. J., and B. M. Ohta. 1988. Special units for Alzheimer's disease patients: A critical look. *Gerontologist*, 28(6):803–808.

Orr, N. 1987. Interview. *American Journal of Alzheimer's Care and Research*, Jan./Feb., 23–28.

Pynoos, J., and C. A. Stacey. 1986. Specialized facilities for senile dementia patients. In *The dementias: Policy and management*, edited by M. L. M. Gilhooly, S. H. Zarit, and J. E. Birren, 111–130. Englewood Cliffs, N.J.: Prentice-Hall.

Raphael, G. B. 1988. Response to questionnaire. Hebrew Home and Hospital, Hartford, Conn.

Robbins, L. J., E. Boyko, J. Lane, D. Cooper, and D. W. Jahnigen. 1987. Binding the elderly: A prospective study of the use of mechanical restraints in an acute care hospital. *Journal of the American Geriatrics Society*, 35(4):290–296.

Sloan, P., and L. J. Mathew. 1988. Personal correspondence. Department of Family Practice, School of Medicine, University of North Carolina, Chapel Hill.

Sorenson, C. 1988. Response to questionnaire. Morningside Manor, San Antonio, Tex.

Teno, J., and R. A. Silliman. 1988. Management of disruptive behavior in cognitively impaired patients. *Clinical Report on Aging from the American Geriatrics Society*, 2(6):16–17.

Tribble, P. 1988. Response to questionnaire. Wesley Homes Budd Terrace, Atlanta, Ga.

U.S. Congress, Office of Technology Assessment. 1987. *Losing a million minds: Confronting the tragedy of Alzheimer's disease and other dementias.* OTA-BA-323. Washington, D.C.: U.S. Government Printing Office.

Verwoerdt, A. 1976. *Clinical geropsychiatry.* Baltimore: Williams and Wilkins.

Widder, B. 1985. A new device to decrease falls. *Geriatric Nursing*, Sept./Oct., 287–288.

Young, S. H., J. Muir-Nash, and M. Ninos. 1988. Managing nocturnal wandering behavior. *Journal of Gerontological Nursing*, 14(5):7–12.

Zgola, J. M. 1987. *Doing things.* Baltimore: Johns Hopkins University Press.

# Chapter 2

# Improving the Quality of Care: The Process of Change

DOROTHY H. COONS

Chapter 1 described a number of changes that health specialists, administrators, or coordinators of dementia care units have been able to accomplish in their efforts to improve the care of persons with dementia. Opinions that there is need for change in long-term care have been pervasive for some time in this country. The growth of the population of the cognitively impaired only adds to the complexities of a system already limited in its potential for change by financial and regulatory measures that discourage innovation and risk taking.

Bringing about change is a slow and intricate process, and at times the roadblocks may seem insurmountable. One of the major problems that nursing homes face is the prevailing pattern of state and federal regulations that have been modeled after those for the acute care setting. The regulations frequently ignore the fact that the goal in nursing homes is not cure, and that the restrictive and inflexible character of the acute care setting that the regulations foster is not appropriate for long-term care facilities (Boling et al. 1983; Brody 1977). Regulations also often fail to recognize that, for the physically and cognitively impaired elderly person, social and emotional deprivation can be as incapacitating as the actual impairments.

A major target of the criticism of the nursing home system has been the poor quality of life offered to the elderly needing care. Developing criteria to define and measure quality of life, however, is exceedingly difficult (Kane and Kane 1982). There are no easy ways to monitor the extent to which residents have autonomy over their own lives, whether they have opportunities to maintain their own lifestyles, and whether they have warm and supportive relationships with the staff.

This chapter presents the point of view that change can occur even with the regulatory and financial restrictions that currently exist in our system of care (Calkins 1988; Koncelik 1976). The extent to which change is possible will vary with the creative and innovative abilities of the change agent, the person or team attempting to bring about change, and with the degree of autonomy with which the agent is invested. The speed and ease with which change will occur depend upon the organizational climate of a facility. Staff members are cautious and slow to change if the system has demanded complete obedience and has been quick to reprimand, slow to praise, and reluctant to accept innovations.

Change may consist of upgrading the skills of aides at the direct service level or improving the quality of activities in an existing facility, or it may be as difficult and complex as establishing a specialized dementia care unit. And even in specialized units, the extent of change that is possible in efforts to meet the special needs of persons with dementia may vary greatly depending upon where they are established. Freestanding units may have more flexibility in design and programing than those in institutional settings. Those based in retirement homes are usually governed by far fewer restrictions than those that are a part of nursing homes.

Policymakers or administrators of long-term care facilities may recognize that there is need for improvement in the care of the elderly, but at the same time they may assume that new methods or new models of care are impossible to implement. If change is needed, it is important that it be viewed as possible and feasible (Edelson and Lyons 1985). This chapter suggests methods for effecting change even with the inevitable roadblocks.

## The Roadblocks to Change

The organizational structure in many long-term care settings tends to discourage individual initiative on the part of the staff. In the hierarchical system, plans, rules, and regulations originate at the top and are handed down through a vertical network of staff levels until they reach the staff members at the bottom, who are expected to obey the rules without discussion. In this system, anyone can easily avoid responsibility because the staff person who is a notch higher on the hierarchical ladder has made the decision. Direct service staff may have ideas that could improve the proposed plan, but they have no opportunities for sharing them with the administrative staff. Rules, written and sometimes word-of-mouth, establish routines over the years that develop a firm hold on staff and make change extremely difficult. Almost as effective as rules in influencing staff behavior are the assumptions made by the staff. They understand that their area is to be neat, clean, and quiet. However, it probably will not be neat, clean and quiet—at least for a while—if a new coordinator decides that residents should have the opportunity to be actively involved in taking care of their surroundings and staff members are to increase the amount of time spent in helping them use their remaining skills. The system dictates certain behaviors for staff members and residents, and the staff realize that it is dangerous to run counter to it. Although many regulations are designed to protect the resident and to ensure efficiency of operation, they may be so restrictive that individual choice or decision making by either residents or staff becomes impossible. Staff may question a regulation but feel powerless to change it.

The pessimism of many administrators, nurses, and aides and their stereotypical view of the impaired older person as someone who is totally incapable and even infantile make it difficult to introduce programs that encourage as much self-care as possible. Specialized training is needed not only to change staff attitudes but also to teach them the skills and techniques they will need to identify remaining capacities and help the older person continue to function.

The low pay scale of many facilities and the inadequacy of staff training programs reinforce staff's feelings that they are in low-status jobs that offer no hope of growth and change. If staff feel inadequate in their work situation or are unsure of themselves as persons, they may interpret any suggestions for change as criticism and an implication that they are doing a poor job.

In facilities giving good custodial care, staff members spend much of their time taking care of residents' bodily needs. The work is usually strenuous and difficult. Staff lift and turn residents; they continually toilet, bathe, and change incontinent residents; they feed those who cannot feed themselves or who refuse to eat without help. Their job is exhausting, but there seem to be no alternatives. To suggest changes would seem to imply that the staff, already overworked, are not doing enough. Added to this dilemma is the fact that in facilities that are understaffed, the provision of residents' basic needs becomes a daily challenge, and staff members have no time to help residents care for themselves.

Much has been written about the difficulty of bringing about change in long-term care facilities, yet many seem to be in a state of more or less constant transition. Administrators and department heads come and go; new policies are implemented and discarded;

new systems of operation are put into practice. Frequently, however, the changes are only organizational in nature, with little emphasis on the philosophy of care or the upgrading of skills. As a result they have little or no impact on the work situation of the direct service staff or the lives of the residents in their care.

## The Role of the Change Agent

Many kinds of health specialists have taken the role of the coordinator or change agent in the development of creative treatment programs in long-term care. Doctors, psychologists, social workers, public health specialists, nurses, and activity therapists have all been represented. In some settings that encourage innovation, aides have been able to introduce new programs at the direct service level with the endorsement and support of, but with little help from, the administrative staff. This wide representation indicates that a common denominator must be the leadership capacity of the change agent rather than the specific academic training the staff person received as a health specialist.

The role of the change agent is difficult and, at least in the beginning, likely to be unpopular; but as a program develops and the residents benefit and the staff gain new knowledge and skills, it becomes an enormously rewarding position. A number of characteristics seem essential for an effective coordinator who is responsible for developing new methods and new programs.

*Studies have suggested that good leaders are not those who are authoritarian and controlling;* they are those who practice good human relations and are skilled at giving support and facilitating interaction (Likert 1975). They are open to others' ideas and get satisfaction from the success of others. The two go hand in hand. The authoritarian person counteracts any questioning of his or her actions or decisions with a reprimand of insubordination. The effective leader welcomes others' points of view and takes prides in the staff members' abilities to analyze and discuss issues.

*Effective change agents must be committed to the need for change.* Few persons will be able to influence others if they are not personally convinced that there are better methods of treatment. The obstacles to change that they will inevitably face will make their efforts short-lived if they are not strongly convinced that the change is needed and possible.

*To have influence, a leader must be willing to take risks.* As mentioned earlier, the role of change agent is an unpopular one, and the changes that must be implemented often lack clear sanctions from the facility or precedents upon which to base judgment. The leader must assume full responsibility for the risks he or she takes. The staff person who shifts the blame onto others when something fails will suffer a swift evaporation of support.

*A change agent must share essential knowledge with others.* To consider aides in long-term care settings, for example, incapable of learning more than basic skills is an attitude that causes everyone to lose. The satisfaction of the leader comes from sharing and teaching rather than from being the sole possessor of knowledge.

While encouraging others to plan and reach decisions, *the leader cannot shirk the responsibility to maintain standards and establish clear expectations for good performance on the job.* The ambiguities of the leader's position when he or she fosters staff development and participation in decision making can easily limit the leader's role to that of enabler— that is, a person who lets staff members grow. This is not enough. The leader needs to make it clear that continued development is expected and then help staff members achieve it.

*In any long-term care setting the effective change agent or coordinator demonstrates to the staff that he or she considers it rewarding to work with older persons.* The leader must be willing to teach the staff new techniques by working directly with residents, and demonstrate by the way he or she personally treats them that they are deserving of respect, consideration, and friendship. Paperwork and administrative duties are often cited as reasons why coordinating staff members are unable to work with residents. Others point to their job descriptions, which may make no reference to duties that directly involve elderly residents. Coordinators striving to be effective change agents but mired in paperwork need to reassess their time and possibly shift some of the paperwork to other staff members. True leadership will not occur from a remote office that shields the coordinator from problems that both the staff and the residents may be having.

*The leader frequently needs to be able to help a staff member recognize success.* The staff who are working with withdrawn or very confused persons may not see the gain they have made when one resident speaks his name or smiles for the first time in months, or when another manages a very simple task such as pouring her milk or picking up her own food tray.

*The effective leader encourages the direct service staff to use their skills and creativity beyond those identified in their job descriptions.* Testing new approaches or new activities can add interest to an otherwise routine and boring job, and at the same time enrich the lives of residents. Staff members need to understand quickly, however, that they are not jeopardized if their ideas are unsuccessful and their plans fail. The failure itself can become a learning process.

*An effective change agent can create a climate of experimentation and growth that is infectious and exciting.* In this climate, the prevailing assumption is that there are always better and more creative methods, and the staff are encouraged to use their own resources to initiate change.

## The Development of Effective Treatment Teams

In describing the importance of treatment teams in the care of the elderly, Baldwin and Williamson Tsukuda (1984) expressed the point of view that no single discipline can meet the diverse and complex needs of the chronically ill elderly. They saw teamwork as a special form of interactional interdependence among health care providers that can help improve the physical, mental, and social functioning of older patients by sharing knowledge and skills. They viewed effective teams as potential change agents who, by their mere existence, "call into question many of the established procedures and relationships of their parent institutions."

The development of effective treatment teams is usually a slow and intricate process proceeding from the determination of goals, to the differentiation of tasks needed to reach objectives, and then to making decisions about who will do which tasks to reach the goals. These procedures require a collaborative approach that is often alien to the systems in which health care professionals have worked (Miller 1988), and time, training, and role models are needed to prepare persons to be effective team members.

Baldwin and Williamson Tsukuda (1984) enumerated the qualities of effective team members as including "the ability to listen, to trust, to be open, and to communicate clearly and effectively, as well as a willingness to give feedback, to live with uncertainty and ambiguity, to take personal and professional risks, and to share power and expertise." Many of these skills and abilities can be acquired through training and the learning process that is a natural part of team growth.

The creation of an effective treatment team involves a revision in the way decisions are usually made. Decisions about the treatment of residents are made at the level where the treatment occurs. In this structure, the team composition of dementia care units might include the coordinating staff of health specialists—the doctor, the unit coordinator, the social worker, the nurse, the activity therapist—

and the direct service staff who become active members of the team. The inclusion of the direct service staff is essential. Their membership on the team will enable them to report upon the changing needs and behaviors of residents, to get assistance with problem solving, and to receive the support that is imperative if they are to function effectively. The structure is not an end in itself but a tool that places the direct service staff in the role of therapists responsible for sharing their knowledge about residents and implementing treatment decisions. At the same time the structure helps coordinating staff members recognize the value of the knowledge and skills that direct service staff possess. This system encourages the staff at all levels to use their experiences and to search for novel and creative solutions to problems (Perrow 1986).

Communication in this system is multidirectional. Ideas and plans are shared both downward and upward among the various levels of the staff and horizontally among the administrative staff and among aides, housekeeping, and dietary staff. Problems are shared in efforts to get help with solutions; and staff members are encouraged to report on successes so that they may receive recognition and others may learn from them (Boling et al. 1983).

Contrary to some interpretations of the shared decision-making structure as exemplified in the team approach, coordinating staff do have authority, and they carry out the responsibilities outlined in their job descriptions. However, the way they carry out those responsibilities and conduct their relationships with the direct service staff differ from the customs in the vertical structure. In the strong and cohesive team, each staff person is valued as an individual and for the special assets he or she brings to the job.

The idea of shared decision making may be threatening to some staff members in supervisory positions. Their positions have vested them with authority. If they interpret this authority as being absolute, they may not be able even to listen to another staff member's opinion. If their satisfaction on the job comes from controlling others, they will find this structure intolerable. They may consider any disagreement as an indication of disrespect, and they may visualize the shared structure as a situation in which everyone is out of control.

Some direct service staff are equally uncomfortable as team members. The fact that they are expected to think through ideas and share in reaching a group decision for which they too must take responsibility is threatening in its own way; many prefer to be told what to do. For the direct service staff to share in decision making, they must be sure that they will not become the scapegoats if there are repercussions from other parts of the facility. They will not feel safe in this new role until coordinating staff have demonstrated their willingness to assume full responsibility for whatever actions are taken.

Membership in a treatment team places expectations on everyone to be a participating, contributing member. Each member grows while testing new techniques and developing better communication skills. Through frequent feedback, standards are maintained and problems are brought into the open so that solutions can be reached. One of the most rewarding benefits is the constant development of the staff. As all staff members become more self-assured, they are able to evaluate current methods objectively and accept change to improve treatment as a normal process of a therapeutic program.

## Special Considerations in Attempting to Bring about Change

Persons attempting to function in the role of change agent need to consider a number of issues. As mentioned earlier, the direct service staff need to be involved in the development of plans for change. Staff members are often willing to undertake much more difficult and demanding responsibilities if they have helped formulate the plans. They are usually in the best position to anticipate problems and suggest solutions.

The staff need time, especially at the beginning, to think over new ideas, consider the problems and possible solutions, and simply to get accustomed to a different approach. The growth and experience of staff members may affect the speed and willingness with which they agree to new ideas. They may reject an idea presented the first, second, or third time it is discussed, then accept it with enthusiasm the fourth time.

It is important that everyone who is to be involved in the development of a plan have a clear understanding of it and of the steps needed to implement it. Even those who are the initiators are not always sure of the decisions reached. Often an oral summary of the plan at the end of a meeting, or a memo afterward describing in detail the steps agreed upon and who is responsible for what phase, helps all the participants clarify their thinking and gives staff members the opportunity to correct any errors in interpretation.

Staff persons need to focus on the development of one phase of planned change at a time. If too many changes are attempted simultaneously, efforts become so diluted that nothing happens, or the efforts in one area may interfere or compete with those in others.

If staff members are to implement new plans, they must have time free from their regular duties to implement them. Occasionally staff members realistically feel they cannot undertake new assignments and still do their regular work. This problem can be solved only if the staff are willing to examine how they spend their time and are willing to share some of their routine tasks with each other until the new program is put into effect.

All staff persons need opportunities to report on the results of their efforts. If a new plan is implemented, it is important that all persons involved have an occasion to tell about their successes. If someone has had problems, he or she should be able to get suggestions and help from others on the staff. This opportunity for feedback establishes that each person is expected to carry out his or her part of the plan, that others value the job he or she is doing, and that the staff recognize and value successes but are on hand to help with problems. If the staff have no opportunity for feedback, they can interpret the silence as a lack of interest on the part of others, and they can easily avoid any further involvement in the plan because it is obviously of little importance.

## The Circular Process of Change

The therapeutic milieu thrives on a circular process of change. Constant evaluation followed by the introduction of innovations as needed and by steps to correct and amend problem areas helps the milieu remain dynamic and vibrant (adapted from Lippitt 1962). The steps in this process include the following:

1. Gaining a clear understanding of the concepts shaping a therapeutic program and recognizing a need for change

2. Developing a plan of action that will clearly designate those staff members to be involved, their specific responsibilities, and a time schedule for the completion of tasks

3. Examining potential roadblocks and taking steps to gain the cooperation of resisting persons or to eliminate or dilute difficult situations

4. Implementing the plan with the expectation that many parts will need to be tested and possibly revised

5. After an adequate testing period, evaluating the total plan, its effectiveness and its weaknesses

6. Stabilizing the phases of the plan that have been successful, to maintain them as an ongoing part of the system

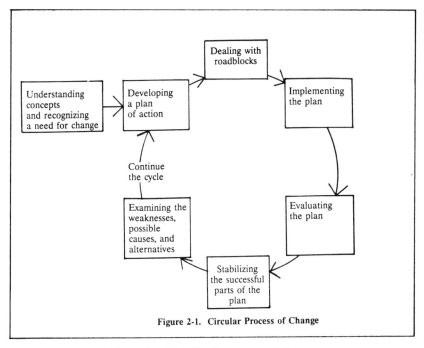

Figure 2-1.  Circular Process of Change

**Figure 2.1.**  The circular process of change

7.  Examining the weaknesses and failures and considering possible causes and alternatives

The cycle continues with the development of a new plan of action that will attempt to eliminate the problems and proceed through the steps followed in the earlier procedure of dealing with roadblocks, putting the plan into effect, evaluating it, and so on (see Figure 2.1).

## Conclusion

Innovation and creativity are essential ingredients in our system of long-term care if it is to achieve and retain vitality. There need to be a constant evaluation of practices and a response to the deficiencies and flaws that exist. The role of change agent is a major factor in the process of change that is a constant requirement for a vital system of care.

The system of the circular process encourages experimentation and innovation. It also helps staff examine all parts of a plan carefully and determine which features are worth retaining and building into the ongoing program. The practice of analyzing why certain parts were unsuccessful and taking steps to correct the flaws helps staff be more objective and avoid the pessimistic attitudes of skeptics who say, "We tried that once, and it didn't work."

This open approach is crucial in creating living units for persons in all stages of dementia. Their needs vary from stage to stage, and it is essential that those designing special units recognize the differences and plan accordingly. Health care providers, at this point, are only beginning to understand the design elements of environments for persons in the middle stages of Alzheimer's disease. It is essential that all parts of the milieu and the various practices in specialized dementia units be subjected to vigorous and continuous testing and evaluation in order to determine the ingredients and the characteristics that will provide the best quality of life for cognitively impaired persons.

## References

Baldwin, D. C., Jr., and R. A. Williamson Tsukuda. 1984. Interdisciplinary teams. In *Geriatric medicine: Fundamentals of geriatric care*, vol. 2, edited by C. K. Cassell and J. R. Welsh, 421–435. New York: Springer-Verlag.

Boling, T. E., D. M. Vrooman, and K. M. Sommers. 1983. *Nursing home management: A humanistic approach.* Springfield, Ill.: Charles C. Thomas.

Brody, E. 1977. *Long-term care of older people.* New York: Human Sciences Press.

Calkins, M. P. 1988. *Design for dementia: Planning environments for the elderly and the confused.* Owings Mills, Md.: National Health Publishing.

Edelson, J. S., and W. H. Lyons. 1985. *Institutional care of the mentally impaired elderly.* New York: Van Nostrand Reinhold.

Kane, R. A., and R. L. Kane. 1982. Long-term care: A field in search of values. In *Values and long-term care*, edited by R. L. Kane and R. A. Kane, 3–25. Lexington, Mass.: Lexington Books.

Koncelik, J. A. 1976. *Designing the open nursing home.* Stroudsburg, Pa.: Dowden, Hutchinson, and Ross.

Likert, R. 1975. *New ways of managing conflict.* New York: McGraw-Hill.

Lippitt, R. 1962. Unplanned maintenance and planned change in the group work process. In *Social work practice*, edited by P. Glasser, 75–95. New York: Columbia University Press.

Miller, P. A. 1988. Teaching process: Its importance in geriatric teamwork. *Physical and Occupational Therapy in Geriatrics*, 6(3/4):121–131.

Perrow, C. 1986 *Complex organizations: A critical essay*, 3rd ed. New York: Random House.

# Chapter 3

# A Model of Residential Living

## DOROTHY H. COONS

Getting my dad to do anything is a major operation. He has to be reminded to pick up food, chew, and swallow. I have to cope with my own anger. Constantly trying to find patience. Doing the best you can and wondering if it makes any difference.

Nowhere in the questionnaire have I mentioned the disbelief I experienced—the unwillingness to accept the fact of this hideous change coming over my sweet, good-natured, capable husband, the frustration he must have felt. . . . My rage and resentment at the demands made upon me. . . . My loving him so much one minute and then so full of hatred the next . . . and my fear and sadness as I watched a beautiful man disintegrate little by little.

These are two of many quotations that appeared in the questionnaires completed by family members who participated in the study *Alzheimer's Disease: Subjective Experiences of Families*,[1] conducted in 1982–83 by the Institute of Gerontology (IoG) of the University of Michigan (Chenoweth and Spencer 1986; Coons et al. 1983). The moving stories tell of the devastating effects the disease has on both the victims and their caregivers. Most families reported that their relative had problems with memory loss, confusion, and disorientation, and about one-third stated that there had been unexplained personality changes. Wandering was also a serious problem for many, especially if it occurred at night. One woman reported that her husband wandered from room to room nightly and that she had gone for more than 18 months without a full night's sleep.

Some families had been quite innovative and resourceful in coping with some of the behavioral changes. Several commented on the need for patience and humor as a means of surviving. For others, however, the experience was long, agonizing, and exhausting to the point that they could no longer think objectively or clearly. Several said that a physician or relative had to make the decision about nursing home placement when they themselves became so debilitated that they could no longer care for relatives. At the time of the study, health professionals, with few exceptions, were ill equipped to recommend coping strategies or methods of reducing some of the difficult behaviors. Families reported also that many nursing homes were not prepared to provide the kind of care needed by Alzheimer's victims.

The dearth of knowledge about how to care for persons with dementia, as illustrated in the family study, led staff members of the IoG to seek direct involvement with Alzheimer's victims, and shortly after the termination of the study of family experiences they began another project that involved working in a nearby retirement home with two small groups of persons with dementia. One group included residents from the home for the aged who were becoming quite disoriented and were having difficulties coping in the large facility. A second group was composed of five residents with severe cognitive impairment from the nursing home.[2] The purposes of this small group work program were to learn more about the characteristics of persons with dementia, the differences in functioning and behaviors of those in various stages of the illness, what capacities still might remain in even the severely impaired, and ways to improve their quality of life.

Both groups became increasingly responsive as the meetings progressed. They seemed to enjoy the companionship and the various activities introduced. Several in the nursing home group were no longer able to communicate verbally, but they joined in the singing with gusto. Some of the most successful sessions with the home-for-the-aged group were the occasions when children from a nearby day-care program joined them. They shared in simple tasks, singing, and games. Both groups demonstrated that they were still able to perform tasks that had been habitual in their earlier lives, such as peeling apples or rolling out dough for pies. Two members of the severely impaired group were especially responsive when a number of antique items were brought to the meeting and placed on the table before them. They were unable to name the items or to comment upon them, but one member reached for an old washboard and went through the motions of scrubbing clothes. Another woman reached for an old black iron that in earlier years would have been heated on a stovetop burner. She pulled her sweater onto the table and began to iron. Both groups responded to humor and light-hearted, joking banter.

## A Recognition of Need for a Dementia Care Unit

At the time when persons from the home for the aged were being selected to participate in the group activities, the administrator expressed concern about approximately a dozen residents who were becoming increasingly disoriented and confused, and who were also in need of far more help with the activities of daily living than the small staff was able to provide. Both the administrator and the staff of the IoG considered them inappropriate candidates for the nursing home that was a part of the facility. They needed little or no medical treatment, and they were physically mobile and active.

After a series of discussions between the administrator and the IoG staff, they reached a decision to design a specialized unit within the home for the aged that would attempt to provide a more supportive, manageable, and appropriate environment for these residents than either their current living situation or the nursing home could offer them. This new area would eventually be named Wesley Hall. The plan called for a two-year experimental/demonstration period, from December 1983 to December 1985, during which the staff of the IoG would be intensely involved. At the end of the two-year period, the staff of the home would assume full responsibility for the unit. The two-year project was based on the concepts from earlier research related to the designing of therapeutic milieus by the IoG, but the project itself was experimental in that one of its purposes was to learn through testing and experimentation the adaptations that would be essential in applying earlier criteria and methods to this special population (Coons 1990).

## The Selection of Residents

In an effort to learn as much as possible about the characteristics of the potential candidates for Wesley Hall, the IoG staff met with staff members from the home's dietary, housekeeping, nursing, social work, and activities departments. They were told the purposes of the special area and were asked to submit lists of names of persons they believed would benefit from living in the new unit. They were also asked to list specific problems residents seemed to be having and some of the resulting behaviors with which the staff were having difficulty coping.

In efforts to choose a somewhat homogeneous population, the selection criteria that were formulated required that residents be having severe memory problems, and be ambulatory, able to feed themselves, not in need of extensive medical care, able to manage some activities of daily living with the help of the staff, and able to follow simple instructions. These criteria would give a general description of the residents chosen for Wesley Hall, all of whom were identified as being in the middle stages of dementia, but much more would need to be known about each person as an individual to design a milieu that responded to each person's needs.

As a part of the selection process, the IoG staff administered mental status tests (Kahn et al. 1960), and the cognitive impairments noticed in observations and interviews were confirmed when residents scored in the category of the severely impaired or on the borderline. Through additional testing, it was determined whether they could still manage familiar tasks and follow simple instructions.

In efforts to determine their special needs, strengths, and problems, the staff spent time with the selected residents, observed them in a variety of situations, and learned to know each person as an individual. Some of the residents seemed uncomfortable with others and spent most of their time in their rooms alone. Those who sat in a lounge after breakfast and lunch seemed to become agitated and bored but were unable to initiate activities except for restless wandering. Two were frequently angry, and one was physically and verbally combative at times. One of the residents had severe spatial problems, making it difficult for her to locate items or to differentiate between one item and another. Most residents had language problems in varying degrees that included difficulty in retrieving words or an inability to form sentences.

Each of the residents selected for the project was aware in varying degrees of his or her surroundings and of the reactions of others. All of the residents seemed to have a close relationship with their families, and only one could no longer recognize members of his family. Before the opening of this unit, all residents were given thorough examinations by the medical director of the home. He diagnosed 10 of the 11 residents as having Alzheimer's disease or multi-infarct dementia. One of the men had brain damage from earlier viral encephalitis. Those who were incontinent were also examined by the Continence Clinic at the University of Michigan to screen for possible infections.

A number of the characteristics of the selected residents identified in this screening period would have direct impact on the choice and design of the physical environment and on the lifestyle to be created in the area. Size would be crucial, because the residents seemed to be overwhelmed by the largeness of the home for the aged and by the numbers of people with whom they had to cope. Most of the residents needed much more help with activities of daily living than originally assessed. Their abilities to do simple tasks would help to determine activities that would be appropriate and therapeutic. Their awareness of others and their positive responses to humor and warmth would provide suggestions for staff approaches and relationships that would help the residents enjoy and feel comfortable in their new home.

## Considerations in Establishing a Dementia Care Unit

### The Selection of the Site

*Issues.* A number of issues need to be considered in selecting an appropriate site for a dementia care unit. If the objective is to establish a small, homelike unit, size becomes a major consideration. In addition to bedrooms for 6 to 15 residents, the unit should include several small congregate areas (e.g., a small dining room, a living room or den that may be used for activities, and a small kitchen for the use of both the staff and the residents). If possible, the congregate areas should be visible to residents when they leave their bedrooms so that they can easily locate the space and can be drawn to areas in which activities are occurring.

If the unit is part of a larger facility, it should be sufficiently separated from other areas that it does not serve as a thoroughfare for the staff, visitors, and other residents. It is desirable to have direct access to an enclosed outdoor area to enable residents to enjoy the outdoors safely when weather permits.

*Applications.* Several wings of the home for the aged were considered as possible sites for the Wesley Hall unit, with the objective in mind that the area would be used to create a residential living model. This model was defined as a setting that would provide the privacy, comfort, and ambience of a home. Every effort would be made to avoid any resemblance to a treatment setting, and the activities and opportunities in the unit would emphasize the capacities of each individual to function and enjoy life.

An area on the fourth floor of the home for the aged was eventually selected as the project site. The unit that would accommodate the two men and nine women chosen for the project had a dozen single-occupancy bedrooms, two baths, and space for a living room, dining area, and small den. The bedroom adjacent to the dining area would be converted to a small kitchen as a part of the renovations. One of the major advantages of the area was that other parts of the home did not have direct access to it, and therefore the unit did not serve as a thoroughfare. The disadvantages were that the unit lacked direct access to the outdoors and the floor plan included a long, institutional-looking corridor with residents' rooms lining each side.

### Physical Renovations

*Issues.* One of the essentials in designing homelike units is the conversion of areas that are institutional in style and character to ones that attempt to individualize personal space, provide furnishings that resemble those in one's home, and compensate for the cognitive and sensory deficits of the impaired persons who will occupy them. Noninstitutional furniture arranged in groupings to encourage socialization together with plants, pictures, and other forms of art can create a warm and friendly environment. Distinctly contrasting colors, increased lighting, and reduction of glare on floors and walls can help persons with sight problems. Carpeting, ceilings of acoustic tiles, and textured wall coverings can help reduce confusing noise.

*Applications.* As part of the renovations in Wesley Hall, the living room, den, and hallway were painted, wallpapered, and carpeted. Ceilings were lowered in those areas and additional lighting installed. Homelike furniture, much of it supplied by family members, was used in the living room and the den. Small square tables with chairs were purchased for the dining area. New toilets, lavatories, a shower, and a tub were installed in the women's bathroom, and the institutional tile on the walls was replaced with contrasting nonglare colored tiles on the lower half of the walls and wallpaper above. The men's bathroom was also stripped of the tiles and then painted and wallpapered. To the extent possible, the arrangement of furniture, pictures, and memorabilia in residents' rooms were as much like that in their former rooms as possible. The major changes were the conversion of one bedroom to a kitchen and the installation of a door between it and the dining area.[3] (See the videotape *Designing the Physical Environment for Persons with Dementia* for details [Coons et al. 1987].)

### The Selection and Training of the Staff

*Issues.* One of the most crucial factors in creating therapeutic milieus in dementia care units is the selection and training of the staff. Both the content and methods of training need to differ greatly from and extend beyond that offered traditionally to prepare the staff to care for the elderly in nursing homes. (See Chap. 7 for a detailed description of training topics and methods.)

*Applications.* All staff members in the facility had opportunities to apply for the positions in the special unit, and the staff were selected both from the nursing and home-for-the-aged sections and from new applicants. Three of those who were eventually chosen had originally observed the meetings of the small groups and had gradually assumed some of the leadership roles. The training and apprenticeship of the staff occurred the month before the opening of the unit.

The staffing pattern during the second year of the project, slightly higher than during the first year, included one full-time and one half-time resident assistant (or aide) on the day shift, one full-time and one half-time resident assistant on the afternoon shift, and one resident assistant on the night shift, one full-time supervisor, and one part-time housekeeper. The medical director of the home also covered Wesley Hall.

Food came from the central kitchen in the home for the aged, and repairs were handled by the home's maintenance department. The cost of both of these services was partially absorbed in the overall budget.[4]

### Preliminary Meetings

*Issues.* Any new endeavor, especially one that deviates from traditional practices, has the potential for meeting with resistance and skepticism. Meetings with organizations or persons that will be affected by or will have the power to interfere with the development of plans can be used to explain the rationale for the changes and answer questions. These efforts can often dilute resistance and attract support and advocates.

*Applications.* At Wesley Hall, the plans to install a small kitchen and to involve residents in household tasks such as washing and drying dishes, setting tables, and preparing snacks with the help of staff did not conform to traditional patterns and had the potential of meeting with rejection by the state's Department of Public Health. To clarify the policies and to get approval for the proposed changes, the administrator and the IoG staff met with persons from the accrediting division of the department to explain the purposes and design of the project. After the presentation and much discussion, the department approved the installation of a small kitchen and the plan to involve residents in household tasks. A similar meeting with the fire marshal helped clarify issues about furniture arrangement and safety measures.

A meeting with a committee from the home's employees' union gave the project staff an opportunity to explain the overall goals of the project and the rationale for changing staff roles and methods of involvement with residents. In the new arrangements, residents would be sharing in many of the tasks ordinarily considered the responsibility of the staff. The union also approved the change.

Before the opening of the special unit, the staff held a number of meetings with the relatives of the selected residents to explain the goals of the project, to solicit their support and involvement, and to answer questions and respond to their concerns. They were asked to complete a questionnaire about their relative's earlier occupation, interests, hobbies, and preferences, with the purpose of helping the project staff get to know each resident as an individual with a past and a personality uniquely his or her own.

In preparation for the move to Wesley Hall, the selected residents, in groups of two or three, were taken on several visits to the unit by staff members who would be working there. They were given a relaxed tour of the area, and then they shared refreshments with the staff. Some seemed to feel comfortable with this preliminary preparation; for others it was confusing and upsetting. All of them responded to the staff and seemed to feel more comfortable with them as they spent time together.

### Planning the Program of Activities

*Issues.* Persons with dementia grow increasingly dependent upon skills and behaviors with which they were familiar in earlier life. Although unable to learn new skills, they can often, with the guidance of the staff, continue to do tasks that have become habitual.

Impairment in persons with Alzheimer's disease seems to be varied, but in almost every person with brain failure there remains a skill or an activity that can still be managed successfully and give pleasure (Gray and Isaacs 1979). A resident may be unable to follow instructions from the staff about how to get dressed, but when clothes are visible and no one interrupts with instructions, the person may be able to get dressed unassisted. A person may seem to have difficulty doing the simplest task and yet can wash dishes and put them in a drainer when the dishwater is ready, dishes are in the sink, and he or she is given a dishcloth and is asked to proceed.

It becomes a challenge for the staff to discover which of the habitual tasks or activities are still possible for the individual to perform. These capacities may vary from day to day or hour to hour, so assumptions cannot be made about what the impaired person can do at the moment. This requires alert, sensitive, and well-trained staff members who can help residents succeed when they are able and help them avoid failure when the task is beyond their momentary capacities. A thorough evaluation of the problems residents may be having, as well as the capacities and qualities that still exist even in very impaired persons, can help the staff develop a milieu carefully targeted to help residents compensate for deficits and avoid some of the situations that cause problem behaviors (Coons and Reichel 1988; Robinson et al. 1987).

*Applications.* Activities in the Wesley Hall project paralleled those in any home setting, and, as in the home, they included self-care and grooming, household tasks, and activities that were fun and exhilarating. They were not viewed or labeled as therapies, but instead were considered a fulfillment of daily needs, an effort to enable persons to use their remaining abilities, and a means of enhancing life for even very impaired persons. These activities enabled residents to continue in the normal social roles that had provided a framework, meaning, and purpose for them in the past. A number of special events were planned for the residents and their families to enjoy together. Children also became regular visitors to the unit, and they shared a variety of activities with the elderly residents, sometimes on a one-to-one basis and at other times with the whole group.

Table 3.1 shows some of the interventions that were introduced over the two-year period of the project. Most of the items were planned before the opening of the unit, but others were introduced and tested later to respond to changes in residents or to fulfill unmet needs. For example, a number of additional visual cues were added when the staff recognized the extent of residents' disorientation and to accommodate the gradual deterioration of some. Alterations were made in all parts of the milieu in efforts to respond to the changing needs of residents and to find better and more appropriate methods to create a good quality of life (Friedman and Robinson 1986).

## The Early Months of the Project

Residents were moved to Wesley Hall during December 1983. The early months were exceedingly difficult and challenging. Many things were known about persons with Alzheimer's disease and other irreversible dementias, and specifically about the residents moving

**Table 3.1.**

**Designing the Milieu to Respond to the Problems and Build on the Assets of Residents**

| Characteristics of Residents | Environmental Interventions |
|---|---|
| They seemed unable to cope with large separated spaces, many people, and disturbing noises | —The unit housed only 11 residents<br>—Congregate living areas were small, open, and clearly visible<br>—The intercom was disconnected |
| They were disoriented | —Visual cues, labels, and symbols were used throughout the unit to assist with orientation<br>—All residents' rooms were furnished with personal furniture and artifacts to give them a sense of ownership and help them identify and locate the space |
| Some had spatial problems | —Plates contrasted with undecorated place mats of primary colors<br>—Toilets, lavatories, and bathtubs contrasted in color with surrounding floor, walls, or countertops |
| Some were incontinent | —Individualized toileting schedules were established for residents who were incontinent<br>—Liquid intake was increased for all residents<br>—Bathrooms were easily accessible and clearly labeled |
| They demonstrated a need for privacy | —Sleeping rooms were single occupancy<br>—Residents had access to their rooms at all times<br>—The small den was available when residents wanted to be alone but away from their rooms |
| They were resistant to controlling or authoritarian staff | —The staff learned to suggest rather than demand<br>—Rigid schedules were avoided (such as bath schedules or breakfast times)<br>—The staff learned to respond to the moods of residents<br>—Staff members wore street clothes to reduce the image of the person in control |

(*continued*)

**Table 3.1.**

**Designing the Milieu to Respond to the Problems and Build on the Assets of Residents (*continued*)**

| *Characteristics of Residents* | *Environmental Interventions* |
| --- | --- |
| They were restless and agitated when they had nothing to do | —Residents were involved in many routine tasks that were familiar to them<br>—The staff developed a repertoire of activities that they could introduce spontaneously when residents seemed bored or restless<br>—Many activities were introduced after the evening meal to reduce evening agitation and restlessness |
| They needed help with activities of daily living | —Much of the staff members' time following the breakfast hours was involved in helping residents continue in self-care activities<br>—Part-time staff persons were added to help with dressing in the morning and undressing in the evening<br>—The staff spent an increasing amount of time in helping residents continue the parts of the activities of daily living they were still able to manage with time and with the staff's guidance |
| They could follow simple instructions and manage familiar tasks | —Opportunities were planned daily that enabled residents to continue in familiar tasks<br>—Several volunteer activities that required only simple instructions were introduced to add variety |
| They were aware of and responsive to their surroundings | —The physical environment offered visual stimulation and interest<br>—A parakeet, a goldfish aquarium, and an outdoor bird feeder were added to create interest |
| They were responsive to warmth, humor, and lightheartedness | —The staff learned to use humor, touch, and lighthearted conversation at every opportunity<br>—Children visited the unit frequently, and the activities they shared with residents were fun and relaxing<br>—Activities such as dancing, ball tossing, and clowning could always lighten moods and bring laughter |

to the area. There were also many unknowns, such as how residents would respond to the setting and to some of the new approaches that had been planned. Wesley Hall was designed not only to provide a more supportive living environment for the residents than was possible in the home for the aged but also to give the staff opportunities to learn more about ways to reduce stress, help residents continue to function and participate in life, and reduce the frequency and intensity of some of the behaviors with which the staff had difficulty coping in the large environment.

In training sessions held before the unit opened it was emphasized that imagination and creativity would be essential. It was anticipated that there would be constant testing of new approaches, methods, and activities. Some would fail, and this could be expected in such a new and untested arena. The failures themselves could provide new knowledge about what was inappropriate for and objectionable to residents. This freedom to use their own talents and ideas was somewhat frightening to many of the staff.

Even with the extensive training and preparation that preceded the opening of the unit, the staff were immediately faced with problems. The area seemed strange and unfamiliar to residents. Several paced incessantly in attempts to find familiar landmarks or to find ways to leave the area.

The doors leading to the stairways had been painted the same colors as the surrounding walls. This served as sufficient camouflage that, even though they were unlocked, they were not used by residents when they first moved to the area. The elevator too was painted to match the surrounding wall, but for some reason this did not serve as a deterrent. Several people during the early months left the area by way of the elevator, to be found later by the staff, lost and frightened in another part of the building. This was very stressful for the staff too, and for a period of time a decorative hanging was placed over the elevator button.

Several of the residents were especially agitated after the evening meal and searched for family members to take them home. During this early period of the project a number of residents were up many times during the night, pacing and restless and at times quite agitated and angry. Efforts to get residents to take baths often met with resistance and anger. For a short period of time one person refused to come to the dining area for meals.

The turmoil during the first few months was stressful and discouraging for the staff, but gradually, as they varied their approaches and found them effective, they became more relaxed and confident. They were also getting to know the residents and learning to anticipate their moods and reactions. At the same time the residents were becoming better acquainted and more comfortable with the staff, and gradually they seemed to accept Wesley Hall as their home.

The initial period in any new project is predictably difficult. Even the most experienced staff persons cannot anticipate the problems that may arise. When the project is designed to test new approaches and interventions, the beginnings can be full of uncertainties and questions. The old ways may seem safer and more predictable in their results. During this period it is especially important that the direct service staff be given much support, reassurance, and special help with problem solving (see Chap. 8 on avoiding staff burnout).

## The Development of an Effective Milieu

Gradually Wesley Hall became a warm and supportive environment for both the residents and the staff. A number of changes were made to help reduce stress and create a more relaxed style.

Arrangements were made with the dietary department to serve breakfast over a period of several hours. The food cart was brought to the area at the usual time but was returned several hours later than usual. Cereal, rolls, bread for toast, and fruit juices were always available in the area. This arrangement enabled residents to have breakfast whenever they awoke. Some came to breakfast in their robes and dressed later with the help of the staff at a far more leisurely pace than in the early months.

For a while very few activities were planned for the period after supper and before residents went to bed. In both the nursing home and the home for the aged, the staff had considered the evening a period for getting ready for bed and nothing more. This was a particularly difficult period of the day at Wesley Hall, because the agitation of several residents disturbed others, who then in turn found it difficult to go to sleep. This situation led the staff to plan a variety of evening activities that could be implemented on the spur of the moment if residents became disturbed. Singing and ball tossing were popular, and a variety of humorous and lighthearted activities became a regular part of the evening's repertoire. Gradually bedtime was moved to a much later hour than in the first several months, and residents retired happier and far more relaxed.

Activities gradually became a natural part of the life of the unit. Activities of daily living occupied much of each morning as staff members worked one-to-one with residents who needed help. Housekeeping and kitchen tasks became an ongoing part of each day.

Frequently one or a small group of residents was involved with the staff in preparing snacks. A volunteer from the retirement home came several times a week to play the piano and lead sing-alongs, and occasionally a resident would begin a song spontaneously and would be joined by other residents and staff members.

Some activities were shared with children when they visited. These occasions were especially enjoyable and pleasant for residents. Family potluck dinners every few months gave residents an opportunity to share a meal with their relatives. The occasions also enabled families to become acquainted with each other and share experiences.

Occasionally residents who were able helped fold flyers and stuff envelopes for the American Red Cross or other organizations. These activities were carefully selected and the tasks were broken down into several simple, repetitive steps.

## Outcomes

The impact of the residential living model was most evident in the response and resulting changes in the behaviors and moods of residents. Some of the more difficult behaviors were never totally avoided, but they occurred much less frequently.

The residents clearly enjoyed humorous situations and light-hearted conversation. Gradually some became able to initiate as well as respond to humorous situations.

> Mrs. Reynolds was a delightful, fun-loving person living at Wesley Hall. Occasionally she seemed depressed and agitated, but she would usually respond to the playfulness of staff. Her son told the staff that his mother seemed more lighthearted than he had ever known her to be. He concluded that her husband, who had been harsh and controlling, had suppressed much of her natural humor.

The staff kept a daily log that reported on the happenings on each of the three shifts. The changes that occurred in night wandering and restlessness over a period of time were documented in the contrasts in staff reports. During the first few months residents were restless at night and were having many problems sleeping. Excerpts from the log during the first month of the project recorded by the resident assistant on the night shift illustrated the problems residents were having (Coons 1987).

12:30   Mrs. Ross came to the dining room with a washcloth. She was rubbing the back of her left leg and seemed to have some discomfort. I put an ice pack on it for a while and she said she felt better. Mrs. Ross went back to bed and I told her to let me know if it started hurting her and she couldn't get to sleep.

1:00    Mrs. Eliot came out fully dressed. I told her the time and she went back to bed.

1:15    Mrs. Jaffe was up wandering around her room. I took her to the bathroom and then tucked her back in bed.

1:35    Mrs. Ross got up again and said she couldn't sleep. We had hot cocoa together, and she helped me make some muffins for breakfast. She did a few dishes and then went back to bed about 2:35.

2:40    Mrs. Monroe was sitting on her bed, about to get up. She was still in her nightgown. I helped her get back in bed, covered her up, and she went to sleep.

3:45    Mrs. Todd came down the hall fully dressed and she had made her bed. I took her to her room and showed her the clock. She told me the correct time and was willing for me to help her get undressed and back in bed.

5:05    Mrs. Leeds was up and getting dressed in her room. I told her how early it was, but she still wanted to stay up.

5:15    Mrs. Todd was standing at her door and clapping her hands, a habit she has started recently when she wants attention. She seems to resent it when I'm helping others. I told her to come to the dining room if she wanted something and didn't see me.

5:20    Mrs Leeds came to the dining room and wanted something to eat. She had several pieces of cinnamon bread and two cups of coffee. Mrs. Ross came in shortly after and sat down with Mrs. Leeds and had some breakfast, then both went back to their rooms.

5:45    Mrs. Todd came to the dining room to find me. She wanted to know if it was time to get up. I feel this was an important step for her and me. Much better than clapping her hands and becoming so angry.

Three months later notes such as "Quiet tonight—no problems" began to appear occasionally in the log. The staff efforts on those nights were devoted almost entirely to carrying out the incontinence schedule.

Six months later Mrs. Todd was still having difficulty sleeping, sometimes getting up eight or more times either to go to the bathroom or to check on the time. A number of interventions were tested. The resident assistant sat with her when she seemed very restless and sometimes rubbed her back to help her relax. When she left the room she would reassure Mrs. Todd that she would check in frequently to see how she was doing. At other times the staff would involve her in making cookies or muffins or preparing vegetables for snacks. She enjoyed these activities, and they seemed to help her relax. Gradually the frequency of her restless periods was greatly reduced.

Four of the residents had been incontinent before coming to Wesley Hall. They were examined to eliminate the possibility of infection, and an individualized toileting schedule was developed for each of the four persons, so that the staff could remind them and, if needed, assist them in getting to the bathroom. This procedure, along with an increase in liquid intake to give the appropriate message to the bladder, helped to reduce incontinence. Adult briefs were never used during the project.

Bursts of anger and combativeness are often some of the most difficult behaviors with which the staff must cope. Often they occur unexpectedly when the staff person may be the least prepared to respond. It is important for the staff to recognize that these behaviors are not stubbornness or nastiness, but a response that the person can no longer control (Mace and Rabins 1981). Weekly staff meetings at Wesley Hall often focused on ways to reduce the explosive anger and on consideration of what might be triggering the incidents. In efforts to reduce the frequency and intensity of the anger, staff gradually adopted a relaxed and unhurried style. They became sensitive to each individual's moods, and they could often avoid an explosive reaction by diversion or by chatting in a light and bantering manner. Often it became essential for the staff to withdraw from the situation and return later.

While no single approach was successful every time, some approaches were consistently unsuccessful. In any case, the staff needed a repertoire of approaches from which to choose. This required imagination and a willingness to try positive, though often nontraditional, ways of helping residents through difficult situations in an effort to enable them to live with a minimum of stress.

There was a change in the appearance of residents who, before coming to the area, had looked confused, ill, out of touch, and depressed. Gradually they became more alert, responsive, well looking, and involved. This led to much speculation by staff about what specific interventions had made the difference. Special efforts were made to help residents be well groomed. Staff members worked with families to provide a variety of attractive clothing. Good hair and nail care was considered essential, as were bathing and dental care. Women wore makeup and jewelry; men were helped to shave regularly. These are all essentials for anyone in feeling well groomed.

The changes went beyond grooming, however. Except for an occasional nap, residents appeared alert and aware of their surroundings. Personality blossomed. They smiled or laughed easily and often. They were quick to establish eye contact with anyone approaching them or to initiate communication.

> Mr. Erickson, a resident at Wesley Hall, at times became agitated and verbally abusive, but the staff had learned to accept this as being beyond his control and to recognize his many appealing characteristics that made him one of the staff's favorites. They told of his response to a small boy who came to visit another resident in the unit. When Mr. Erickson saw him coming down the hall, he jumped up from his chair, walked up to him and, with a big smile, reached out to shake his hand and said, "I'm glad to meet you. Just call me Uncle Jim." This disarming gesture and many others like it gave the staff a sense of the person Mr. Erickson had been before his illness.

Certainly the constant interchange with the staff must have been a major factor in increasing these residents' responsiveness. The shared activities provided occasions for conversation or light banter. When the staff were giving residents help in any self-care activities they explained the steps involved, encouraged, reassured, complimented, and reminisced or laughed together about any funny incident that might have occurred. This constant stimulation in a relaxed and undemanding milieu seemed to be effective for even the most impaired residents.

## Conclusion

The residential living model encompasses the concept of "home," a place where one belongs. Verwoerdt (1976), in his delineation of the requirements for maintaining human dignity, stresses the need for privacy and an acceptance of territoriality, that is, the need for space to call one's own and over which one has control. That space is individualized in furnishings, color, and accessories to help the person feel at home and achieve a sense of familiarity. The quality of special units can perhaps be measured by how comfortable residents feel and how much they accept the unit as their home.

It is predicted that it will be into the next century before biomedical research will be able to identify the cause of and the appropriate clinical treatment for Alzheimer's disease. In the meantime the health care system needs to alter markedly its therapeutic efforts toward this vulnerable population (Baro 1983).

The residents at Wesley Hall demonstrated that persons with dementia can respond to and benefit from a therapeutic milieu that is sensitive to their needs and responsive to their moods. At the same time, the project gave convincing evidence that staff can learn to work effectively and gain great satisfaction in providing a positive and supportive quality of life for impaired persons. The residential living model, as tested in the Wesley Hall project, offers a vital and effective alternative to custodial care and a new dimension in the continuum of care.

## Notes

1. The study was supported by the AARP–Andrus Foundation.
2. Both units were part of the Chelsea United Methodist Retirement Home in Chelsea, Michigan, that later became the site of the Wesley Hall project.
3. Costs for the renovations, the purchase and installation of kitchen equipment, and the purchase of furniture for the Wesley Hall unit beyond that donated by family members totaled approximately $25,000.
4. The actual cost to residents of Wesley Hall in December 1985, the end of the second year, was $42.65 per day per person, as compared with $29.70 in the home for the aged and $60 in the nursing home.

## References

Baro, F. 1983. Paper presented at the International Symposium sponsored by the Kellogg International Scholarship Program on Health and Aging, Ann Arbor, Mich.

Chenoweth, B., and B. Spencer. 1986. Dementia: The experience of family caregivers. *Gerontologist*, 26(3):267–272.

Coons, D. H. 1987. Designing a residential care unit for persons with dementia. Washington, D.C.: Congressional Office of Technology Assessment, Contract #633-1950.0.

Coons, D. H. 1990. Residential care for persons with dementia: A link in the continuum of care. In *Dementia care: Patient, family, and community*, edited by N. L. Mace. Baltimore: Johns Hopkins University Press.

Coons, D. H., B. Chenoweth, C. Hollenshead, and B. Spencer. 1983. *Final report of the project on Alzheimer's disease: Subjective experiences of families*. Ann Arbor: Institute of Gerontology, University of Michigan.

Coons, D. H., and W. Reichel. 1988. Improving the quality of life in nursing homes. *American Family Physician*, 37(2):241–248.

Coons, D. H., A. Robinson, B. Spencer, and L. Green. 1987. *Designing the physical environment for persons with dementia.* A 20-minute slide/tape or videotape. Photomotion Producers. Distributed by Terra Nova Films, Chicago.

Friedman, A., and A. Robinson. 1986. *Wesley Hall: A special life.* A 29-minute film or videotape. Innerimage Productions. Distributed by Terra Nova Films, Chicago.

Gray, B., and B. Isaacs. 1979. *Care of the elderly mentally infirm.* London: Tavistock Publications.

Kahn, R. L., A. I. Goldfarb, M. Pollack, and A. Peck. 1960. Brief objective measures for the determination of mental status in the aged. *American Journal of Psychiatry*, 117(Oct.):326–328.

Mace, N. L., and P. V. Rabins. 1981. *The thirty-six-hour day.* Baltimore: Johns Hopkins University Press.

Robinson, A., B. Spencer, S. Weaverdyck, and S. Gardner. 1987. *Helping people with dementia in activities of daily living.* A 22-minute slide/tape or videotape. Photomotion Producers. Distributed by Terra Nova Films, Chicago.

Verwoerdt, A. 1976. *Clinical geropsychiatry.* Baltimore: Williams and Wilkins.

# Chapter 4

# Dementia Care Units in Nursing Homes

NANCY L. MACE, M.A.

$M$any nursing homes are establishing units that are specifically intended for people with Alzheimer's disease and related disorders. Yet nursing homes are often criticized for providing care that is inadequate, impersonal, and overly medical with little emphasis on fostering a meaningful life for the chronically ill. Will this change with the creation of dementia care units? The same factors that have created these problems may inhibit the development of innovative dementia-specific care in nursing facilities. Most authorities agree that the existing nursing home model is inappropriate, perhaps harmful, to many residents including those with dementia, but the model has proven resistant to change. This chapter will describe the characteristics of the dementia care units this author has observed or surveyed and outline the factors inhibiting the growth of effective units.

## Characteristics of Dementia Care Units in Nursing Facilities

This section will discuss dementia-specific units in nursing facilities in the United States, emphasizing trends and issues in their development. This chapter focuses on dementia-specific units only in *nursing facilities*. Comparisons will be made with American non-nursing facilities and units visited in Belgium, England, Canada, and Australia. Information has been gathered from published and un-published sources, program literature, and multiple site visits in all five countries. Although this chapter will describe excellent programs in other countries, it is important to keep in mind that all five countries struggle with similar difficulties of adequate funding, adequate staffing, and patient needs and that many residential facilities abroad—like those in the United States—fall far short of the ideal. Nevertheless, it appears that the funding and regulatory systems in the other four countries are more likely to foster a few good experimental dementia-specific programs than are those of the United States.

In 1988–89 Coons and Mace surveyed 17 dementia care units, 12 of which were in nursing facilities in the United States, and the results of that survey are presented in this chapter.[1] Efforts are now under way to develop objective measures for determining the impact of care on a person with dementia. At present, however, estimates of benefit remain subjective. For the purposes of this chapter, a "successful" unit is defined as one that brings about positive patient change and generates staff reports of job satisfaction. Table 4.1 lists the common areas of patient change.

Dementia care units have developed in response to (1) the rising number of people with dementia in nursing facilities, many of whom have behavioral problems that distress the staff and other residents, (2) the perceived risk to a physically vulnerable resident if a resident with dementia becomes combative, (3) the market response to an increasing public awareness and demand for specialized care, and (4) a humanitarian desire to improve the quality of life for people with dementia. Dementia-specific care units are not new. A few facilities, notably the Hebrew homes, established such units more than 20 years ago (Edelson and Lyons 1985) and have considerable expertise in care.

This growing interest in dementia care units has been accompanied by research (Mathew et al. 1988; Sloan, no date; Kwon and White 1988; U.S. Congress, Office of Technology Assessment 1987). Ohta and Ohta (1988) pointed out that there are a wide variation and range in special units: "These units vary tremendously. . . . Often times these differences . . . appear to place special units in direct opposition to each other. Nonetheless, without exception, their proponents have hailed the success of the units."

## The Benefits of Dementia-specific Care

Dementia-specific care has the potential to benefit (1) the resident with dementia, (2) other residents of the facility, (3) the resident's family, (4) the staff, or (5) the facility owners or stockholders.

Although studies have been begun, measuring the impact on the resident with dementia will be challenging. Mathew and colleagues

**Table 4.1.**
**Patient Change**

Decrease in wandering

Decrease in episodes of agitation

No screaming or a decrease in screaming

Few or no drugs needed to control behavior[a]

Improved orientation

Decrease in socially unacceptable behaviors

Weight gains or improved eating

Decrease in depression[b]

Greater ability to sleep through the night

A sense of humor

A happy, relaxed appearance

The formation of friendships

Reduction or elimination of incontinence[c]

The initiation of interpersonal exchanges

Decrease in hallucinations[b]

*Notes:* Changes observed/reported in residents with dementia in dementia-specific nursing facility units, adult day-care, dementia-specific domiciliary units, and dementia-specific residential units in the United States, England, Canada, Belgium, and Australia. No program reported all changes in all residents. Each change has been observed in at least three residential settings (U.S. Congress, Office of Technology Assessment, 1987).

[a] Depending on the patient population, about half will need very low doses of neuroleptics.

[b] In part through appropriate psychiatric treatment.

[c] Usually through an individualized scheduled program.

(1988) compared a dementia care unit with two other mixed units through observation, examination, and chart review. They found no differences in mental status scores, functional scores, behavior scores, use of psychotropic medication, use of PRN medication, recent falls, recent hospitalization, weight loss, sleep problems, or decubiti. Because of the variation among inputs in different dementia-specific units, studies of other units might produce different results.

Observations of change in patients' behavior and of subjectively observed evidence of quality of life have been published (Miller 1977; Greene et al. 1985; Cleary et al. 1988; Sawyer and Mendlovitz 1982; Haugen 1985; Coons 1987; Hall and Buckwalter 1987; Benson et al. 1987; Pynoos and Stacey 1986). Bullock and colleagues (1988) found a decline in agitation, anxiety, combativeness, insomnia, restlessness, stripping, uncooperativeness, withdrawn behavior, and yelling. Greene and colleagues (1985) found a decline in ten behavior variables in six patients. Table 4.1 lists behaviors reported by the Office of Technology Assessment (1987) as changed in at least three sites. In addition, reduced verbal and facial expression of anxiety may be observed; residents are often more cooperative with activities of daily living (ADL); there may be a decline in the amount of time the patient is awake but appears "tuned out" (not observing or participating); there may be decreased perseveration or decreased function in language, and praxis may appear to increase slightly when the patient is more relaxed. Some programs claim to prolong ambulation. This may be because these programs rarely use physical or chemical restraints.

Of the nursing homes that responded to the survey questionnaire, all reported that patients showed less agitation, anger, and irritability; 90 percent reported that patients paced and wandered less and smiled more often. Eighty percent reported that combativeness, apathy, and yelling had declined and that social communication with the staff, laughter, humor, and involvement in activities had increased. Ninety percent reported that residents had gained weight. The number and consistency of these observed changes support the hypothesis that change in patient quality of life, but not in underlying neurological function, does occur in the middle stages of the illness when certain types of care are provided. Some changes are more commonly observed than others. (Eight other behaviors were reported as improved by only some of the facilities.) There are several possible explanations for this. What is interesting at this point is the consistency with which programs report some declines in negative behavior and some gains in positive, socially appropriate behavior.

### Unit Affiliation

The for-profit sector is expanding its dementia-specific services. Ohta and Ohta (1988) reported one major chain with more than 40 units. Kwon and White (1988) found that two-thirds of the 99 units they examined were proprietary. There is no reliable evidence that one sector can or cannot provide good dementia care, but the factors described later in this chapter may inhibit the development of good care in certain sectors.

### Size

The survey found unit size to range from 8 to 47 beds; Ohta and Ohta (1988) found a range of 10–49; Kwon and White (1988) found an average of 31.6 beds. Few nursing facility programs in the literature and only one visited by this author were smaller than 20 residents. With one exception, the most successful units were small or composed of subunits. American programs face several problems: (1) obstacles to converting existing plants to dementia care, (2) regulatory design limitations (particularly fire), (3) a belief that larger units and their staffing patterns are most cost-effective, and (4) little motivation to make changes that include financial risk and that may conflict with regulations. Some architects (Cohen and Weisman, in press; Calkins 1988) are experimenting with designs intended to address both the need for small units and cost-effectiveness.

### Residents

Although these units are often called "Alzheimer's units," they usually accept residents with any dementia. Some units accept residents because their behavior problems cannot be managed elsewhere; other units do not accept residents with certain behaviors, particularly combativeness. The survey indicated a considerable range in the abilities and needs of residents: programs reported that 70–100 percent were ambulatory or independent with a wheelchair, 50–100 percent needed minimal help with feeding, 5–80 percent needed minimal help with dressing. However, some programs reported that as many as 70 percent wandered, up to 50 percent needed total help with meals, and as many as 95 percent needed total help with dressing. Programs reported a range of 30–85 percent needing help with toileting.

Some international programs accept people who can no longer live alone but are still able to provide much self-care. However, in the United States most residents must meet Medicaid standards, which require a high level of functional dependency or physical illness. Families report that these requirements are an obstacle to admission for the very confused but physically able victim of dementia.

Some programs transfer residents when they feel they "can no longer benefit" from the program. Kwon and White (1988) found that the two most common discharge criteria were nonresponsiveness and certain (aggressive) behaviors. Four of the 17 units surveyed keep residents until death. The care of these residents is time-consuming and changes the character of the unit, yet the residents continue to need special care. One facility transferred more impaired residents to a step-down unit.

## Management

Although the literature says little about the role of management in a dementia care unit, the successful units visited by the author in nursing facilities all reported that the full support of management is essential. Management goals influence the outcome of the units. If marketing strategies are the dominant factors, they will affect the units accordingly. Several units visited by the author reported serious problems because of conflicting goals of staff and management. If units are to change enough to generate patient benefit, management must also change. Considerable staff stress is created when staff members are trained for a kind of dementia care that management does not understand or support.

> One administrator visited the dementia unit at 10:30 a.m. and, finding beds unmade, instituted disciplinary action. The unit had made bed making a scheduled therapeutic activity for some residents. For others, bed making was attended to when there was a lull in patient care activities later in the day.

## Unit Leadership

In the international programs and the programs that are not part of nursing facilities, unit leadership may be provided by a nurse, social worker, psychologist, or occupational, physical, or rehabilitation therapist. In the United States the medical/nursing mandate of Medicaid requires nurse leadership. The level and kind of nursing skills possessed by some nursing facility staff are inadequate to meet the diverse care needs of people with dementia. In every nurse-led unit that the author visited in which residents have made noticeable psychological gains, the nurse leadership has had additional training in psychiatry, community nursing, or human behavior.

Leadership style (hierarchical versus team) also appears to be critical to success.

> A purpose-built, carefully planned facility was experiencing high levels of staff conflict and little patient change. Staff and administration told this author that the nurse-leader had extensive nursing facility experience but lacked experience in a psychosocial team model. She was uncomfortable trusting the opinions of aides and the occupational therapist and frequently overruled them. She tended to use neuroleptics to manage residents' restlessness, rather than seeking nonpharmacological ways to reduce their distress.

Units find that by the middle stages of the disease, residents need the attention of those with nursing skills. However, in all of the successful programs reported or observed by the author, there were also found professionals expert in enabling improved psychosocial function (social workers, psychologists, and psychiatrists) and professionals skilled in enhancing function (physical, occupational, activity, or recreation therapists). These professionals had a greatly expanded role in patient care and in unit leadership. However, primary discipline varied and skills overlapped. Several programs reported confusion over the leadership roles between these disciplines and nursing. Some units (not nursing facilities) have successfully used recreation therapists, psychologists, or social workers as unit leaders.

Professional consultation is infrequently used, although outside expertise may be the only way to relieve a resident's distress.

> One woman, confined to a wheelchair, spent much of her day screaming or moaning. Consultation with a physical therapist determined that the wheelchair was painful for her to sit in for long hours. A new wheelchair was prescribed and the staff were instructed on how to make her comfortable with pillows. Her moaning stopped and she was then able to participate in some activities.

### Staff

To compare systems in the survey, staff-patient ratios were estimated by including only the staff members providing direct hands-on care. Activity, social work, or other staff time spent directly with residents was included, but staff time spent doing paperwork, administration, supervision, wheelchair washing, and so on was excluded. Some programs had made few if any changes in staff levels. However, programs in this survey, and in those units visited that reported patient gains, consistently identify levels close to one staff person per five residents on the day shift. This is a much better ratio than many nursing facility units have. Kwon and White (1988) found that more than 90 percent met or exceeded the staffing level required for skilled nursing facilities in their state. Ohta and Ohta (1988) reported a range on the day shift of $1:3-1:12+$. We found a day-shift range of $1:3$ to $1:7.3$, with a mean of $1:5$. Better ratios reflect a universal experience that little can be accomplished when staffing is low. Good dementia care is staff-intensive; programs in some states that rely heavily on Medicaid reimbursement will be unable to offer low ratios. Improved staff ratios, however, are probably necessary to improve care for most of the residents using nursing facilities.

Although direct care ratios are increased for the day shift, evening and night shifts fare less well. In the survey there was a range of 1:3.3 to 1:9 on evenings and 1:3.6 to 1:21.5 on nights. Ohta and Ohta (1988) reported a range of 1:3–1:16 on evenings and 1:3–1:25 on nights. Few activities are planned in the evenings, although this is a time when residents become restless. When the staff are limited, residents are put to bed early. When the second shift is adequately staffed, programs offer evening activities and allow residents to stay up later, reducing behavior problems and helping to restore normal sleep patterns.

Night shifts are often short staffed and are assigned non–patient care duties. When the night shift is able to spend time with residents (toileting, comforting, offering a cup of warm milk), the need for soporifics is reduced. Successful programs report that residents can resume sleeping through the night (Coons 1987).

### Staff Support

Successful programs provide training, support, role modeling, daily report, and in-service training for staff. The staff members have considerable autonomy and are encouraged to participate in problem solving. A key to good care appears to be a changed role for aides. Within a traditional system, aides have a set amount of time in which to complete specific tasks of personal care. (Taken to an extreme, personal care can be delivered assembly-line fashion, with each aide repeating the same tasks on each resident.) The aide is successful if he or she is efficient and fast.

In good dementia care, the aide has fewer patients but may be responsible for all aspects of care for them. The aide has much more flexibility as to the times by which certain tasks must be completed: some residents may come to breakfast in robes if they wake up late; beds may not be made until there is a lull after lunch. The aide is successful if his or her residents are relaxed, are cheerful, and participate in some parts of tasks.

Some facilities rotate staff members to prevent burnout, although there are clinical advantages in a stable staff. Some successful units do not rotate staff and staff reported high job satisfaction.

Higher staff ratios (Ohta and Ohta 1988), greater autonomy, volunteering onto the unit, administrative support, and training are credited by good units with reducing staff turnover. Training alone produced limited change in patient care practices and can increase staff stress. Some successful units reported in response to the survey that management changes have a greater impact on burnout rates than does rotation or the difficulties of caring for people with dementia.

The author interviewed aides who had worked on the same special unit for 20 years. They liked their work and were proud to be asked for advice. Unit leadership continued to provide support, autonomy, and ongoing training.

One facility that had provided training but made no management changes reported that the staff were "bored out." In others, aides reported higher job satisfaction than in previous positions.

Another facility had a direct care ratio of 1:2.5. During the visit, all but one resident were sitting in a dayroom while a volunteer gave a slide show. One resident was pacing. Staff were congregated at the end of a corridor, smoking and griping. They reported "nothing to do until lunch." The unit followed the traditional model in which the aides have little role in activities. Morning ADL were accomplished in the traditional way: aides did most of the work for the residents, and had not been trained to encourage and assist the residents to do for themselves. Aides had little autonomy and did not contribute their opinions about patients' abilities or needs.

A high staff level is not, by itself, a solution to the problems of dementia care. Although this unit was overstaffed with aides, no investment had been made to increase time for occupational or activities therapy. The aides ratio could have been raised to 1:5 and the difference invested in more professional recreational or activity therapy. The activity being offered was poorly conceived and served merely as a time filler. With a 1:5 aide ratio in which aides have an active role in therapeutic activities (Zgola 1987; Coons 1990), small groups of residents could be involved in focused tasks with the assistance of the aides and under the direction of a recreation specialist.

On international and non–nursing facility units we observed changes in the traditional staff roles to provide more staff time with residents. The housekeeping staff may take over some tasks aides traditionally do; the housekeeping staff on a few non–nursing facility units this author observed have been trained to interact with the residents. Paperwork may be shifted so that the charge nurse spends more time with the residents, thus providing more professional time in role modeling. One large facility trained non–patient care staff (maintenance, secretarial, kitchen) to spend one hour a day as a companion to one resident. This raised total patient/staff contact time without making a significant impact on other services. On these units (and on one American nursing facility unit) it was observed that work hours had been shifted so that an extra aide worked 11 a.m to 7 p.m., assisting with two meals and activities. On another unit professional activity time was from 11 a.m. to 7 p.m., helping to cover the evening hours. Some programs split a shift between two part-time employees so that one covered morning ADL and one covered the evening "sundowning" period. Although these changes may not be right for other facilities, incentives are needed to encourage experimentation.

In sum, staffing practices on successful units are good management practices, higher staff ratios, and increase in specific professional skills. These would benefit other populations in the facility as well. Unique to dementia is the kind of training given staff.

### Programing

All the units surveyed developed individual care plans for residents. Units commonly reported using small group activities, music, and one-to-one activities to increase stimulation. A total of 19 other activities to provide stimulation were listed by the 12 programs. Facilities most commonly reported a quiet area, one-to-one care, and "conveying a calm atmosphere" as interventions to reduce stress. Twenty-five other activities were listed. The same activity was often listed by one facility to reduce stress and by another to increase stimulation. Twenty-two different activities were listed as daily activities; the most common were exercise, housekeeping, walks outside, and music. Zgola (1987) and Coons (1987) described similar dementia programing. Successful units structure programing to meet individual preferences and to respond to functions that are spared or impaired; they reduce the periods of idleness for the resident but present a low-key, flexible day. ADL and all other activities are considered part of the therapeutic plan; activities are planned for their specific therapeutic and pleasurable qualities and not as time fillers for the residents. Activities are planned by professionals and carried out by the aides under the supervision of the therapist. The most successful units observed had independently developed similar approaches to programing. Some have advanced theories of programing (Rader 1987; Hall and Buckwalter 1987). Although these theories may indicate disagreement, what they actually *do* in daily living is remarkably similar.

### The Use of Chemical and Physical Restraints

In discussing drug use, small doses of neuroleptics prescribed to relieve specific psychiatric symptoms must be distinguished from larger, detrimental doses used to subdue the resident. Two of the U.S. programs visited by the author (one was a nursing facility) used no neuroleptics. Both had one actively hallucinating resident who might have benefited by intervention.

In comparing a dementia-specific unit with two other units, Mathew and colleagues (1988) found a higher use of both routine (53.8 percent of residents) and PRN neuroleptics and less use of physical restraints on the dementia care unit.

Pynoos and Stacey (1986) reported that 45 percent of patients with organic brain syndrome (OBS) are treated with tranquilizers, and that as the length of residency increased, so did the use of psychotropic medication. Beers and colleagues (1986) found that more than half the residents of 12 facilities were receiving psychoactive medication, with 26 percent receiving antipsychotics. In the survey it was found that both physical restraints and neuroleptics were used: all but one nursing facility used PRN behavior-controlling medication. Half the facilities reported that more than half their residents received PRN medication. Seventy-five percent of the facilities said this use had declined since their residents came on the unit. Bullock and colleagues (1988) reported four residents (out of 13) who received no psychoactive medication. Dosage levels for those who received medications were low. This unit was providing excellent care to a severely behaviorally disturbed group. Seventy-five percent of the facilities reported that residents needed medication to sleep. This is not surprising, given the low staff ratios at night. However, all facilities said the use of sleeping medications had declined since residents first entered the unit. Some of the units the author visited used no sedatives for sleep (Coons 1987).

Half the facilities reported using physical restraints, with a range of 2.5–15 percent (mean 11.8 percent) of residents restrained. In contrast, in the dementia unit of one state mental hospital, in some domiciliary facilities visited, and in some international facilities, no physical restraints were used. Nursing homes argue that they must use restraints to compensate for poor staffing ratios, fire regulations that restrict locked doors, and fear of liability if the patient falls. Restraints are probably not required for patient care; the problem involves the system rather than the patient.

### The Role of the Physician

Physicians set a standard for quality of care on the unit and provide specialized care for these vulnerable patients. Programs that have ongoing close support from a physician who is skilled in geriatric medicine emphasize that this resource is essential (see Chap. 14).

A unit in which the residents were cared for by their private physicians reported, "We have a lot less trouble with Dr. Peters's patients than with other residents—he comes out when we call, he doesn't overprescribe."

However, many physicians caring for residents of nursing homes do not understand how active involvement on their part would benefit their patients. Nursing facilities complain of difficulty involving physicians, and some have found alternative solutions.

When asked about physician involvement, one administrator said, "Our head nurse knows a lot. She keeps a close eye on the residents and she has persuaded most of our private physicians to go along with her."

### A Model of Care

People with dementia need safety and physical care, treatment of excess disability, reduction of stress, increase in stimulation, time spent in meaningful activities, and the restoration of those elusive elements, quality of life, dignity, self-esteem, self-actualization, happiness, friendship, and maximum function (Coons 1990; Mace 1990; Miller 1977). The factors controlling American nursing facilities place unequal emphasis on these needs. The nursing facilities are tied to a medical/nursing model. A unit with a good nursing model with strong psychosocial components is effective with people with dementia. However, when the form is not driven by a medical funding system, the tendency of many programs to use a psychosocial model indicates that this may be the dominant need.

Hall and Buckwalter (1987) emphasized the need for reduction of stressors. Individual patients respond to different stressors, however, and an individual problem-solving approach (Mace 1990) with trained staff is essential if patient stress is to be reduced. For example, the human environment is a more powerful stressor than the aspects of the physical environment being targeted by many facilities.

Most of the programs surveyed sought to increase resident stimulation. Here also, adequate staff and an investment in professional expertise are necessary.

Visitors to a unit often cause stress to the staff as well as to the residents. In these situations this author has occasionally observed the staff ignoring a resident who appeared to want to participate in the conversation or a staff member who overlooked a resident's need to focus on visitors.

> In one international unit a woman resident joined the tour of visitors. She proudly showed the visitors (who included a high-ranking local official) every laundry chute and broom closet, including one in which three large roaches lay dead. When the group reached the dayroom, the lady fluffed up a dozing gentleman as well as all of the pillows. The administrator cheerfully supported her sense of belonging. Roaches represent a sanitary issue, but the administrator was not so embarrassed that he failed to meet the woman's psychosocial need to be a part of things.

Quality of life is easily observed but difficult to teach. Therefore, programs must be able to hire enough professional staff who are adequately trained to serve as role models for direct care providers.

> An administrator was showing the author through a facility. She knocked on a resident's door and when there was no answer, entered the room. The resident was standing at her sink, trying to wash stool out of her panties. She was visibly upset. The administrator promptly entered the room, leaving the author outside, and assisted the resident (although this was technically an aide's responsibility). She emerged in a few minutes with a relaxed resident and continued on the tour.

Pynoos and Stacey (1986) emphasized the resident's total loss of autonomy. Autonomy for the dementia patient is challenging to provide within the nursing home "system." Whether resident autonomy will be implemented or will remain only in the prospectus is determined by the administration's willingness and ability to provide higher staff ratios and to take the perceived economic and safety risks. Successful programs report that a flexible approach results in gains in efficiency. No facility visited or reviewed had experienced a serious accident caused by giving residents more autonomy. In a more normal setting, residents tend to use their old skills correctly. In one setting we observed that residents were permitted to use a hand-operated lawn mower and garden tools in the outdoor area. There were no accidents or inappropriate uses of these familiar tools.

Whether or not these elusive qualities will be real parts of the care plan depends on leadership. But many administrators have been trained only for the tasks of management, quality assurance, and cost control. Most have had no training in psychology or human relations as these apply to people with dementia or to the staff. For example, a key element in the best programs is the restoration of pleasure (see Chaps. 3 and 10).

> A group of nursing home administrators were overheard laughing about another private-pay facility whose administrator bemoaned the fact that his chef had quit. The group thought it ridiculous for a nursing home to have a chef. For them, the goals of care included safety, cleanliness, nutrition—all things measurable by inspectors—but they did not consider the pleasure impaired people might obtain from good food to be a major goal of care.

It is not easy to reduce the anxiety, stress, and sheer terror that people with dementia face sufficiently that they can experience pleasure, but when we do, what really improves the quality of life is things like good food, succeeding at a task, understanding a joke, music, children, puppies and kittens, or feeling that one belongs in the place where one lives enough to show it off to visitors. These things often get lost within our system.

### Safety

American nursing homes emphasize fire safety and safe physical care. Concern over fire safety is reflected in numerous regulations. Neither physical care nor fire safety concerns are entirely logical. For example, practices such as use of medication to control behavior, extensive use of physical restraints, low staff ratios, and the institutional environment increase risks of falls, combativeness, wandering, decubiti, and concurrent illness. Overuse of neuroleptics is a significant cause of falls (Beers et al. 1988). It may be more difficult to evacuate heavily drugged residents or free those in restraints in the event of fire than to unlock an exit door.

In some other countries, a number of the dementia-specific units have approached these issues with equal concern but different assumptions, essentially focusing on fire *prevention* and giving quality of life greater weight in the equation.

### The Physical Plant

More has been written about the physical plant than other aspects of dementia-specific care. In the United States, dementia-specific units have often emphasized changes in the physical plant over staff changes. In visits and in the survey there was found to be wide variation among physical plants, but the variability was only within certain limits. Some changes in the plant are less costly, are easier to make than persuading staff or management to change their behavior, or will not conflict with regulations. They are highly visible and are consistent with the concept of the physical plant as a key marketing tool. The literature has extensive information about an appropriate physical environment for people with dementia or with sensory impairment (Hiatt 1986). This author found physical plants that did not utilize knowledge about sensory loss and human use of space, and some showed much greater concern with regard to the physical plant (theories that color will influence mood, floor plans to reduce wandering, etc.) than with psychosocial needs.

Of the 12 facilities surveyed, renovation/new building costs ranged widely from $4,100 to $150,000, probably reflecting these differences in emphasis. All but one nursing facility we observed retained the double-loaded corridor with double rooms and dominant nursing station (with limited variations, such as a lower desk surface), although non–nursing facility units and international units are exploring other designs.

Although the physical plant can contribute significantly to resident function and to staff convenience, the survey found programs with numerous positive patient changes in a range of settings, including some that were grim, cheerless, and institutional in design. These programs had staff trained to work with people with dementia and offered programing designed for this population. These inputs may more directly affect patient well-being than physical plant in the absence of good staffing and programing. Regulations and cost were often reported to limit those models that are thought to benefit people with dementia.

However, modifications of the plant in nursing facilities have not been logical. There were programs taking opposite interventions: while some report using uniform or pastel colors, others report using high contrasts and wallpaper. Some remove all mirrors and pictures, others deliberately introduce them; some report laying out interesting items to encourage "fiddling" (a distressing term), others report bolting things in place. The author visited two new purpose-built facilities that retained strong institutional cues. Both had poor lighting, shadows and glare were major problems, there were high background noise levels, and the outside area was barren. None of these problems would have been expensive to correct or would have violated building codes. One facility caring for quite impaired residents had striven for positive change by purposely increasing sensory stimulation in the physical plant. Rooms and corridors were decorated with memorabilia, and a sign reminded the staff and visitors to use these decorations to trigger reminiscing. The decorations included photographs of people, mirrors, and trompe l'oeil painting. It was reported that although residents occasionally talked to themselves in the mirror, this decor had not caused problems.

Kwon and White (1988) found that fenced exterior areas were added by 32 percent of facilities. This author saw two gardens that used the natural grade of the land to create a barrier that still did not give the appearance of restriction. Planting was lush and paths looped around and behind plants, giving one the impression of having walked somewhere. One facility used old-fashioned lawn furniture; one used a gazebo. The entrances to these gardens were shaded, so people were not blinded as they exited the building. We visited a number of programs that did not use their outside areas; the staff reported that "the residents might eat the grass," "someone has to be out there to watch them." These are autonomy-risk issues, which, if not overcome by administration, will not be overcome by a new plant.

One U.S. nursing facility observed was without a nurses' station; in another, the station was inconspicuous. Although some international and non–nursing facilities omit or reduce the nurses' station, some states require them.

Many facilities use institutional bathing equipment and long dining tables that seat eight with matching waterproof plastic chairs. These send cues of "institution." Many units retain high-glare floors. A few nursing facilities have used carpeting; some have had serious odor problems. Others, with better staff ratios, toileting schedules, and washable carpet tile, have found that carpets reduce noise and cushion falls yet remain odor-free. Nurses' uniforms are the topic of lively debate. Some people believe uniforms are essential in helping cognitively impaired persons to identify the staff, although small units have found that residents learn to recognize staff members without the uniform to cue them. While nonuniforms and carpeting may be preferable, it is unlikely that either issue will have nearly as significant an impact as the unit's overall philosophy.

The study indicated that the most common changes in dementia-specific units were an egress-control system and furnishings that included some of the residents' possessions. The egress-control devices ranged from $25 magnetic catches operated by an electrical circuit to high-cost devices worn by the residents and detected by a light beam at the door. Kwon and White (1988) reported that 44 percent of the facilities had added egress-control devices. The staff and families reported that their stress level is lower when they do not need to watch doors constantly. Emergency exits and doors to stairs, closets, and offices also pose problems. Some Australian programs hung curtains over exit doors. Some units have camouflaged fire escapes with paint to match the surrounding wall or have set a large plastic plant in front of emergency exits. These solutions would not be acceptable under American fire safety standards. Some facilities fear that their status as a non-IMD (Institution for Mental Disorders) will be challenged, and some report state restrictions. Most report long—and therefore costly—negotiations with fire and health authorities. This author observed considerable variation, and apparent unpredictability, in what fire and health authorities would allow.

Fewer than half the programs surveyed reported problems with architectural or fire safety regulations, although many of the other facilities visited did report such problems. More of the surveyed programs might have done so if they had attempted changes such as eliminating the nurses' station or introducing sitting rooms between patient rooms and the doors. Some facilities are seeking "home for the aged" licensure to avoid these regulations.

Some problems are created when architects do not understand dementia.

> One purpose-built unit contained a cul-de-sac out of sight of the nurses' station. One resident repeatedly disappeared into it and crashed against a cart, bringing staff running.
>
> On one unit a decorator had used a bright color to outline all doors, including those that patients were not supposed to use. The bright color drew residents' attention to all doors indiscriminately.

Programs report that closets, toilets, and sinks in resident rooms cause problems when residents can no longer use them independently. Some facilities believe the American families expect a private half-bath.

Some good ideas fail because, while the idea was good, some basic fact of human nature was overlooked.

> One program designed "busy" alcoves that did not work out as planned. These alcoves were away from the center of activity on the unit and were furnished with toys and a radio that did not work. People do not usually stop to examine or become involved with things partway down a corridor, and the items themselves were inappropriate and may have sent negative messages.

The debate over wandering space is international. Some advocate a racetrack design so that the resident can wander endlessly. Others seek to discourage wandering. The programs surveyed by Kwon and White (1988), by Ohta and Ohta (1988), and by Mace and Coons gave mixed reports. Aimless wandering and desperate efforts to leave are in part artifacts of an impoverished environment that should be changed. However, some people with dementia do appear to need to walk.

> In a program outside the United States, in which residents were relaxed and involved in activities, one young male resident walked past the author many times during the day. His walking was not pressured and he smiled and tipped his cap, but he clearly did need to walk much of the day. He was the only such person observed in successful units.

Space to walk is probably important, but a design that encourages wandering over more therapeutic interventions is probably misdirected (Coons 1988).

Visual cues are also the subject of impassioned debate. There is no evidence that color consistently affects mood or assists in orientation. Nevertheless, programs have tried color cues. Some report that signage helps with those residents who can still act on written information. Symbols may fail because of the loss of the ability to abstract. The author saw many orienting devices on or near resident doors, such as a large alcove beside the door that contained meaningful objects. With one exception, nursing facilities did not use assorted chairs so that residents could identify one as "mine." Only two American nursing facilities visited used resident furniture (excluding mattresses) extensively in resident rooms to aid in orientation or to help the resident feel at home. One successful unit reported trying this and removing the furniture when it did not seem to help. Few bathrooms or toilet rooms offered cues and color contrast.

Most nursing facilities are continuing to use double rooms. Costs and existing plant and regulatory limits on the size of single rooms are cited as reasons. Regulations on room size assume that residents would spend most of their time in their room, although dementia programs try to have them out of the room except for "quiet" times and for sleep. A few programs cling to the unproven idea that double rooms encourage friendships.

Nursing facility furnishings—draperies, bedspreads, chairs, tables—are marketed for the purpose and tend to support the institutional image. Some non–nursing facility units use carefully selected fire- and stain-resistant furniture from the general market.

### Costs

It is impossible to get comparable data on costs from one country to another or from one kind of licensing to another. Required paperwork, overheads, staff roles and deployment, resident level of impairment, and salaries complicate estimates. However, the programs surveyed report an astonishing range of costs—some more than double others. Wesley Hall, a home-for-the-aged unit described in other sections of this book, cost $42.65 per patient day in 1985 when the two-year project ended. Two purpose-built dementia care units, neither of which seemed to the author to offer the ideal model of care or to demonstrate significant patient changes, reported costs in excess of $140 per patient day in 1988. One New York facility visited reported fees between $160 and $200 per day in 1989. Units in the survey reported costs ranging from $42 per day to $90.42 per day, with a mean of $61.36 per day.

Kwon and White (1988) found that four-fifths of the units surveyed noted a rate for private-pay patients that was higher than the Medicaid rate. Mathew and colleagues (1988) found that 92 percent of the patients in the dementia care unit they surveyed were private pay, significantly higher than the two comparison units. Only two of the facilities surveyed by Mace and Coons reported that unit costs were higher than on other units in the nursing facility, although many this author visited reported higher costs. The percentage of private-pay residents per unit ranged from none to 100 percent, with a mean of 53 percent. Two units in the survey and several that were visited reported that they accepted no Medicaid residents.

Units in the study reported that a new physical plant or major renovations, increased staffing, and increased food costs were the most common sources of cost increases. A major chain also reported, in addition to an increase in food costs, the loss of revenue of one patient room per unit converted to a dayroom. Other nursing facilities reported increased costs due to unreasonable regulations and vast amounts of paperwork. An examination of those changes that might be cost-effective is clearly needed.

## Policies and Expectations Inhibiting Innovation in Nursing Facilities

### Diverse Expectations of the Nursing Facility

The nursing facility is expected to meet the care needs of multiple, diverse groups. At any one time a nursing facility may be providing care to short-stay patients recuperating from an acute episode; old, frail, long-stay patients; bedfast patients who require total care; dying patients; and some who are mentally ill or mentally retarded as well as physically impaired.

The nursing home population has grown older: in 1980, 25.7 percent of the residents were over 85; in 1990, 31.6 percent will be over 85, and they will be sicker (American Health Care Association 1988). In 1985, 91 percent of residents needed assistance in bathing, 63 percent required assistance in transfer, and 55 percent were incontinent; 67 percent of those over 85 had cognitive impairments (U.S. Department of Health and Human Services 1987). Medicare now reimburses hospitals based on the patient's diagnostic grouping. This has led to earlier discharges from hospital and, therefore, admission to the nursing home of people who need more intensive nursing. Many facilities are providing intravenous care, postsurgical care, and stroke rehabilitation.

### A Medically Driven System

Forty-eight percent of most nursing home care is borne by the federal/state Medicaid system (U.S. Congress, Office of Technology Assessment 1987). (Medicare contributes only a small fraction to the total nursing home payment.) If a facility accepts any Medicaid or Medicare residents (almost all rely on Medicaid for a portion of residents), it must meet Medicaid standards for all residents. This funding system essentially shapes care in nursing facilities. Medicaid defines a nursing facility as "an institution which is primarily engaged in providing to residents *skilled nursing care and related services for residents who require medical or nursing care, rehabilitation services for the rehabilitation of injured, disabled, or sick persons, or on a regular basis, health related care and services* to individuals who because of their mental or physical conditions require care and service (above the level of room and board) which can be made available to them only through institutional facilities, and is not primarily for the care and treatment of mental diseases" (U.S. Congress, Omnibus Budget Reconciliation Act [OBRA] 1987, part 2, sec. 1919a). Thus, American nursing home care is a *medically driven* system. To the extent that care of people with dementia does not require primarily medical, rehabilitation, or nursing care, facilities that seek to provide specialized care must work against the system.

In conflict with this emphasis on medical care is the expectation that the nursing facility be a home. With many roles, it is difficult to determine what expectations are reasonable and should be met. If the nursing facility is to care for those with dementia, which needs is it expected to meet: Custodial? Medical? Psychosocial? Mental health? Support of the family?

## Public Ambivalence about the Provision of Mental Health Care

Although most of the dementing illnesses are not psychotic diseases, the need for a psychiatric role in the care of people with dementia is clear: Rovner and colleagues (1986) and Chandler and Chandler (1988) found high rates of psychiatric symptomatology in people with dementia. Yet there is virtually no reimbursement for mental health care in nursing facilities. Instead, a facility in which more than half the residents are identified as mentally ill (and are not demented) loses its Medicaid-eligible status (U.S. Department of Health and Human Services, Health Care Financing Administration [HCFA] 1986). The status of facilities that provide mental health services to people with dementia is unclear, but several facilities have told the author they have terminated agreements with outside mental health providers to avoid the risk of decertification.

The 1987 OBRA requires that all nursing facility residents be screened to prevent inappropriate placement of those who are mentally ill or mentally retarded. Federal regulatory language (U.S. Department of Health and Human Services, HCFA 1989) requires that the state provide treatment regardless of site of residence, but no federal funds are allocated for this. The impact of this legislation on dementia will not be clear for some time, but the confusion itself may discourage mental health input in dementia-specific units.

### Custodial Reimbursement Rates

Reimbursement rates and salaries have not kept pace with the increased severity of resident illness or the need for mental health services. Medicaid reimbursement in some states reflects an expectation of custodial, rather than therapeutic or homelike, care. Although the 1987 OBRA put into law standards of care including requirements that the nursing facility ensure that the resident "attain or maintain the highest practicable physical, mental, and psychosocial well-being," no additional funding was allocated to carry this out. Some existing dementia-specific units are now limited to private-pay patients, but most people with dementia will outlive their funds and need Medicaid. Units that accept Medicaid patients must maintain enough private patients and charge them a high enough rate to offset their losses on Medicaid patients.

### Inadequate Physician Services

The medical care system focuses on acute, high-technology interventions; few physicians have been trained in the management of chronic geriatric disease. Several factors, including reimbursement, ageism, and lack of trained nursing facility staff, have made medical care in the nursing facility unattractive to physicians. People with dementia are highly vulnerable to excess disability from concurrent illness and medications (Larson et al. 1985). Without adequate medical interventions, the efforts of the staff to reduce behavior problems and maximize function are severely hampered.

### Staff Shortages and Limited Staff Training

Staff shortages also hamper the development of expert care. At present there is a nursing shortage; in addition, because of low salaries and low prestige, nursing facilities often cannot compete with local hospitals for nurses. The problem is so serious that federal law grants exceptions to facilities that cannot recruit the minimum number of nurses required by law (U.S. Congress, OBRA 1987; U.S. Department of Health and Human Services, HCFA 1989). Most nurses have not been trained in geriatrics. Many of those working in nursing homes have had no training in the psychosocial skills essential to care for this population.

Aides, who make up more than two-thirds of the staff (Pynoos and Stacey 1986), are unskilled labor drawn from the bottom of the labor pool. They have a high turnover and present serious management problems. Often they have had no training in patient care. The 1987 OBRA requires that aides receive 75 hours of training, but this is inadequate to prepare them for the multiple demands of the job.

Social work and activity therapy are both essential to successful dementia care. Much of the devastation of a dementing illness is its attack upon one's ability to relate to others, to sustain roles, to maintain purpose and identity, and to control behavior. Social work and activities therapy professionals have the skills to compensate partially for these losses for part of the course of the dementia. However, the medically driven nursing home system de-emphasizes these nonmedical skills. They are rarely budgeted for more than a few hours a week. Pynoos and Stacey (1986) found that only 4 percent of staffs are comprised of "therapeutically oriented staff (OT, PT, social workers, speech pathologists, pathologists and audiologists, and activities workers)." Even private-pay dementia-specific nursing facilities have sometimes failed to invest equally in psychosocial and therapy skills. When dementia-specific programs do hire qualified professionals, the leadership hierarchy may not change: social workers and activity therapists often do not share leadership roles with nurses. Thus, they lack the power to change effectively the lives of their patients.

### Market Forces and Regulations

Nursing homes in the United States are primarily a for-profit industry. In 1985, 75 percent of the nursing facilities in the United States were for-profit; 41.4 percent were affiliated with chains (American Health Care Association [AHCA] 1988). Nursing facilities require high capital outlays: in 1985 the industry reported construction costs of $25,000 per bed (AHCA 1988). For this reason, large units are preferred as more cost-effective, although most experts believe that small units (15 beds or less) are preferable for people with dementia.

In addition to being dependent on two (federal and state) funding systems, the industry is heavily regulated. Some states have controlled rising nursing home (Medicaid) costs by restricting the number of new facilities built: the average occupancy level nationwide is 92.5 percent (AHCA 1988). High occupancy rates and extensive regulation limit free-market forces and discourage small, innovative models for dementia care. There is no incentive to risk major changes and considerable incentive to continue successful strategies with a new marketing approach—Alzheimer's. However, a for-profit industry alone cannot be blamed for failure to be innovative. Economic forces can encourage, as well as discourage, innovation in a for-profit system. The same pressures affect the smaller number of nonprofit facilities.

The regulatory system is frequently cited as the reason facilities continue to follow the established models. As discussed in Chapter 6, the regulatory system is complex and cumbersome, and allows a range of interpretations among individual inspectors. Individual regulations prohibit changes that would benefit the person with dementia; in addition, the complexity of the regulations is itself a powerful disincentive to making changes. A fiscally responsible administrator will stick to models known to be acceptable and risk no innovations that may not be accepted by future inspectors. Even having a long-established record for the quality of its care does not protect a nursing facility from being penalized for a plate of food left for a slow eater.

### Fear of Liability

The acute medical care system has experienced a dramatic increase in the number of lawsuits and the size of payments to claimants. There have been fewer awards in long-term care, but the *fear* of law suits on the part of the states and the facilities limits innovation.

The chronic dementing illnesses are fatal, and their symptoms place the victim at considerable risk of accident and concurrent illness. It may not in all cases be possible to avoid all risk and still maintain quality of life for the patient. For example, nursing homes report that state inspectors have required that unsteady residents not be permitted to ambulate (Orr 1989), although the risks of using restraints in some cases outweigh the risks of ambulation. Regardless of the infrequency of such incidents, the fact that such fears circulate limits innovation. Although families can sign waivers, facilities fear that the courts will not uphold them.

### Lack of Models

Finally, nursing homes launching special care units do not have good models to emulate. Few people have observed any models outside the United States, and some of the best American models have not been licensed as nursing facilities. The explosion of interest has generated a group of "experts," many of whom are aggressively contradicting one another, and another group that is arguing that not enough is known about dementia-specific units to proceed.

It is within this climate that the development of dementia-specific units in nursing homes must be viewed. Domiciliary licensed facilities and international facilities do not operate under the same constraints. A nursing facility license is the only access to public funds for care, and care is too expensive to support more than a few private facilities. Because Medicaid/Medicare regulations are often used as a model for state licensure requirements, the same factors affect the model of care even in the few all-private facilities. Given these limitations, it is not surprising that most facilities seek ways to superimpose the special services these patients need onto the existing system. Although dementia care units will be seen to vary widely within certain parameters, few venture to make changes that are restricted by the forces described above.

However, these problems do not entirely explain the failure to develop a few highly innovative dementia-specific units in the United States. A few units have been established that rely entirely on private payment. These programs can hire quality staff and contract with geriatricians; they do not fall under federal certification restrictions. Many states, however, incorporate federal standards into state licensing requirements that must be met by all facilities operating in the state (see Chap. 6).

The private, dementia-specific facilities this author visited reported difficulty meeting state licensure. They retained major components of the traditional physical plant and a nurse-led hierarchical management approach. They hired qualified social workers and activity therapists, but these professionals consistently reported that they lacked power within the system. Although activities time was commonly increased, the approach and goals of therapy remained inappropriate for people with dementia.

Such facilities raise many more questions than answers about the factors that influence dementia-specific units. The answers will clearly not be simple to determine or to implement.

## Conclusion

The factors that inhibit change within nursing facilities and the characteristics that this book identifies as being desirable for people with dementia are the same factors that apply to all nursing homes and to most residents of nursing homes. People with dementia may be the most reactive victims of a defective system: it is those with dementia who most often scream, become combative, or require restraints and drugs to control, but others suffer as well. While these patients need certain unique features in dementia-specific units, the changes advocated for the system will benefit all residents.

Other nations are struggling with the same problem—too many people with dementia, not enough money, and facilities providing mediocre care. However, some have been able to create and sustain a few excellent model dementia-specific units.

What is remarkable is not the failures within our system—failures that have been repeatedly documented over 20 years and that apply to all residents—but that so many nursing facilities have effected some changes resulting in improved quality of life for these very difficult patients. The programs surveyed and visited had not been able to make all the changes that might be ideal, yet most reported some evidence of improved quality of life for their residents with dementia. Contrary to the common assumption, people with dementia are highly responsive to their physical and psychosocial environments (Lawton 1981). Our findings support the observation that even small changes can result in improved psychosocial function for the patients, and excellent care results in dramatically improved quality of life.

Many have condemned the marketing approach of some facilities to dementia-specific units, and this chapter has criticized many facets of nursing facilities in the United States. However, the target for criticism is not correctly the individual facility—the administrator, director of nurses, or the aides who are daily caring for difficult people under circumstances that are greatly limiting. If change is to occur, it must occur within the system—those who write regulations, those who enforce them, the American public that supports a medical model of care, and a for-profit system devoid of incentive to change. The implication is not that individual nursing facilities do not provide excellent dementia-specific care. The argument is that the system discourages the growth and success of focused, fine-quality programs and that those who succeed do so in spite of negative pressures. The United States urgently needs a few model units with nursing facility licensure. They will need waivers of some regulations, financial resources, and leadership willing and able to take the risks inherent in trying a new model. Their goal must be to demonstrate the changes in patient psychosocial function that this book has shown to be possible despite a deteriorating disease source.

## Note

1. All references in this chapter to "the survey" refer to this 1988–89 survey of dementia care units by Mace and Coons.

## References

American Health Care Association. 1988. Long-term care data book, source cited, National Center for Health Statistics. Washington, D.C.: American Health Care Association.

Beers, M., J. Avorn, S. B. Soumerai, D. E. Everitt, D. S. Sherman, and S. Salem. 1988. Psychoactive medication use in intermediate-care facility residents. *Journal of the American Medical Association*, 260(20):3016–3020.

Benson, D. M., D. Cameron, E. Humbach, et al. 1987. Establishment and impact of a dementia unit within the nursing home. *Journal of the American Geriatrics Society*, 35(4):319–323.

Bullock, K. M., L. E. Reilly, and D. S. Nies. 1988. An initial evaluation of the Eastern State Hospital special care unit. Unpublished paper.

Calkins, M. P. 1988. *Designing for dementia: Planning environments for the elderly and the confused.* Owings Mills, Md.: National Health Publishing.

Chandler, J. D., and J. E. Chandler. 1988. The prevalence of neuropsychiatric disorders in a nursing home population. *Journal of Geriatric Psychiatry and Neurology,* 1(Apr.):71–76.

Cleary, T. A., C. Clamon, M. Price, and G. Shullaw. 1988. A reduced stimulation unit: Effect on patients with Alzheimer's disease and related disorders. *Gerontologist,* 28(4):511–514.

Cohen, U., and G. D. Weisman. 1991. *Holding on to home.* Baltimore: Johns Hopkins University Press.

Coons, D. H. 1987. Designing a residential care unit for persons with dementia. Washington, D.C.: Congressional Office of Technology Assessment, Contract #633-1950.0.

Coons, D. H. 1988. Wandering. *American Journal of Alzheimer's Care and Research,* 3(1):31–36.

Coons, D. H. 1990. Residential care for persons with dementia: A link in the continuum of care. In *Dementia care: Patient, family, and community,* edited by N. L. Mace. Baltimore: Johns Hopkins University Press.

Edelson, J. S., and W. H. Lyons. 1985. *Institutional care of the mentally impaired elderly.* New York: Van Nostrand Reinhold.

Greene, J. A., J. Asp, and N. Crane. 1985. Specialized management of the Alzheimer's disease patient: Does it make a difference? *Journal of the Tennessee Medical Association,* Sept., 559–563.

Hall, G. R., and K. C. Buckwalter. 1987. Progressively lowered stress threshold: A conceptual model for care of adults with Alzheimer's disease. *Archives of Psychiatric Nursing,* 1(6):399–406.

Hall, G. R., M. V. Kirschling, and S. Todd. 1985. *Sheltered freedom: The creation of an Alzheimer's unit in an intermediate care facility.* Iowa City: University of Iowa Hospitals and Clinics.

Haugen, P. K. 1985. Behavior of patients with dementia. *Danish Medical Bulletin, Journal of the Health Sciences,* Special Supplement Series, no. 1, 62–65.

Hiatt, L. G. 1986. Environmental design and mentally impaired older people. In *Alzheimer's disease: Problems, prospects, and perspectives,* edited by H. J. Altman, 309–320. New York: Plenum Press.

Kwon, O. J., and B. J. White. 1988. Physical aspects of specialized units for Alzheimer's patients in long-term care facilities. Refereed paper for American Association of Housing Educators, Oct.

Larson, E. B., B. V. Reifler, S. M. Sumi, C. G. Canfield, and N. M. Chinn. 1985. Diagnostic evaluation of 200 elderly outpatients with suspected dementia. *Journal of Gerontology,* 40(5):536–543.

Lawton, M. P. 1981. Sensory deprivation and the effect of the environment on management of the patient with senile dementia. In *Clinical aspects of Alzheimer's disease and senile dementia,* edited by N. E. Miller and J. D. Cohen, 227–249. New York: Raven Press.

Mace, N. L. 1990. The management of problem behaviors. In *Dementia care: Patient, family, and community*, edited by N. L. Mace. Baltimore: Johns Hopkins University Press.

Mathew, L., P. Sloan, M. Kilby, and R. Flood. 1988. What's different about a special care unit for dementia patients? A comparative study. *American Journal of Alzheimer's Care and Research*, 3(2):16–23.

Miller, E. 1977. The management of dementia: A review of some possibilities. *British Journal of Sociology and Clinical Psychology*, 16:77–83.

Ohta, R. J., and B. M. Ohta. 1988. Special units for Alzheimer's disease patients: A critical look. *Gerontologist*, 28(6):803–808.

Orr, N. 1989. Personal communication.

Pynoos, J., and C. A. Stacey. 1986. Specialized facilities for senile dementia patients. In *The dementias: Policy and management*, edited by M. L. M. Gilhooly, S. H. Zarit, and J. E. Birren, 111–130. Englewood Cliffs, N.J.: Prentice-Hall.

Rader, J. 1987. Dealing with agenda behavior: A method for decreasing confusion, wandering, restlessness and combativeness in the elderly. Benedictine Nursing Center, Mt. Angel, Oreg. Unpublished paper.

Rovner, B. W., S. Calanek, L. Filipp, et al. 1986. Prevalence of mental illness in a community nursing home. *American Journal of Psychiatry*, 143:1446–1449.

Sawyer, J., and A. A. Mendlovitz. 1982. A management program for ambulatory institutionalized patients with Alzheimer's disease and related disorders. Paper presented at the annual conference of the Gerontological Society, Nov. 21.

Sloan, P. No date. Report in progress.

U.S. Congress. 1987. Omnibus Reconciliation Act, Public Law 100-203, Dec. 22, subtitle C, part 2, sec. 1919a.

U.S. Congress, Office of Technology Assessment. 1987. *Losing a million minds: Confronting the tragedy of Alzheimer's disease and other dementias*. OTA-BA-323. Washington, D.C.: U.S. Government Printing Office.

U.S. Department of Health and Human Services. 1987. Advance data. Use of nursing homes by the elderly: Preliminary data from the 1985 National Nursing Home Survey, no. 135, May 14.

U.S. Department of Health and Human Services, Health Care Financing Administration. 1986. Pub. 45-4, State Medical Manual, part 4, Services, sec. 4390, Sept.

U.S. Department of Health and Human Services, Health Care Financing Administration. 1989. Federal Register, Feb. 2, 42CFR, part 405 et al. Medicare and Medicaid: Requirements for long-term care facilities; final rule with request for comments.

Zgola, J. M. 1987. *Doing things*. Baltimore: Johns Hopkins University Press.

# Chapter 5

# Architectural Planning and Design for Dementia Care Units

GERALD D. WEISMAN, M. ARCH., PH.D.,
URIEL COHEN, D. ARCH., KEYA RAY,
M. ARCH., AND KRISTEN DAY, B. ARCH.

This chapter focuses on the architectural planning and design of care units for people with Alzheimer's disease and related dementias. Attention is turned first to the potential therapeutic role of the architectural environment and to a conceptual framework for analysis, planning, and design. The second section of the chapter presents more detailed guidelines for the planning and design of dementia care units; the topics reviewed include program and location, key dimensions of the environmental experience, spatial organization of the unit, and design criteria for selected activity areas. Two prototypical designs—each illustrating one possible integration of these guidelines—are presented in the third section. The chapter concludes with a discussion of some of the major unresolved issues in the architectural planning and design of dementia care units.

## The Therapeutic Role of the Architectural Environment

The success of architectural planning and design efforts for special user groups, such as people with Alzheimer's disease and related dementias, depends upon two fundamental and interrelated assumptions. First, it should be recognized that the role of the physical environment need not be limited to the simple provision of shelter; the environment represents a potentially important, albeit frequently underutilized, therapeutic intervention. Furthermore, it must be recognized that the physical environment does not exist in isolation; rather, the physical setting is an integral part of a larger, complex system. To realize their therapeutic potential, settings such as dementia care units must be designed, and must function, in concert with the social and organizational dimensions of the larger systems of which they are a part. This section, therefore, presents a conceptual framework that reflects the interaction of these complex systems and explicitly incorporates therapeutic goals within the model.

### Conceptual Framework: The Environment As a Complex System

The environments inhabited by people with dementia and those who care for them constitute a complex system composed of organizational, social, and architectural factors that interact in multiple ways. This is no less true for people residing in dementia care units than for those in the community. For purposes of analysis, programming, and design, environments of people with dementia can be conceptualized in terms of a five-part framework (see Figure 5.1).

First and foremost are *people with dementia*, defined in terms of their physical, functional, and emotional needs as determined by the characteristics of their disease (see Chaps. 3, 12, and 14).

Second is *therapeutic goals*. In response to the nature and needs of people with dementia, many authors present therapeutic goals such as "preservation of dignity" or "maximizing independence." Such goals, while clearly abstract in themselves, provide guidance and direction for subsequent decisions regarding organizational and social planning as well as architectural design.

The final three components of this project framework are the *organizational, social,* and *physical environments* within which people with dementia live. The organizational context is conceptualized in terms of the policies and program of a dementia care unit. The social context is represented by family and friends who serve as informal caregivers and by the staff. The physical setting is defined in terms of the unit's materials and finishes, furnishings and equipment, and sensory and spatial properties.

While the primary goal of this chapter is to present guidelines for the design of the physical settings of dementia care units, architectural variables cannot be considered in isolation; the other dimensions of the framework must be taken into account as well. Whether or not a person with dementia will experience a facility as sufficiently private is a consequence not only of building design but also of organizational policy and the behaviors and attitudes of other residents, staff members, families, and friends. Furthermore, the environment—as defined in physical, social, and organizational terms—will over time

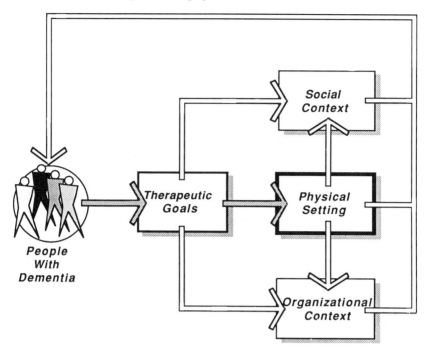

**Figure 5.1.** A conceptual framework for environments for people with dementia

have an impact, positive or negative, upon people with dementia. With the emergence in recent years of the field of environmental psychology (e.g., Holahan 1982; Gifford 1987) has come the realization that the environment is more than a background variable the influence of which needs to be controlled; there is increasing evidence of the impact of the environmental context upon human behavior. Principles for design not only respond to the therapeutic goals that reflect the nature and needs of people with dementia but may also, over time, influence them as well.

### Therapeutic Goals

A review of the literature on dementia and design (Rand et al. 1987) reveals a variety of therapeutic goals intended to provide direction in the creation of appropriate and supportive environments. To the extent that such goals specify desired relationships between people with dementia and their social, organizational, and physical environment, they can provide an important basis and direction for policy, programing, and design decisions for dementia care units.

The following set of goals has been distilled from our review of the literature and has proved useful in both the analysis and the design of environments for people with dementia.

*Safety and security.* Ensuring that users sustain no harm is the first imperative of any therapeutic environment. As emphasized by Calkins (1988), people with dementia are potentially vulnerable as a consequence of not only cognitive impairment but also physical disabilities related to the process of aging as well as the dementing illness. Thus, it is essential to ensure the physical safety and psychological security of people with dementia. In addition to life-saving issues (e.g., fire-retardant construction, adequate emergency exits), the physical environment may impact the safety and security of people with dementia in less obvious ways. Thus, design problems might include the absence of adequate grab bars, an unsecured gas stove, or, on a larger scale, floor plan configurations that thwart staff supervision of residents.

*The support of functional ability.* Both Mace (1987) and Peppard (1986) emphasized the importance of maintaining those abilities not totally impaired by dementia. Support of the highest level of functional ability can have important and positive implications for the sense of competence and self-esteem of people with dementia. This goal can be furthered both by the provision of prosthetic devices that compensate for limited ability (e.g., handrails in corridors to facilitate walking) and by spaces or equipment that support familiar activities of daily living (e.g., modest cooking or housekeeping facilities).

*Awareness and orientation.* Program, policy, and design should all assist people with dementia in "knowing where they are" in spatial, temporal, and social terms. Disorientation brought on by confusing, illegible, and unpredictable environments can be decreased. Clear paths to desired destinations, differentiation or elimination of repetitive forms, and physical landmarks are among the possible interventions.

*Environmental stimulation and challenge.* People with dementia may not be able to process high levels of stimulation without experiencing overload and distress; conversely, many institutional settings represent a degree of sensory and social deprivation that is clearly not therapeutic. The physical environment can provide "unobtrusive" stimulation (e.g., views to the outdoors, color schemes, things to touch) that does not overwhelm residents.

*A positive social milieu.* Providing opportunities for social interaction and maintaining some degree of challenge might slow the atrophy of skills, reduce deprivation, and enhance the quality of life (Lawton et al. 1984). The physical environment can provide opportunities for involvement, from places for passive viewing of activities to an arena for participatory activities (e.g., a domestic kitchenette).

*Privacy and control.* People with dementia should, to the greatest extent possible, have the ability to make decisions and to take responsibility for their own lives and environments. "Personalization" of one's own space can foster a degree of individuality. Control over social and environmental stimuli can be supported by places for retreat and reflection offering a lower degree of sensory input.

*Adaptability to the changing needs of people with dementia.* It is essential to respond to the changing needs of residents and evolving therapeutic approaches, and to determine the level of ability a given therapeutic facility is capable of handling. A flexible design can provide a better fit between varying levels of residents' competence and the environmental demands to which they are exposed.

*The healthy and familiar.* Patients with dementia are confronted with an ongoing series of changes in themselves and their world. Thus, it is important to maintain, to the extent possible, their ties to the familiar. Patterning the facility after familiar environments—the home and the past—can provide a "soft transition" to the institution (Mace and Rabins 1981). "Things from the past" and "homelike environments" are directions for many design applications.

## Guidelines for Planning and Design

The following guidelines for the planning and design of dementia care units are the product of an iterative process of development and are based upon the existing, albeit limited, literature on dementia and design, site visits to dementia care units, and consultations with experts in the field.[1] Given the newness of the field, the limited research, and the small number of significant demonstration projects, these guidelines are best viewed not as inflexible directives but as an effort to expand and stimulate thinking on the relationships between dementia and design; thus, they are hypotheses amenable to, and requiring, implementation and validation.

The following presentation of guidelines is organized in a clear hierarchy of environmental scale, from location and site concerns to micro-scale issues. Broad issues of philosophy, policy, and location are considered first. These are followed by principles that deal with environmental "characteristics" or "experiential qualities" and then principles for the overall spatial organization of dementia care units. The final set of principles focuses on individual activity areas.

It should be noted that only limited attention is given here to those architectural features—for example, colors, materials, finishes, square footage allocations—that most people associate with the relationship between the environment and human behavior. While such variables may be quite important, their impact upon people with dementia is not always simple or direct; rather, it comes through the contribution of features and general attributes of the environment such as accessibility, stimulation, or privacy. Furthermore, such environmental attributes are typically most helpful in understanding and defining the therapeutic potential of physical settings.

### Policy and Planning Decisions

The first sets of decisions to be made in the planning and design of a dementia care unit are not fundamentally architectural in character; they are most clearly in the province of facility administrators and staff. However, their implications for the design of the physical setting are profound and pervasive. These key decisions are briefly reviewed here to ensure that they are consciously and carefully considered in the overall planning and design process and are not simply made by default.

*Expanding the continuum of care.* Living options for people with dementia are typically conceptualized in terms of a small number of familiar environments: one's own home in the community; group homes; long-term care facilities. It is critical to recognize, however, that what currently exists is not synonymous with what is possible. Indeed, some of the most creative and important approaches to the planning and design of dementia care units (see Chap. 3) demonstrate that new living options are both necessary and possible.

As illustrated in Figure 5.1, the environment of dementia care units is defined by the interaction of organizational factors (i.e., policy, program, and services), the social environment (i.e., formal and informal caregivers) and the physical setting. By combining these three subsystems in new and creative ways, it is possible to expand the continuum of care available to people with dementia. In long-term care facilities, for example, environments for people with dementia can be made less restrictive and more homelike. This approach might result in the de-emphasis or elimination of the nursing station, creation of more shared spaces for social contact, and reduced use of hard, institutional materials and finishes such as tile, terrazzo, or vinyl.

*Tapping local resources.* It is essential to recognize that a dementia care unit is not an independent entity; rather, it exists in a larger environmental context that can provide important opportunities.

Among the most important local resources are those family members and friends who may serve as informal caregivers and thus make significant contributions to the social environment of a dementia care unit. Decisions regarding the location of such a unit can either strengthen or weaken these ties.

Proximity or easy access to specialized medical facilities can alleviate the need for the costly provision of these services within a dementia care unit. In addition to possible economic benefits, the removal of such services from a unit can reduce its institutional or "medical" character and create a more homelike and familiar environment.

*Smaller groups of residents.* The transition from the small-scale residential environment to a larger-scale group living situation can be stressful for anyone, often especially so for people with dementia. New residents may be overwhelmed by a complex and unfamiliar environment (Peppard 1986) and may experience confusion, frustration, and feelings of helplessness. They are often removed from their everyday social support network of family and friends as well as the familiarity of their home, neighborhood, and, in some cases, community.

Such problems may be ameliorated by the creation of smaller groups of residents, more on the scale of "family" as opposed to "institution." Group size in institutional settings is often defined solely in terms of the number of residents under the supervision of a staff member (e.g., the number of residents in the nursing unit of a traditional long-term care facility). However, it is possible to break such functional groups down into smaller social groups, often referred to as "households," "families," or "clusters."

To emphasize further the concept of social groups, activity areas should be contiguous to a cluster of residents' rooms. Such areas can then become the center of "household" activities, with these households functioning as self-contained units accommodating common functions such as dining. Staff-resident ratios need not necessarily be higher in such cluster arrangements than in typical nursing units. Indeed, some authors and administrators have suggested the creation of smaller groups of residents intensifies and enhances resident-staff relationships and contributes to a perception among staff members that tasks are more manageable.

A variety of architectural strategies can be employed to reinforce spatially the organization of residents into smaller groups. Shared spaces can be created for each such grouping; these spaces can serve the traditional functions of dining room, living room, or kitchen and can be so described and named (see Figure 5.2).

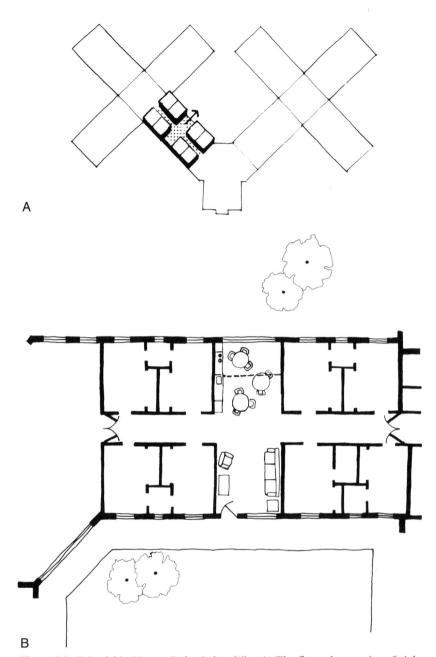

A

B

**Figure 5.2.** Friendship House, Cedar Lakes, Wis. (A) The floor plan consists of eight identical and identifiable modules of "households." (B) Each "household" includes eight double rooms. In most cases, two resident rooms share a bath. At the center of each household is a "living room" and a "dining room/kitchen" located to either side of the central corridor

## The General Attributes of the Environment

As emphasized in the introduction to this set of guidelines, one's experience of and behavior in a particular environment are often most strongly influenced not by the specific architectural features of the setting but by its more general qualities. In the planning and design of dementia care units, four such attributes appear to be particularly salient: image, negotiability, familiarity, and stimulation. In each case it should be remembered that these attributes are a function not only of the physical environment but also of the interactions of physical, organizational, and social subsystems. Thus, the creation of a more homelike environment requires appropriate furnishings and finishes, patterns of ongoing activity typical of residential settings, and policies and programs supportive of such residential activities.

*A noninstitutional image.* It has already been stressed that, because of the many changes confronting people with dementia, it is important for them to maintain their ties to the healthy and familiar. A dementia care unit patterned after the outside community and its residential imagery—rather than after the medical model of the hospital and nursing home—can assist people with dementia in retaining these ties.

Breaking down the monolithic character typical of many hospitals and nursing homes is a necessary first step in creating environments more in keeping with the scale of human beings. Externally, this can be achieved by creating smaller interconnected units as opposed to a larger monolithic structure (see Figure 5.3); internally, it can be achieved by breaking down the organizational as well as the physical structure of the people with dementia (see "Smaller Groups of Residents"). The reduced use of materials like ceramic tile and stainless steel, typically selected for their indestructibility, can reduce the institutional ambience; avoiding a totally uniform visual appearance throughout the facility can also contribute to this goal.

*More negotiable environments.* While considerable attention has been directed in recent years to the creation of "barrier-free environments" (ANSI 1980), truly accessible or "negotiable" settings for people with dementia must respond to additional demands. Dementing illnesses may often exacerbate common age-related problems in performing seemingly simple tasks such as knitting, fastening buttons, or closing snaps. It may be equally difficult to utilize a variety of "control devices" in the microenvironment such as appliance dials, door handles, or telephones. Such difficulties reflect a variety of factors (Mace and Rabins 1981); these include apraxia (whereby messages

**Figure 5.3** Wesley Woods Geriatric Hospital, Atlanta, Ga. The wood siding exterior, pitched shingle roof, articulated units within the overall plan, and sitting on a gentle hill surrounded by trees introduce the human scale and minimize the institutional image. Designed by Preston Stevens, F.A.I.A.

from the brain may not be transmitted to hands and fingers), tremors, muscle weakness, and vision problems.

In addition to the more familiar requirements for barrier-free design (ANSI 1980), a variety of strategies may be employed to mitigate hazards and overcome barriers to negotiability in dementia care units. Pastalan (1979) proposed the concept of redundant cuing, whereby the same information is presented via several sensory modalities; at the micro scale, light switches can be made conspicuous through color as well as form.

Objects in the microenvironment of the dementia care unit can often be designed with enhanced anthropometric fit to compensate for the decreased abilities (e.g., hand-eye coordination or visual acuity) of people with dementia. Examples would include lever-action handles instead of doorknobs or pressure-plate light controls instead of the common switch. Koncelik (1976) proposed the use of objects of self-correcting design in the microenvironment; such objects might include door locks with recessed tumblers to "guide" the key, thus directing and correcting the movements of people with dementia.

*Things from the past.* While people with dementia often cannot remember recent events (Gwyther 1986), their long-term memory remains relatively intact until the later stages of the disease. Furthermore, the emotional components of memory may remain even after other components are lost (Coons 1985). The utilization of familiar objects—things from the past—can provide opportunities for the exercise and celebration of these remaining capabilities.

The use of things from the past can assist in the retention of ties to the healthy and familiar through the creation of more personalized and homelike environments, particularly for people newly relocated to dementia care units. Articles and events from the past provide people with dementia the opportunity to reflect upon past experiences and environments (Rapelje et al. 1981); such emotions and memories often serve to stimulate social interaction. In particular, the ability of residents to bring some of their own belongings and furniture to the unit can foster a more familiar environment. Links to the past may be created in a variety of ways. Objects from the past may be dispersed throughout the public areas of a unit or aggregated in a "museum" area.

*Sensory stimulation without stress.* Levels of sensory and social stimulation in environments for people with dementia may differ dramatically from those most commonly encountered in home environments. In some instances, there may be a virtual absence of stimulation characterized, for example, by monochromatic, repetitive spaces with little or no ongoing activity. In other cases, people with dementia may be bombarded by very high levels of stimulation including intercoms, alarms, or bright lights glaring on polished surfaces.

Attention must be paid, therefore, to regulating the character and intensity of stimulation in dementia care units. The goal, in Mace's (1987) terms, is "stimulation but not stress." Among the design strategies available for such regulation are two complementary approaches also employed for negotiability: the *amplification of the message* and the *dampening of extraneous stimuli*. Message amplification can be achieved by heightened contrast or redundant cuing, while dampening might include the use of sound-absorbing materials, the elimination of intercoms, or the "painting out" of doors to service spaces.

## Building Organization

In contrast with the preceding set of general environmental guidelines, this group is more physical in character, focusing on architectural rather than policy and program variables. Specifically, the common theme of the following guidelines is the arrangement of spaces relative to one another, to provide areas for specialized activities, define levels of privacy, or ensure views to the exterior.

*Family clusters.* Relocation to an institutional setting often presents people with dementia with major discontinuities in their social, organizational, and physical environments. Such transitions, and the overwhelming complexity and unfamiliarity they present, can be extremely stressful (Peppard 1986). Further confusion results when people with dementia are expected to carry out their normal patterns of behavior in a new setting to which they cannot easily relate. It is important, therefore, to create a physical and social environment that can aid in orienting people with dementia and in facilitating their adjustment to the new environment. Moreover, the social structure of "family clusters" should be supported through a physical organization of space that allows for the creation of independent territories for each family.

A necessary first step in the creation of such family clusters would be the grouping or clustering of residents' rooms. In addition, a rich mix of residential activities should be provided to emulate as closely as possible those found in homes. Together with providing opportunities for the full range of residential activities, the environment should allow a clear identification of different activity areas to help orient people with dementia. As in most single-family homes, the activity areas for family clusters should be contiguous to the cluster of residents' rooms. This would help define a public space at the scale of the family cluster for "household" activities (see Figure 5.4).

*Opportunities for meaningful wandering.* Wandering is one of the many difficult behaviors attributed to people with dementia. Gilleard (1984) and Coons (1988) identified three types of wandering behavior most commonly found among people with dementia: (1) wandering as a consequence of disorientation, which may be as much a result of an illegible environment as it is of an incapacitated resident; (2) habitual activity stemming from previous experience; and (3) restless seeking of activity, typically found in environments that provide very little to engage residents.

To reduce wandering from disorientation, the design should ensure that the environment is easily read and the people do not get lost. Thus, repetitive modules should be avoided and memorable and unique landmarks should be introduced to provide residents with orientation cues.

Recognizing and accepting wandering as a habitual activity for some residents, walking paths should allow for more than mere physical exercise. Such paths should allow residents opportunities for passive involvement in activities without requiring them to participate, thus exposing them to social/sensory stimulation (see Figure 5.5). Coons (1988) contended that in a rich and supportive environment that provides residents with opportunities for involvement and participation, wandering behavior actually subsides.

*Positive outdoor spaces.* Outdoor spaces can provide unique and relatively inexpensive settings to meet a wide range of needs, pro-

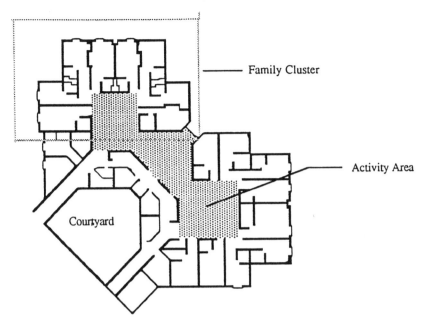

**Figure 5.4.** The generic butterfly plan, by Preston Stevens, F.A.I.A. The butterfly plan represents a relatively recent and innovative plan organization. It is intended to provide communal areas adjacent to each "family" of 12 residents and to avoid the typical institutional corridor. These common spaces can be used for a variety of "residential" and "family" activities

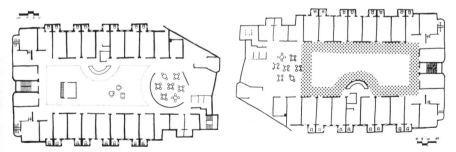

**Figure 5.5.** Philadelphia Geriatric Center. The continuous indoor loop serves as a wandering path. In addition to being a continuous loop, the path allows views to activity areas, thereby exposing residents to ongoing activities and the stimulation they generate

viding variety and choice by allowing opportunities for both socializing and retreat within a safe and controlled environment. The
outdoor environment is an excellent tool for enhancing a nonmedical,
noninstitutional, positive image for residents, staff, and families.
Such spaces also provide an important link with natural elements.

Wheelchair-accessible raised planting beds can provide residents
with opportunities for gardening. Water features, such as pools,
fountains, and waterfalls, located in well-landscaped outdoor spaces
can provide visual, tactile, and auditory stimulation, while places for
pets might establish links with the past. Outdoor spaces should,
however, be simple and safe from physical and perceptual obstacles
to movement and ambulation, and they should allow for easy
surveillance. Enclosures should be defined as unobtrusively as possible (e.g., by plants or building mass) so as not to be either obvious
or disturbing to residents. Recognizing the physical frailty of elderly
dementia patients, outdoor spaces should have a positive microclimate
that ensures protection from excessive sun or harsh winds.

Large, undifferentiated open spaces may be counterproductive
and disorienting for people with dementia. Open spaces should
therefore be differentiated by means of alcoves that can provide both
settings for group activities and places for solitude and retreat. Such
spaces can serve as interest points along an outdoor walking path,
aid in spatial orientation, and create an outdoor environment offering
a rich mix of activities.

### Activity Area Guidelines

This final set of guidelines focuses on several of the most important
spaces within a dementia care unit; these include residents' rooms,
common areas, and places for visiting. While areas for other activities
such as entry and staff work are of course also significant, space
limitations preclude a detailed consideration of them here.[2]

*Residents' rooms.* In the single-family homes in which most Americans reside, the bedroom constitutes the most private region of the
house, where the activities of sleeping, grooming, dressing, and
bathing take place. In traditional long-term care facilities, however,
residents' rooms must serve as the setting for a broad range of public
as well as private activities. The occupants of these rooms, therefore,
are forced to relinquish the right to privacy that most people take
for granted. Also lost is the clear identification of function that can
prompt and support appropriate patterns of behavior. The planning
and design of a dementia care unit, therefore, must heed the
traditional role of the bedroom as well as eliminate conflicts between

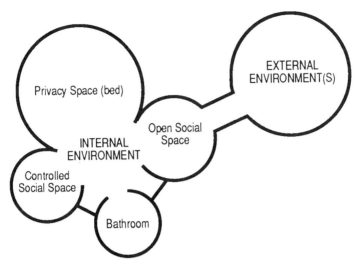

**Figure 5.6.** The "sitting room" concept, after Koncelik (1976). Koncelik's conceptual diagram for the organization of a resident's room in a long-term care facility includes both "controlled" and "open" social spaces as buffers between private and public areas

those functions that are relatively public and those that remain fundamentally private (see Figure 5.6).

*Common areas for each family.* The design of public areas within the dementia care unit should support the social structure of family clusters through the physical organization of space. The continuum of spaces should ideally range from the essentially private resident room to the shared public areas of activity within each family cluster. In the design of these common areas, one should bear in mind the goal of increasing social interaction among residents as well as providing opportunities for individuality, privacy, and control.

One appropriate technique for establishing common areas involves the centralization of various activities at the core of each family cluster. This activity core becomes the public center of the cluster, much as the living room, dining room, and kitchen represent the core of family homes. Activity areas should be established adjacent to, but not interrupted by, circulation paths (Howell 1980). This makes activities highly visible, thereby encouraging use, but does not force participation or lead to disruption. When possible, it is desirable to carve small subspaces out of larger activity areas to create alcoves for passive participation or retreat, again in recognition of residents' need for privacy.

Finally, common areas should be roughly complementary to those

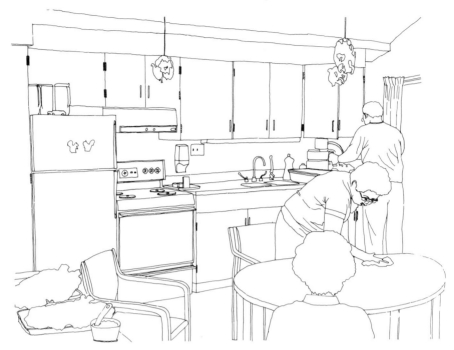

**Figure 5.7.** This example shows a truly small dining area with its own kitchen, used for preparing beverages and snacks for 16 residents. The domestic ambience of this setting maintains ties to the heathy and familiar, while the residential scale facilitates social interaction among residents

found within homes in terms of both scale and ambience. These domestic qualities will reinforce the residential nature of the space and highlight the ordinary activities of daily living, some of which might be as simple as food preparation in a small kitchenette or family activity around the dining room table (see Figure 5.7).

*Dining areas.* While there is no evidence to suggest that meals are as highly anticipated by people with dementia as they are by the general population, there is evidence that stress can accompany this activity (Snyder 1984; Hiatt 1981; Roach 1985), often as a consequence of the loss of ability to feed oneself and increased difficulty in the manipulation of utensils. Large, undifferentiated dining areas often provide overstimulation as a consequence of too much noise and too many people, leading to agitation and confusion. Mealtimes, however, can still hold the potential for being social as well as nutritional activities. Maintenance of the eating patterns developed over an individual's lifetime can provide continuity with the past and increase the scope for reminiscence.

Spatial organization that breaks dining spaces into separate sub-rooms or zones can reduce the institutional image associated with a dining hall seating large numbers of people at long tables. Intimate dining areas with smaller tables seating family-size groups of two to six people can evoke associations of home, be comfortable for residents, and be more manageable for staff. Noninstitutional furniture together with a residential decor can help create a domestic ambience, de-institutionalize the space, and evoke associations of home.

*Places for visiting.* Visits from family and friends are an important component in the lives of people residing in dementia care units. It is therefore important for these facilities to provide spaces for visiting other than residents' rooms, crowded dayrooms, or corridors that do not readily accommodate such activities. It is reasonable to assume that, at least in the early stages of the disease, residents might benefit from environments that offer opportunities for private conversations. Environments supportive of visitors' needs might encourage more frequent visits, which would likely prove beneficial to residents, family members, and the staff. To this end, residents and their visitors should have the opportunity to meet and converse in small, intimate settings.

Persons with dementia may become passive. Visiting can then become a very frustrating time for family members, who might find conversation difficult. Spaces for visiting might remedy this situation by including things from the past to act as catalysts for conversation with people with dementia, whose long-term memory may be relatively intact. It would also be useful for such spaces to offer "something to do." Places for visiting can have links to the outside to enable visitors to take a walk with a resident, or can provide simple games that residents and visitors could play together (see Figures 5.8 and 5.9).

## Prototypical Design Applications

The guidelines presented above are meant to be suggestive, not dogmatic. As such, they can clearly be combined in many different ways, to respond to varying contexts. To illustrate the great freedom and variation inherent in the use of such guidelines, two prototypical design applications have been developed.[3] Both schemes of course represent "ideal" solutions and would have to be tempered by the realities of organization, resident mix, site, facility, and program.

The first such application reflects both the preceding guidelines

**Figure 5.8.** Outdoor Courtyard, Shorehaven, Oconomowoc, Wis. This outdoor court-yard in a long-term care facility is easily accessible from public spaces for visiting. The paved paths of the courtyard and the beautiful landscape make it an ideal spot to take a walk for "something to do" with residents

and knowledge derived from the Wesley Hall experience (see Chap. 3). The criteria used in designing the freestanding home (Figure 5.10) include the following:

1. Creation of small, homelike clusters
2. Avoidance of long, double-loaded corridors
3. Absence of the institutional nursing station
4. Inclusion of single-resident rooms to provide privacy and to enable each room to be furnished with personal furniture and memorabilia
5. Presence of common activity areas with clearly differentiated and comfortably scaled zones that are easily visible to residents when they leave their rooms
6. Existence of safe walking areas both indoors and outdoors
7. Inclusion of baths and toilets that ensure privacy
8. Provision of an environment that supports and encourages normal everyday activities and a continuation of normal social roles.

**Figure 5.9.** An activity corner in a day-care center. This activity center provides "something to do" to spark interaction during visiting. It includes spaces for simple crafts that visitors can do together with the residents, as well as things from the past to trigger remembering

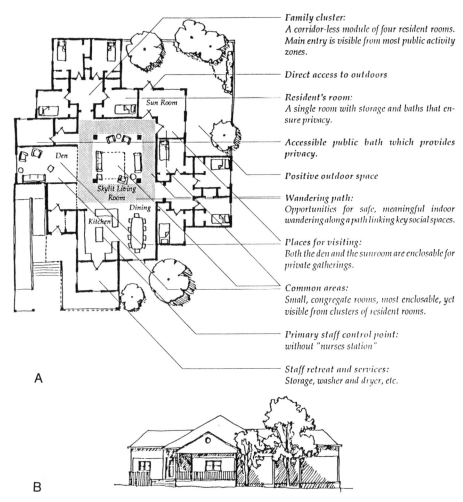

**Family cluster:**
*A corridor-less module of four resident rooms. Main entry is visible from most public activity zones.*

**Direct access to outdoors**

**Resident's room:**
*A single room with storage and baths that ensure privacy.*

**Accessible public bath which provides privacy.**

**Positive outdoor space**

**Wandering path:**
*Opportunities for safe, meaningful indoor wandering along a path linking key social spaces.*

**Places for visiting:**
*Both the den and the sunroom are enclosable for private gatherings.*

**Common areas:**
*Small, congregate rooms, most enclosable, yet visible from clusters of resident rooms.*

**Primary staff control point:**
*without "nurses station"*

**Staff retreat and services:**
*Storage, washer and dryer, etc.*

**Figure 5.10.** A freestanding group home with residential scale and domestic features for eight residents. (A) Floor plan. (B) Entry facade. Designed by U. Cohen, G. D. Weisman, J. T. Dicker, G. C. Meyer, and B. Robison

This model, offered here as a freestanding home, could also be used in the designing of dementia care units within retirement and nursing homes.

The second application (Figures 5.11 and 5.12) illustrates the restructuring of a nursing unit of the sort typically found in long-term care settings. Except for the double-occupancy rooms, the plan follows the criteria applied to the freestanding home.

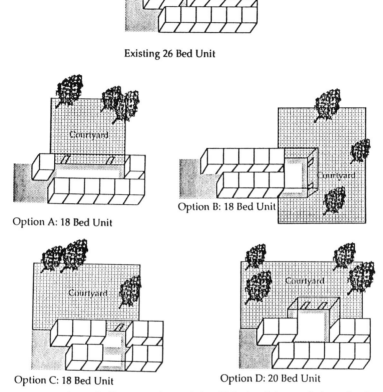

**Figure 5.11.** Schematic diagrams of an existing 26-bed unit in a typical nursing home, and four design approaches for adding "quality of life" attributes during a conversion

## Conclusion: Unresolved Issues

Recognizing the newness of this field and the limited literature addressing dementia and design, it is impossible to identify all the important areas of research that still need to be investigated. However, it is useful to point out some examples of unresolved questions to suggest potential directions for inquiry into the design-dementia relationship. The following examples have been organized in a hierarchy according to environmental scale.

*Policy and planning decisions.* An important issue at this level concerns the limited nature of the present continuum of care. What are the innovative alternatives to the traditional housing modes available to people with dementia (e.g., home, day-care, group home, long-

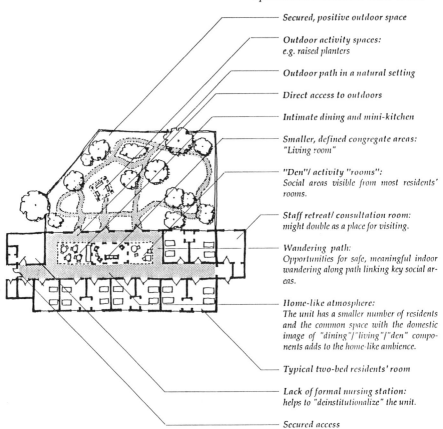

Secured, positive outdoor space

Outdoor activity spaces:
e.g. raised planters

Outdoor path in a natural setting

Direct access to outdoors

Intimate dining and mini-kitchen

Smaller, defined congregate areas:
"Living room"

"Den"/ activity "rooms":
Social areas visible from most residents'
rooms.

Staff retreat/ consultation room:
might double as a place for visiting.

Wandering path:
Opportunities for safe, meaningful indoor
wandering along path linking key social areas.

Home-like atmosphere:
The unit has a smaller number of residents
and the common space with the domestic
image of "dining"/"living"/"den" components adds to the home-like ambience.

Typical two-bed residents' room

Lack of formal nursing station:
helps to "deinstitutionalize" the unit.

Secured access

**Figure 5.12.** The floor plan of a nursing unit converted into an 18-person unit.
Designed by U. Cohen, G. D. Weisman, J. T. Dicker, G. C. Meyer, and B. Robison

term care facility)? More specifically, how can the range of services
be increased while maintaining or improving the residential nature
and affordability of the housing options available to people with
dementia?

More general questions involve the overall impact of the facility,
as well as its proper attitude and philosophy. What are the effects of
the environment on residents' affect, emotions, behaviors, and general sense of well-being? How can the environment help residents
continue to use their remaining capacities to the maximum? What is
the impact of the environment of a long-term care facility on a
resident's spouse and family members? More specifically, can an
environment with greater residential and humane attributes affect
the satisfaction, frequency, and duration of visits of spouses and

other family members? If so, does an increase in the frequency and duration of visits improve the quality of life for residents, either directly (i.e., more participation) or indirectly (i.e., more visitors, contributing to a homelike environment)?

*General attributes of the environment.* The whole territory of sensory stimulation and sensory underload/overload, as it relates to people with dementia, is relatively unexplored. In designing environments for this population, is it preferable to use soft earth tones and pastels, presumably for their soothing effect, or should primary colors be employed, with the objective of enhancing legibility and wayfinding? The behavioral effects associated with various colors are not clearly known, and the research findings are conflicting.

*Building organization and activity spaces.* There is still a great need for research at the scale of the interior of the facility. Residents' rooms exemplify one such area of inquiry. What is the proper function of the resident's room? In congregate living arrangements for people with dementia, is it preferable to provide multiscale common areas for social interaction, reducing the resident's room to only minimal, bedroom status, or is it better to provide spaces for social interaction within the resident's room, perhaps to the exclusion of more common areas?

It is the authors' intention that this chapter, and the hypotheses it presents, will generate further research into these issues, thereby increasing the likelihood of success in designing to support this special population.

## Notes

The research upon which this chapter is based was supported by the Retirement Research Foundation and previous funding from the Health Facilities Research Program of the American Institute of Architects and the Association of Collegiate Schools of Architecture.

1. See Cohen et al. 1988b.
2. For a discussion of these additional activity areas, see ibid.
3. Design prototypes were developed by project architects James T. Dicker (AIA) and George C. Meyer (AIA); Bill Robison; and other members of the project team.

## References

American National Standards Institute. 1980. *Specifications for making buildings and facilities accessible to and usable by physically handicapped people,* ANSI 117.1. New York: American National Standards Association.

Calkins, M. P. 1988. *Designing for dementia: Planning environments for the elderly and the confused.* Owings Mills, Md.: National Health Publishing.

Cohen U., G. Weisman, K. Ray, V. Steiner, J. Rand, and R. Toyne. 1988a. *Environments for people with dementia: Case studies.* Washington, D.C.: Health Facilities Research Program of the American Institute of Architects and the Association of Collegiate Schools of Architecture.

Cohen U., G. Weisman, K. Ray, V. Steiner, J. Rand, and R. Toyne. 1988b. *Environments for people with dementia: Design guide.* Washington, D.C.: Health Facilities Research Program of the American Institute of Architects and the Association of Collegiate Schools of Architecture.

Coons, D. H. 1985. Alive and well at Wesley Hall. *Quarterly: A Journal of Long-term Care,* 21(2):10–14.

Coons, D. H. 1988. Wandering. *American Journal of Alzheimer's Care and Research,* 3(1):31–36.

Gifford, R. 1987. *Environmental psychology.* Newton, Mass.: Allyn and Bacon.

Gilleard, C. J. 1984. *Living with dementia: Community care for the elderly mentally infirm.* Philadelphia: Charles Press.

Gwyther, L. 1986. Treating behavior as a symptom of illness. *Provider,* May, 18–21.

Hiatt, L. 1981. Designing therapeutic dining. *Nursing Homes,* Apr./May, 33–39.

Holahan, C. 1982. *Environmental psychology.* New York: Random House.

Howell, S. 1980. *Designing for aging: Patterns of use.* Cambridge, Mass.: MIT Press.

Koncelik, J. A. 1976. *Designing the open nursing home.* Stroudsburg, Pa.: Dowden, Hutchinson, and Ross.

Lawton, M. P., M. Fulcomer, and M. Kleban. 1984. Architecture for the mentally impaired elderly. *Environment and Behavior,* 16:730–757.

Mace, N. L. 1987. Programs and services which specialize in care of persons with dementing illnesses—Issues and options. *American Journal of Alzheimer's Care and Research,* 2(3):10–17.

Mace, N. L., and P. V. Rabins. 1981. *The thirty-six-hour day.* Baltimore: Johns Hopkins University Press.

Pastalan, L. A. 1979. Sensory changes and environmental behaviors. In *Environmental context of aging,* edited by T. Byerts, S. Howell, and L. A. Pastalan, 118–126. New York: Garland.

Peppard, N. R. 1986. Effective design of special care units. *Provider,* May, 14–17.

Rand, J., V. L. Steiner, R. Toyne, U. Cohen, and G. Weisman. 1987. *Environments for people with dementia: Annotated bibliography.* Washington, D.C.: Health Facilities Research Program of the American Institute of Architects and the Association of Collegiate Schools of Architecture.

Rapelje, D., P. Papp, and L. Crawford. 1981. Creating a therapeutic park for the mentally frail. *Dimensions in Health Service,* Sept., 12–14.

Roach, M. 1985. Reflections in a fake mirror. *Discover,* 8:76–85.

Snyder, L. H. 1984. Archetypical place and the needs of aging. In *Institutional settings: An environmental design approach,* edited by M. Spivak, 52–62. New York: Human Sciences Press.

# Chapter 6

# Public Policy and Dementia Care Units

KATIE MASLOW, M.S.W.,
AND NANCY L. MACE, M.A.

Although the number of nursing home units that are specifically intended for persons with dementia is increasing in the United States, existing governmental policies may constrain the development and use of high-quality dementia care units. Some governmental regulations for nursing homes conflict with the best current thinking about how nursing home units for persons with dementia should be designed and operated. In addition, reimbursement through public programs is often too low to cover the cost of care in the units. At the same time, many people are concerned about nursing homes that claim to offer specialized dementia care but actually do not offer any special services and use the concept of specialized dementia care as a marketing tool. Because of those concerns, at least two states have developed licensing regulations for dementia care units, and other states are considering doing so. This chapter describes the various governmental policies that affect nursing homes. It discusses existing nursing home regulations that may constrain the development and use of state-of-the-art dementia care units, and it considers the pros and cons of changing federal or state nursing home regulations to encourage or control the development of such units.

The perspective of the authors is that there is still considerable disagreement among experts about what constitutes good nursing home care for persons with Alzheimer's disease and related disorders, and that it is therefore too early to develop comprehensive governmental regulations for dementia care units. Such regulations would hinder the kind of experimentation with alternative methods of care that in the past decade has produced many exciting new ideas and approaches to caring for these patients. On the other hand, there is

107

a need to protect desperate families from fraudulent claims of some nursing home operators that they are offering specialized dementia care.

The chapter concludes that, at this time, government can best support the development and use of high-quality dementia care units by the following means:

1. Funding research and demonstration projects on appropriate care for persons with dementia

2. Granting waivers of certain regulatory requirements on a facility-by-facility basis to nursing homes that want to experiment with various forms of care

3. Funding research to evaluate dementia care units

4. Mandating certain minimum requirements that must be met by nursing homes that claim to offer dementia-specific care

5. Supporting public education about Alzheimer's disease and related disorders and about alternative treatment settings for persons with these conditions

6. Sponsoring forums for discussion and eventual development of consensus about what constitutes good nursing home care for persons with Alzheimer's disease and related disorders

## Governmental Policies That Affect Nursing Homes

Nursing homes are among the most highly regulated entities in this country. Federal, state, and local governmental regulations affect virtually all aspects of nursing home care. Governmental policies for inspections and for the training and supervision of surveyors affect the interpretation of existing regulations. In addition, the amount of Medicaid nursing home payments determines to a great extent what resources facilities have to care for their residents.

The development and use of high-quality dementia care units may be constrained by regulatory requirements, inspection policies, payment levels, or a combination of the three. People who want to facilitate the establishment of high-quality dementia care units should be aware of the various kinds of governmental policies that may interfere with their objectives. To change governmental policies that interfere with the development and use of such units, it is necessary to target the policies that create the problem. It is pointless, for example, to lobby for changes in Medicare and Medicaid nursing home regulations if the primary problem is inspection policies or payment levels, and vice versa. The following sections identify the types of nursing home regulations and the inspection and payment policies that create the framework within which dementia care units are currently developed and operated.

### Federal Regulations for Medicare and Medicaid Certification of Nursing Homes

The legislation that created the Medicare and Medicaid programs gave the federal government authority to set standards for nursing homes that choose to participate in the programs. Nursing homes must be certified as meeting these standards to receive Medicare or Medicaid payment for any of their residents. As of 1986, 13,420 of the 16,388 nursing homes in this country (82 percent) were certified for Medicare, Medicaid, or both. Those facilities accounted for 93 percent of all nursing home beds in the country (U.S. Department of Health and Human Services 1988). The Veterans Administration (VA) also uses Medicare and/or Medicaid certification as a criterion for selecting the non-VA nursing homes in which it places eligible veterans (Mather et al. 1987).[1] Thus, the regulations for Medicare and Medicaid certification of nursing homes have a strong and pervasive influence on the whole nursing home industry.

The standards for Medicare and Medicaid certification of nursing homes have been changed several times in the past two decades, most recently as a result of nursing home reform legislation passed by Congress in 1987. Before that legislation, there were two sets of standards for nursing homes: one set (called "conditions of participation") for skilled nursing facilities (SNFs), and another set for intermediate care facilities (ICFs). The 1987 legislation eliminated the distinction between SNFs and ICFs, effective October 1990. A single set of standards for Medicare and Medicaid certification of "nursing facilities" is being developed by the federal Health Care Financing Administration (HCFA) and will go into effect in 1990.

Medicare and Medicaid standards pertain to a facility's physical plant; staff credentials; levels of staffing and staff-resident ratios; in-service training; patient assessment; patient rights; patient admission, transfer, and discharge policies; nursing procedures; activities; social services; administration and storage of drugs; nutrition and food services; use of restraints; handling of patient funds; record keeping; and many other areas. The new standards are expected to focus more than previous standards on the outcomes of care for residents.

### State Licensing Requirements for Nursing Homes

Each state licenses nursing homes on the basis of state standards. In general, these standards pertain to the same areas covered by the federal Medicare and Medicaid standards for certification, and some states use the federal standards for state licensing purposes. Other states use different standards that may be more or less stringent. In some states, the licensing standards for nursing homes are incredibly detailed and complex.

In 1984 the Institute of Medicine's Committee on Nursing Home Regulations surveyed state licensing and certification agencies. Agencies from 47 states responded to the survey. Of those, more than half said their state's licensing requirements for ICFs were more stringent than the existing federal Medicare and Medicaid standards for ICFs, about one-quarter said their state's licensing requirements were about the same as the federal standards, and one-quarter said their state's licensing requirements were less stringent. More than one-third of the state licensing and certification agencies said their state's licensing requirements for SNFs were more stringent than the federal standards for SNFs, about one-third said their state's requirements were the same, and about one-third said they were less stringent (Institute of Medicine 1986).

Inspections for state licensing purposes are generally conducted by the same state agency and at the same time as inspections for Medicare and Medicaid certification (Institute of Medicine 1986). It is the authors' impression that many people who work in nursing homes and have experienced the inspection process do not distinguish between state licensing requirements and federal requirements for Medicare and Medicaid certification. In some respects this distinction is not important, because the federal Medicare and Medicaid regulations include a requirement that facilities must have a state license, so the federal regulations in effect incorporate state licensing requirements. On the other hand, for people who want to facilitate the development and use of dementia care units and perceive obstacles in the existing regulations, the distinction is very important. If the obstacles are caused by a state licensing law or by the regulations that implement it, one must seek a solution at the state level. For example, one might seek a change in the law or the regulations or a waiver for a particular facility. If the obstacles are caused by a federal law or the regulations that implement federal law, one must seek a solution at the federal level, either in changes to the law or regulations or in waivers for certain purposes.

## Local Governmental Regulations

Many counties and other local governments also license nursing homes. Local governmental regulations, particularly building codes, may interfere with the implementation of innovative physical design concepts in some jurisdictions. Likewise, sanitation and food service facility regulations may limit the implementation of some generally accepted ideas about how food should be prepared for and presented to persons with dementia. For example, the regulations may require that nursing homes give residents food at a temperature that is too high for a resident to pick up in his or her fingers. Clearly, the solution to the problems that arise from local law and local regulations must be sought at the local level.

### Inspection Policies and Procedures

Most nursing home inspections are conducted by the state licensing and certification agency. That agency generally conducts inspections for state licensing proposes. The federal government delegates to states the responsibility for inspecting nursing homes for Medicare and Medicaid certification, and the state licensing and certification agency generally performs those inspections. The federal government also conducts some nursing home inspections to evaluate the states' inspection procedures. In addition, various state agencies conduct what are called "inspections of care," in which the quality and appropriateness of care received by each Medicaid-covered resident is reviewed (Institute of Medicine 1986). Last, the VA inspects annually all non-VA nursing homes that it uses, and a VA social worker or nurse is supposed to visit each veteran placed in a non-VA nursing home monthly to review the quality and appropriateness of the care the veteran receives (Mather et al. 1987).

A recent study of nursing home regulation in New York, Virginia, and England (Day and Klein 1987) identified two different regulatory models. In one model, the regulatory agency regards the nursing home operator as an "amoral calculator who will risk breaking the rules for a profit." In this model, if the nursing home fails to meet standards, the failure is seen as deliberate. The surveyor is seen as a policeman, and the inspection process is formal, legalistic, and adversarial. In the other model, the regulatory agency regards the nursing home operator as fallible but well intentioned. The nursing home's failure to meet standards is regarded as an accident. The surveyor is seen as a consultant, and the inspection process is informal, cooperative, and consensual.

Whether a given survey agency is more like one than the other of these two models affects the way its surveyors conduct inspections. Nursing home regulations are not completely clear or precise, so the preconceptions of the survey agency and its surveyors can easily

influence their interpretations of existing regulations. Those preconceptions are also likely to influence the way a survey agency and its
surveyors respond to experimentation and innovative treatment
methods, including dementia care units.

In addition to the differences among survey agencies, individual
surveyors may differ in their interpretation of regulations. The
amount and type of training and supervision surveyors receive vary
in different states (Institute of Medicine 1986). In states where
surveyors receive very little training or supervision, individual surveyors may differ greatly in their interpretation of the regulations.
Even in states where surveyors receive considerable training and
supervision, their interpretations of the regulations may vary. Day
and Klein (1987) pointed out that many nursing home surveyors are
nurses and social workers who consider themselves professionals
capable of independent judgment and discretion in interpreting the
regulations.

That individual surveyors interpret nursing home regulations
differently is confusing for everyone. Sometimes it benefits a particular dementia care unit. For example, the authors have heard about
instances in which an individual surveyor has interpreted regulations
that could be obstacles for a dementia care unit in a way that made
them not obstacles. Conversely, surveyors sometimes interpret regulations that are not obstacles in a way that makes them obstacles.

Sometimes, some nursing home operators in a state regard certain
regulations as obstacles to developing or operating a dementia care
unit, whereas other nursing home operators in the same state do not
regard those regulations as obstacles. This may occur because of
differences in the way individual surveyors interpret the regulations.
Those differences in turn may reflect the surveyors' opinions about
the nursing home operators. If a surveyor regards some nursing
home operators as having bad intentions and deliberately failing to
meet standards and others as having good intentions and accidentally
failing to meet standards, the surveyor may interpret the regulations
less rigidly in the latter facilities and may react more positively to
experimentation and innovative treatment methods in those facilities.

The relative impact on dementia care units of nursing home
regulations versus surveyors' interpretations of the regulations is
unknown, and it probably varies among states and among different
facilities in the same state. Clearly, however, if obstacles to the
development and use of high-quality dementia care units arise from
questionable interpretations of regulations by survey agencies or
individual surveyors, the solution does not lie in changing the

regulations. Efforts should be focused instead on the training and supervision of individual surveyors.

### Medicaid Payment Levels

In 1986, Medicaid paid 41 percent of the total cost of nursing home care in the United States (U.S. Congress 1988), but because Medicaid requires nursing home residents to contribute their own resources to the cost of their care, a larger proportion of all residents are covered by Medicaid. Long-stay residents are more likely than short-stay residents to be covered by Medicaid (U.S. Department of Health and Human Services 1987a), and persons with dementia are likely to be long-stay residents (Keeler et al. 1981; Liu and Manton 1983). Therefore, although no data are available on the proportion of nursing home residents with dementia that are covered by Medicaid, it is undoubtedly more than half and may be much higher.

Medicaid payment levels are low in most states. In 1985, they averaged $49.93 per day for SNFs and $39.57 per day for ICFs (U.S. Department of Health and Human Services 1987b). These rates limit the resources nursing homes have to care for Medicaid-covered residents, including residents with dementia. Many people believe that providing care in dementia care units is more costly than providing it in regular nursing home units. If this is true, the low level of Medicaid payments is a greater problem for dementia care units than for nursing homes generally.

Private-pay patients and their families can be and are being charged more than Medicaid pays for nursing home care in general. In 1985, the average payment by private-pay patients was $61.01 per day for skilled-level care and $48.09 per day for intermediate-level care (U.S. Department of Health and Human Services 1987b). In many nursing homes, the higher rates paid by private-pay patients actually subsidize the care of Medicaid patients.

Dementia care units frequently have a majority of private-pay patients, and some have only private-pay patients. Some people can afford to pay privately for care in such a unit, but for many persons with dementia access to this type of care, especially for prolonged periods, depends on the availability of Medicaid funding.

The authors believe that some concerns and complaints about nursing home regulations that interfere with the development and use of dementia care units are not really about the regulations. Instead, they are about the difficulty of meeting the regulations and simultaneously providing the additional staff, services, and design features that the unit operator considers essential for persons with dementia. In these instances, increased Medicaid funding for care for persons with dementia would be a more appropriate solution than changing the regulations.

### Other Governmental Policies That Affect Nursing Homes

Several other governmental policies affect nursing homes in ways that are directly or indirectly relevant to the development and use of dementia care units. For example, federal Medicare policies and federal and state Medicaid policies are currently creating strong financial incentives for hospitals to discharge patients earlier. As a result, nursing homes are caring for sicker people. At the same time, states have implemented policies to limit the supply of nursing home beds. As the number of very sick people that need nursing home care increases and bed supply remains constant, some types of patients that previously were cared for in nursing homes will have to be cared for in other settings. Several states have implemented case-mix reimbursement policies that create financial incentives for nursing homes to admit very severely ill and physically impaired patients rather than less severely ill and cognitively impaired patients. In some of these states, the persons with Alzheimer's disease and related disorders who probably are most appropriate for dementia care units—those in the middle stages of the diseases—may be precisely the patients who are no longer cared for in nursing homes. Nursing home preadmission screening programs that have been implemented in many states may have the same effect of screening out persons with Alzheimer's disease and related disorders who are in the middle stages of the disease.

As this chapter goes to print, the federal Medicare and Medicaid regulations for nursing homes that have been written to implement legislation passed by Congress in 1987 are being finalized. It is unclear how those regulations will affect the development and use of dementia care units. It is also unclear whether changes in state licensing requirements will occur in response to changes in the federal Medicare and Medicaid regulations, what such changes would be, and how they would affect dementia care units.

The impact of the federal preadmission screening and patient assessment regulations that were at least partially implemented by most states in 1989 is also unclear. Although the law specifically exempts people with a primary diagnosis of Alzheimer's disease and related disorders, many factors can influence the real effect this law will have on people with dementia. These factors include the diagnostic sophistication in the region, fiscal pressures on nursing facilities to admit or not to admit behaviorally disturbed patients, regulations that, for example, limit the use of drugs or restraints, the intent of the individual states to serve or not to serve people with dementia, and the number of personnel available for screening. In fact, the impact of the law on people with dementia may differ greatly from state to state.

### The Regulation of Private-pay Facilities

Nursing homes that have only private-pay residents are exempt from federal regulations for Medicare and Medicaid certification and related inspections. They are, however, subject to state licensing requirements that may be as stringent as or more stringent than the federal regulations and to local governmental nursing home regulations. Thus, private-pay facilities do not escape government regulation.

### Nursing Home Operators' Fears about Challenging Regulations and Surveyors

Nursing home operators are often very reluctant to challenge regulations and surveyors' interpretations of regulations for fear that the surveyors will be annoyed and will cite the nursing home for violations of other regulations. Because of the complexity and rigidity of nursing home regulations in most jurisdictions, virtually all nursing homes—even very good facilities—are deficient or out of compliance with one regulation or another at any particular time. Given those fears, some operators are reluctant to innovate. The authors have heard many operators say that they prefer to "keep a low profile," hoping to "keep the surveyors off their backs."

## What Types of Governmental Regulations Interfere with the Development and Use of Dementia Care Units?

The preceding section described the types of nursing home regulations and governmental policies other than regulations that may interfere with the development and use of dementia care units. This section discusses some of the regulations that may cause problems, including regulations about the physical design of nursing home units; locked units; use of restraints; diet and meal schedules; and residents' involvement in activities such as cooking, washing dishes, setting tables, and other activities that may be therapeutic.

As discussed earlier, federal regulations for Medicare and Medicaid certification of nursing homes are the same for all states, but state licensing requirements differ. As a result, regulations that interfere with the development and use of dementia care units in one state may not exist in other states. People who want to facilitate the development of dementia care units in a state must be knowledgeable about the licensing requirements in that state.

### Regulations about the Physical Design of Nursing Home Units

Many people who want to set up dementia care units complain that regulations about the physical design of nursing homes make it impossible for them to create the environment they regard as most therapeutic. An analysis of regulations that affect nursing homes in the Wisconsin Administrative Code (Cohen et al. 1989) pointed out that the regulations were written primarily with the needs of physically impaired rather than cognitively impaired patients in mind. They tend to encourage large nursing home units, modeled after hospital units, with patient rooms located on long, straight corridors with few social spaces. Regulations that specify the number of square feet per patient room and require 8-foot-wide corridors and nursing stations with visual access to all patient rooms were said to create the greatest challenges or obstacles in designing dementia care units.

These findings agree with complaints the authors have heard about regulations in other states. The complaints generally focus on regulations that make it difficult to create a noninstitutional, homelike care setting. The regulations in question often pertain to security and the need to assure rapid evacuation of patients in the event of a fire. These objectives, of course, are important in the care of persons with dementia. In general, however, they can be achieved without requiring a hospital-like design for the facility.

There may be consensus now about some regulations that are obstacles to developing the best possible physical environment for the care of persons with dementia. There is disagreement about other regulations, however. The source of the disagreement is differences of opinion about the best environment for the care of persons with dementia. Some dementia care unit "experts," operators, and staff complain, for example, about regulations that limit the amount of open space in nursing home units, because they consider open space a necessary component of the ideal care setting for persons with dementia. Others are not bothered by regulations that limit open space, because they think that persons with dementia become agitated in large open spaces.

Likewise, some people complain about regulations that require a nursing station on every unit, because they believe those regulations discourage the development of small homelike units for as few as 12 patients. Others might argue that a nursing station is needed on each unit, and problems with these regulations arise only when the specific requirements for a nursing station interfere with design concepts for the unit. In addition, of course, having a nursing station for every 12 patients probably increases costs significantly.

In instances where there is disagreement about whether certain regulations interfere with the development of the ideal physical environment for care of persons with dementia, it is probably better in the short term for individual facilities to seek a waiver of the regulations that are troublesome than to try to change the regulations. Once it is clear which design features create the best care environment, nursing home regulations should be changed to require those features.

### Regulations about Locked Units

Some people who want to set up dementia care units complain that fire safety regulations for nursing homes do not allow them to lock the units and thereby make it impossible for them to keep residents from wandering away. In the authors' experience, this problem is eventually resolved, but sometimes only after extensive meetings with the survey agency and local fire marshal in which methods of securing the unit are considered. Often, the agreed-upon solution is a two-step lock that cognitively unimpaired persons can open easily but cognitively impaired persons usually cannot. In some cases, however, agreement about a method for securing the unit is not reached until one or more residents wander away from the unit and become lost, become injured, or even die. Then the danger of not securing the unit becomes obvious and outweighs arguments against locked units.

Nursing home operators in several states have told the authors that they believe that having a locked unit would make their facilities IMDs (institutions for mental disease) according to federal criteria and thus jeopardize Medicaid reimbursement for their residents. Having locked wards is one of the ten indicators the federal government uses to determine whether a facility is an IMD (Gattozzi and Goldman, no date). The authors do not know whether having a locked ward is sufficient reason in itself to establish that a nursing home is an IMD.

### Regulations about the Use of Restraints

Overuse of restraints to restrict wandering and to control residents' behavior is a widely criticized aspect of the care provided for persons with dementia in many nursing homes. Some people say, usually without elaboration, that "the regulations encourage overuse of restraints." The authors are not aware of any regulations that literally encourage the use of restraints, and in fact the wording of regulations about restraints that we have seen specifically limits their use. For example, the latest version of the federal regulations for Medicare and Medicaid certification includes a requirement that "the resident has the right to be free from any physical restraint imposed or psychoactive drug administered for purposes of discipline or convenience, and not required to treat the resident's medical symptoms" (U.S. Department of Health and Human Services 1989, p. 5363).

On the other hand, nursing home operators and staff are afraid—often realistically—that they will be cited for deficiencies if residents fall or wander off. They may overuse restraints to protect themselves, even though the regulations about restraints discourage overuse. In this situation, it is probably not specific regulations that cause the problem, but rather a general regulatory climate that discourages risk taking. As discussed in Chapter 4, it may be impossible to improve the quality of life of nursing home residents with dementia without taking some risks.

With respect to the overuse of restraints, the solution does not seem to lie in changing existing regulations. Instead, facilities should (1) devise effective methods for securing dementia care units; (2) develop procedures for informing families and other responsible parties about the alternatives for handling resident wandering and behavioral problems and obtain their informed consent, when appropriate, for not using restraints; and (3) educate survey agencies and surveyors about the goals of care for persons with dementia and about alternative methods by which wandering and behavior problems can be managed (see Chaps. 9 and 13 for descriptions of alternative methods).

### Regulations about Diet and Meal Schedules

Some people who want to set up dementia care units complain that regulations do not allow them to offer residents appropriate foods on the schedule that they think is best. Sometimes, they want to offer primarily finger foods, so that even quite severely impaired residents can feed themselves. They may also want to serve only one food at a time, to place no utensils on the table, or to offer small meals five or six times during the day or evening, rather than three larger meals. Anecdotal evidence indicates that surveyors sometimes cite or threaten to cite facilities for each of these practices.

Regulations about diet and meal schedules are generally intended to ensure that residents receive a nutritionally adequate diet and that they do not go hungry between meals. It may be that some surveyors oppose changes in the diet and meal schedules because they do not believe it will be possible to ensure that residents' nutritional needs are being met if the changes are made. In addition, there may be specific federal, state, or local government regulations that prohibit one or more of the changes. We have not found such regulations, however, in the latest version of the federal regulations for Medicare and Medicaid certification. Those regulations require "at least three meals daily"; menus that "meet the nutritional needs of residents in accordance with the recommended dietary allowances of the Food and Nutrition Board of the National Research Council"; and food "prepared in a form designed to meet individual needs (U.S. Department of Health and Human Services 1989, pp. 5367–5368). There is no prohibition of finger foods or more frequent meals, and there is no requirement that the resident eat with utensils.

### Regulations about Residents' Involvement in Activities That Could Be Regarded as Work

Some people who want to set up dementia care units say that regulations stop them from letting residents help with cooking, washing dishes, setting tables, and other activities that could be regarded as work. The latest federal regulations for Medicare certification and the previous version of these regulations allow work that is therapeutic. According to the latest regulations, residents have a right either to perform or to refuse to perform services for a facility (U.S. Department of Health and Human Services 1989).

Some state licensure laws or regulations that implement them may prohibit residents from participating in activities that could be regarded as work. In many cases, however, the concept that residents cannot participate in such activities is probably a surveyor's erroneous interpretation of the regulations.

### Other Regulations That May Interfere with the Development and Use of Dementia Care Units

There are hundreds and perhaps thousands of nursing home regulations, many of which might be an obstacle to someone's concept of how a dementia care unit should be staffed and operated. Some possibilities are regulations that require certain types of staff, certain staff-resident ratios on specific shifts, and certain medication procedures. Some people think, for example, that the staff-resident ratio on the evening and night shifts should be higher for a dementia care unit than for a regular nursing home unit because they think persons with dementia are more likely than other nursing home residents to be up at night. If sufficient funds were available, staff could be increased on the evening and night shifts and be kept at the required levels for the day shift.

## Should Government Adopt Comprehensive Regulations for Dementia Care Units?

The preceding discussion suggests the complexity of the existing regulatory situation for nursing homes, including the different types of regulations that may affect the development and use of dementia care units and the confounding effects of differences in surveyors' interpretations of these regulations, as well as the low level of Medicaid nursing home payments that limits the overall resources nursing homes have to care for their residents. In many cases, it is not clear whether the obstacles that confront people who want to set up dementia care units are specific regulations, surveyor interpretations, or payment levels. In some cases, it is not clear whether the troublesome regulations are federal, state, or local. When one adds to this complexity the current lack of consensus among experts about what constitutes good nursing home care for persons with dementia, one can only conclude that caution is necessary in developing comprehensive new regulations for dementia care units.

There would be at least two benefits from developing comprehensive regulations for dementia care units, assuming it were possible to do so. First, the regulations would control the proliferation of nursing home units that do not offer specialized dementia care but nevertheless use the designation "special care," "special Alzheimer's care," or "special dementia care" as a marketing tool. As of early 1989, at least two states, Texas and Iowa, have developed voluntary programs for licensing dementia care units. In these states, nursing homes can apply for a special license or certification for their dementia care unit, in addition to their general nursing home license. The states have developed standards for these units. However, nursing homes do not have to have a special license or certification status to operate a dementia care unit. In Iowa, four months after the licensing law went into effect, no nursing homes had applied for a special license (Hall 1989). The Iowa Task Force on Alzheimer's Disease and Related Disorders has asked the governor to make the licensing law mandatory.

Several other states are considering developing regulations for dementia care units. For example, the Arkansas legislature has mandated the development of regulations for a special license for the units.

A second benefit of developing comprehensive regulations for dementia care units would be the possibility that Medicaid payment levels might be increased for the units. At present, some states are providing grants to a limited number of nursing homes that have dementia care units. For example, Massachusetts has a pilot program that has provided grants for eight such units. Likewise, New York has awarded grants to twenty nursing homes for dementia care units and programs. It is unlikely, however, that Medicaid payments would be increased generally for nursing home residents in dementia care units in the absence of comprehensive regulations that define who is eligible for care in the units, what unique services are necessary, what staff members are needed, what physical design characteristics distinguish the units from other nursing home units, what special activities or other procedures are needed, and many other factors. Regulations in all these areas are probably a prerequisite for increased Medicaid funding for dementia care units.

Despite the potential benefits of developing comprehensive regulations for dementia care units, there are several important reasons for not doing so at this time. First, experts disagree about many aspects of nursing home care for persons with dementia. Whose ideas would prevail if comprehensive regulations for dementia care units were developed now? Second, implementation of comprehensive regulations at this time would limit experimentation with innovative care methods. People with good ideas might not be able to meet all the standards and thus would not be able to test out their ideas. Last, some units that are now providing good care for persons with dementia might not meet all the new standards and might be put out of business.

These arguments do not imply that no changes should be made in existing regulations, but simply that we are not yet ready for comprehensive regulations. The question of changing certain regulations to facilitate the development and use of high-quality dementia care units requires further evaluation. As discussed in the previous section, some of the regulations that people perceive as troublesome are physical design regulations intended to ensure the security and safety of nursing home residents. Other regulations are intended to ensure that residents receive a nutritionally adequate diet and are free from exploitation. These regulations may not achieve their objectives. In fact, it is often said that regulatory procedures are generally more effective in preventing the worst abuses than in ensuring good care. One wonders, in this context, whether it would be wise to change existing regulations—for example, to decrease the required size of residents' rooms, eliminate the requirement for a nursing station on small nursing home units, allow locked units generally, or eliminate existing regulations about diet and meal schedules. A more desirable approach at this point probably is to allow waivers of the regulations on a facility-by-facility basis to test new methods of care for persons with dementia.

## Broader Issues That Affect the Development and Use of Dementia Care Units

The chapter has focused thus far on the nursing home regulations, inspection procedures, and Medicaid payment levels that constrain the development and use of dementia care units. Several broader issues are implicated as well. These issues also underlie and explain some of the potentially troublesome regulations. They are mentioned briefly here and discussed at greater length in Chapter 4.

Comparison of U.S. policy with that of other countries provides some perspective. All industrialized nations are facing increasing numbers of people who are living into old age and who need long-term care. Not all of this care can be provided by families. The cost of this care is of serious concern internationally. We know of no country that has solved the problems of long-term geriatric care, and none of the countries we have visited is providing ideal care; many, in fact, have facilities that provide mediocre care. Some nations, however, have created an atmosphere in which a few model dementia-specific units have flourished, and they offer a supportive climate for the development of more innovative programs.

Among the factors that create or inhibit good dementia-specific care are the following:

*Funding for services.* In the United States, public funding for services is tied to poverty and the individual's needs. In Great Britain, funding is tied to social service needs, and impoverishment is not required. Many countries consider a minimal level of care to be the right of every citizen.

*Qualified medical personnel.* The United States is only now beginning to encourage the training of geriatricians and allied medical professionals with a focus in geriatrics. Great Britain expects to have enough geriatricians by 1990 (Stoline and Weiner 1988).

*Impact of free-market forces on a for-profit industry.* The United States has a large percentage of for-profit facilities but has weakened the market pressures that encourage good-quality care.

*Fragmentation of funding.* Funding for acute care, long-term care, and mental health care in the United States comes from different sources. In nations where all care needs are paid for from the same purse, greater opportunities exist to provide a balanced package of care.

*Goals of care.* All nations must balance the goal of enhancing quality of life with goals of prolonging life and providing protection from illness or injury. These decisions are not always rational, and they vary from country to country. The United States sometimes seeks to ensure safety even when risks are low, and as a result quality of life suffers greatly.

*Liability.* The fear of liability seems, so far, to be particularly American. Efforts to avoid any possible risk of suit in the care of people with debilitating diseases can result in severe restrictions on patients' freedom and quality of life.

Every nation struggles to arrive at a balance that is in agreement with national values. Large, culturally diverse nations such as the United States may find this more difficult, and some policies may have developed for narrow populations or without serious attention to their long-term impact. The federal government can support careful examination of the impact of policy and encourage consensus conferences that work toward nationally acceptable compromises.

## Conclusion

Certain federal, state, and local governmental regulations may restrict the development and use of high-quality dementia care units. These regulations should be identified and waived on a case-by-case basis for facilities that want to provide special care for persons with dementia. The authors believe that government could be persuaded to provide waivers for this purpose and that this approach is preferable at this time to making across-the-board changes in existing regulations for nursing homes.

In addition, government should fund research on the methods and appropriate settings for care for persons with dementia. The scope of this research should not be limited to small changes in the prevailing methods of nursing home care in this country. It should also include the alternatives that are suggested by the preceding discussion of broader issues that affect the development and use of dementia care units.

Specialized care units have the potential to provide good care for some persons with dementia. They also provide a laboratory for developing better methods of care for all persons with dementia. Governmental policies should be made to support both those functions.

## Note

1. The VA also has its own standards for VA nursing homes, but those standards and related inspection policies are beyond the scope of this chapter.

## References

Cohen, U., G. D. Weisman, K. Day, and K. Ray. 1989. *Environments for people with dementia: Regulatory analysis.* Milwaukee: School of Architecture and Urban Planning, University of Wisconsin.

Day, P., and R. Klein, 1987. The regulation of nursing homes: A comparative perspective. *Milbank Quarterly,* 65(3):303–307.

Gattozzi, A., and H. Goldman. No date. *Information summary for state and local government officials: IMO classification.* Rockville, Md.: National Institute of Mental Health.

Hall, G. 1989. Chairwoman, Iowa Governor's Task Force for Alzheimer's Disease and Related Disorders. Personal communication, Jan. 12.

Institute of Medicine. 1986. *Improving the quality of care in nursing homes.* Washington, D.C.: National Academy Press.

Keeler, E. B., R. L. Kane, and D. H. Solomon. 1981. Short- and long-term residents of nursing homes. *Medical Care,* 19(3):363–369.

Liu, K., and K. G. Manton. 1983. The characteristics and utilization pattern of an admission cohort of nursing home patients. *Gerontologist,* 23(1):92–98.

Mather, J. H., M. Goodwin, and J. R. Kelly. 1987. The U.S. Veterans Administration health care delivery system: One health care system's approach to quality assurance. *Danish Medical Bulletin, Journal of the Health Sciences*, Special Supplement Series, no. 5, 54–60.

Stoline, A., and J. P. Weiner. 1988. *The medical market place*. Baltimore: Johns Hopkins University Press.

U.S. Congress. 1988. *Medicaid source book: Background data and analysis*. Washington, D.C.: U.S. Government Printing Office.

U.S. Department of Health and Human Services. 1987a. Discharges from nursing homes: Preliminary data from the 1985 National Nursing Home Survey. *Advancedata*, no. 142. Hyattsville, Md.: National Center for Health Statistics.

U.S. Department of Health and Human Services. 1987b. Nursing home characteristics: Preliminary data from the 1985 National Nursing Home Survey. *Advancedata*, no. 131. Hyattsville, Md.: National Center for Health Statistics.

U.S. Department of Health and Human Services. 1988. Nursing and related care homes as reported from the 1986 inventory of long-term care places. *Advancedata*, no. 147. Hyattsville, Md.: National Center for Health Statistics.

U.S. Department of Health and Human Services, Health Care Financing Administration. 1989. *Federal Register*, Feb. 2, 42CFR. Medicare and Medicaid: Requirements for long-term care facilities; final rule with request for comments.

## Chapter 7

# Training Direct Service Staff Members to Work in Dementia Care Units

### DOROTHY H. COONS

The training of direct service staff in traditional nursing homes has focused almost totally upon the physical and health care of residents and upon compliance with facility requirements and state and federal regulations. Legislation passed by Congress in 1987 and now moving toward implementation in the states will require all nurses aides employed for more than four months in nursing homes to have satisfactorily completed a 75-hour state-approved training and competency evaluation program. Training must cover basic nursing skills, personal care skills, mental and social needs, basic restorative services, and resident rights. This core of information is essential in providing good treatment in any care setting for the physically and mentally impaired elderly. In attempts to improve the quality of life, some states have required that training give particular attention to the psychosocial needs of residents. The staff are taught communication skills and are helped to understand and empathize with older persons (Barney et al. 1981).

Responding to psychosocial needs is of primary importance in caring for persons with Alzheimer's disease and other dementias. This chapter describes the topics and training methodology that were developed for, tested, and found effective in preparing the staff to work in the Wesley Hall project and in a number of other dementia units that have since been established.

The selection of the staff is of prime importance. Skills and approaches can be taught, and many staff members can learn to develop an understanding of impaired persons. There is a decided advantage, however, if staff members are carefully screened and selected on the basis of their sensitivity to the needs of dementia victims and of their abilities to respond to and communicate with persons who have severe language problems. It is also helpful if staff members working in dementia units are flexible and imaginative enough to be able to improvise on the spur of the moment and respond to the constantly changing needs, moods, and abilities of residents. Some people work exceedingly well with alert but physically impaired persons, while others enjoy and find it challenging to work with persons with dementia. Staff persons need to be helped to recognize where in a facility they can make the greatest contribution.

## The Role and Style of an Effective Trainer

The role and style of the trainer are important in any educational series, but they are especially so in the training of direct service staff who may be uncomfortable in classroom situations and unconvinced that the training will enhance their skills and make their jobs more rewarding. It is essential that the trainer be well-prepared and knowledgeable about the various topics to be presented and familiar with lecture content, the audiovisuals, and exercises to be used.

The trainer can help relieve some of the stress and tension that trainees experience by opening the first session with an exercise that enables them to share something about themselves or their ideas about aging, for example (see Figures 7.1 and 7.2). This also establishes the expectation that the training will be participatory and that all will have opportunities to contribute to the sessions.

The challenge for the trainer is to establish a relaxed and friendly climate but to maintain a pace that provides for good learning and averts boredom. Injecting humor from time to time can help reduce tension, but humor must be handled carefully. If trainers can direct the humor toward themselves and acknowledge their own flaws or show that they have experienced some of the same difficulties that the trainees have had on the job, this may help to open up communication.

Throughout the training series, it is crucial that the trainer treat the trainees with dignity and respect and encourage participants to express their own ideas. The trainer serves as an enabler, as well as a teacher, who helps the participants to recognize their own potential and abilities.

## Suggested Training Topics

The training sessions described here are designed to help staff members understand the unique characteristics of persons with

---

### GETTING TO KNOW YOU

Please complete the following items. You and your partner will share this information and then use it to introduce each other to the total group.

1. Name _____

2. How long have you worked at your present job? _____

3. What sorts of things do you enjoy doing most? _____

4. What are your special interests or hobbies? _____

5. What sorts of things make you laugh? _____

6. What special skills do you have? _____

7. Describe an older person that you have especially enjoyed.

   _____

   _____

   _____

8. If you had a whole day with nothing you had to do, how would you spend it?

   _____

9. What would you like to have accomplished by the time you are 80?

   _____

Please introduce your co-worker and select two items from the above list to tell about him or her.

---

**Figure 7.1**

Alzheimer's disease or other irreversible dementias. The staff also need to be taught how to assess residents' strengths, needs, and capacities and then be given the skills to assist residents to continue to function maximally. A further goal in the training is to teach the staff how to examine their own approaches and other factors in the environment that may be causing some of the difficult behaviors.

The training is most beneficial when trainees are given practical hands-on assignments between meetings that are directly related to

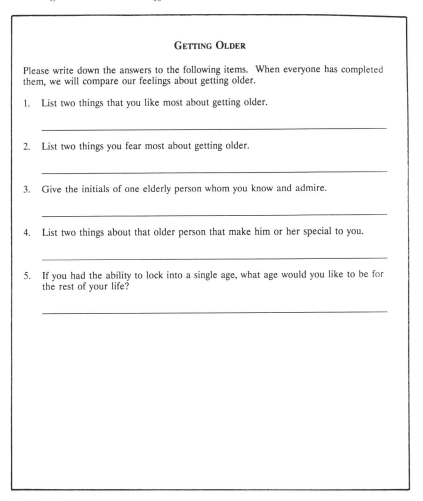

Figure 7.2

the session they have just completed. The assignments may involve evaluating practices in their work situations if they are currently employed or visiting with residents. This expectation that they will spend time talking with residents also legitimizes social interactions between the staff and the residents—interactions that are considered a waste of time in some settings. At the beginning of the session following the hands-on experience, the staff need time to discuss the results of their assignment.

The following topics are suggested as essential in preparing staff to undertake the difficult and challenging responsibilities involved in staffing dementia care units. If trainers have less time for training than the 12 sessions recommended, they will need to select the topics they feel will be most useful or combine several sessions. Some of the sessions could be offered after the opening of a dementia unit if the staff can be released for blocks of time.

### 1. Dementia: An Overview

This session describes the symptoms that occur in dementia and the possible progression of the disease over time. It cites some of the reversible dementias and potential causes. There is a description of the behaviors that may occur and some of the possible causes beyond the dementia itself. This session is also an occasion to point out that one of the purposes of a dementia care unit is to provide maximum freedom for residents. The unit is therefore designed to be accepting and tolerant of behaviors that would be disruptive and disturbing to residents in other units. The session emphasizes that, even with the changes that dementia produces, the person is still a human being with a history, a personality, and individuality. This statement presents a crucial point of view about impaired persons that can help shape the thinking of the staff and their attitudes toward dementia victims. It can also clarify the rationale for some of the later training sessions (Cohen and Eisdorfer 1986; Cummings and Benson 1983; Mace and Rabins 1981; see Chaps. 12 and 14).

### 2. Characteristics of a Therapeutic Milieu in a Dementia Care Unit

Session 2 identifies the features of the environment that are crucial in the establishment of dementia care units. It presents some of the specific changes from traditional practice that need to occur, such as the relaxing of daily schedules, an emphasis on helping residents continue in the activities of daily living and in simple tasks that make up the pattern of everyday life, and a discarding of the caretaker role for the staff. This can lead to a discussion of the benefits of enabling residents to have breakfast over a period of several hours and to take baths when they are relaxed and willing. This also gives an opportunity to discuss the problems that may arise when traditional patterns and routines are disrupted and possible solutions. Session 2 attempts to prepare the staff for the next session on changing staff roles (Coons 1990; Friedman and Robinson 1986; see Chaps. 1 and 3).

### 3. Changing Staff Roles

This session introduces the idea that a staff person in the role of custodial caretaker only increases the dependency of elderly persons and prevents their continuing to manage the tasks that they are still capable of doing. Acknowledging that staff members have no choice in how they function if a facility is understaffed or if caretaking is standard practice and the expectation of the administration, the session describes the staff roles—enabler, friend, and sharer of tasks—that are preferable in dementia care units. In the roles of enabler and sharer of tasks, the staff help residents to continue to do as much as possible for themselves or to share with the staff in whatever steps they are able to handle successfully. In the role of friend, staff members respond to the social and psychological needs of individuals (Coons 1987a).

### 4. Activities and Opportunities for Residents

Session 4 identifies a variety of activities that appeal to impaired elderly persons and help them maintain contact with and involvement in the world around them. The activities parallel those of everyday life and include many tasks that had become habitual before their illness and that are still possible for them, if the tasks are carefully selected by the staff and instructions are appropriately given. A number of fun and lighthearted activities are also identified (Friedman and Robinson 1986; Mace 1987; Zgola 1987; see Chap. 10).

### 5. Assessing the Strengths, Needs, and Abilities of Residents

This is a very important session, because it de-emphasizes diagnoses and problem behaviors. From the perspective of the residents' strengths and needs, the staff usually begin to view even difficult persons in a more positive way. As a result, the staff's methods of communicating become more supportive and accepting and less controlling and hostile. This, in turn, helps reduce the problem behaviors. This session is most useful if staff members have opportunities to consider specific residents with whom they have been having problems and time following the meeting to work with those they have discussed and evaluated (Whyte and Booth 1989; Coons 1990; Coons 1987b; Zgola 1987).

This training session helps the staff learn to work well with the cognitively impaired, but it is also a very effective training technique

---

EXERCISE
PROBLEM BEHAVIORS

Please think about the persons with whom you or your staff work. Select one person
who has been especially difficult for the staff to work with.

What words or sentences would you use to describe that person's behavior?

---

**Figure 7.3**

to use with intact persons with whom staff are having problems. The
first part of the session deals with the problem behaviors that staff
persons have observed. In small groups trainees are asked to list the
behaviors on the form shown in Figure 7.3, and a discussion follows.
Part 2 of the session asks trainees to consider the resident's strengths
and needs (Figure 7.4). This is followed by a discussion of how the
staff might build on the resident's strengths and respond to his or
her needs. The session is even more effective if there is time to role-
play staff approaches and if the trainer is sufficiently familiar with
the resident in advance of the session to develop a role-playing
situation.

---

### STRENGTHS AND NEEDS OF A RESIDENT

If we can look at the strengths and needs of specific residents, we can often help them through difficult times and help them avoid some of the behaviors that result when the staff are not aware of them as individuals. If a resident is seen as being a "problem," his or her attributes are often ignored.

As you think of Mr. or Mrs. _____ (a resident who is not always easy to work with) what would you identify as his or her strengths and special needs?

| Strengths | Needs |
| --- | --- |
|  |  |
|  |  |
|  |  |
|  |  |
|  |  |

**Figure 7.4**

One of the most satisfying features of this training session is that trainees themselves are able to solve problems and present alternatives. Two case studies illustrating the impact the session can have on both the staff and the residents whom they may consider to be difficult problems are presented later in the chapter.

### 6. The Use of the Technique of Task Breakdown

This session helps staff focus on the remaining skills and capacities of impaired persons. It teaches trainees the technique of task breakdown, which requires that they examine a specific task, determine the steps involved in completing it, and evaluate the difficulty of the various steps. The purposes are to help the staff recognize how difficult a specific task may be for impaired persons and the points at which a resident may need help to proceed. As a part of the session, the staff can be asked to analyze the steps involved in activities of daily living such as getting dressed or the simple household task of setting the table. The session also helps the staff begin to understand the differences in the way tasks need to be structured for persons with varying degrees of impairment to enable them to remain active (Robinson et al. 1987).

### 7. Developing a Repertoire of Approaches

Too frequently the staff in treatment settings follow a pattern of communication that varies little from day to day and seldom takes into account the feelings or moods of residents. If they are consistently unsuccessful with a resident, causing a reaction of anger or combativeness, it may not occur to the staff that there may be other approaches that will enable the resident to respond in a more positive manner. The purpose of session 7 is to help staff members examine their own styles and learn a variety of new ways of communicating with residents. The staff can often develop their own repertoire of approaches if they are asked to think about how they would like to be approached if they were in the role of resident (Robinson et al. 1988; see Chap. 9).

### 8. Responding to Difficult Behaviors

This session is related to session 7, but it examines the potential causes of some of the difficult behaviors of residents from a broader perspective. Staff members are asked to consider the physical environment and the various activities offered as well as staff interventions and approaches that might be triggering these behaviors. One of the objectives in both sessions 7 and 8 is to help the staff realize that a number of steps can be taken to change behaviors that are far more therapeutic than the use of physical restraints and overmedication (Robinson et al. 1988; Gwyther 1985; see Chaps. 9, 12, and 13).

### 9. The Importance of the Physical Environment

The effects of the physical environment are often overlooked. While the direct service staff seldom have opportunities to alter it to any extent, they may be able to compensate for its deficits and use the positive aspects effectively if they become able to evaluate it. The session considers the impact of a small homelike setting that offers privacy. It presents a discussion of ways in which the physical environment can de-emphasize illness and can create feelings of individuality, a sense of ownership, and continuity with the past (Coons et al. 1987; Calkins 1988; see Chap. 5).

### 10. Compensating for Sensory Loss in Old Age

Session 10 describes the sensory losses that result from normal aging and ways in which the physical environment can help compensate for those losses. The major focus is upon ways in which the staff can communicate more effectively with persons who have hearing or visual problems (Pastalan 1976; see Chap. 13).

### 11. Involving Families

This session suggests the possible roles that families may take in treatment settings to enhance the lives of relatives who are living there. It presents ways in which the staff can gain insight and knowledge about residents from families and methods they can use to help families feel more comfortable on visits. The session also points up the value of viewing families as partners rather than adversaries. Everyone benefits by keeping family members informed about the progress of their relatives and gaining their assistance in solving any difficult problems the staff may be having in working with them (Metzelaar and Coons 1986; see Chap. 11).

### 12. Developing a Cohesive Staff Team

Session 12 addresses the need to develop a cohesive staff team of persons who are able to share and plan together and work toward common goals. By sharing both problems and successes, the staff can help one another gain new knowledge and skills and avoid burnout. The session demonstrates problem-solving techniques that can be applied on the job. The need for effective communication and feedback is stressed.

The training series is directed toward giving the staff the practice, skills, and the understanding they need to work with persons with dementia. Many of the methods used, however, are designed to help the staff learn to think through and analyze situations and seek solutions as problems arise. Through the acquisition of new knowledge and skills, staff members can experience continuous growth that can provide job satisfaction and inevitably improves the quality of life for both residents and staff (see Chaps. 2 and 8).

## Training Methodology

The selection of the content and training methods for preparing the direct service staff to work in dementia care units is of special importance and warrants careful consideration. Staff members need to acquire not only an understanding of dementia and its possible progression but also an awareness that persons with dementia still have capacities that the staff can identify and help them continue to use. It is important to convey throughout the series the ultimate feeling of optimism that the staff can help cognitively impaired persons continue to function and enjoy life.

Training may seem boring and a waste of time for some staff members and stressful to others. It is desirable to use methods that will help trainees relax and enjoy the experience. They also need to feel that they have the capacity to contribute to the learning process and that they are experiencing personal growth.

People learn in many different ways. Some are able to listen to lectures and absorb the content; others may grasp information only by reading. Some may learn by viewing films or videotapes. Others may find that only by actually experiencing situations will they absorb information and understand concepts. Effective training uses all of these methods over a period of time so that trainees are given opportunities to learn by whatever method or combination of methods is best for them (Coons and Metzelaar, in press). A number of training methods are described below that have been effective in training both administrative and direct service staff to work in dementia care units.

### Lectures

Lectures, one of the most frequently used teaching methods, are important in transmitting information. They should be brief and concise, and should be accompanied by written handouts giving the same information so that trainees may review the material apart from the session.

### Audiovisual Materials

Audiovisual materials, such as videotapes, films, and slide/tapes, help trainees visualize what is being presented in lecture form. They can illustrate techniques and staff approaches and clarify the concepts presented in lectures. The audiovisuals need to be selected carefully. A few of the current videotapes on Alzheimer's disease and other dementias build a very negative and derisive image of cognitively impaired persons. Audiovisuals can be realistic and still demonstrate the humanity of the individual and the capacity of even severely impaired persons to enjoy life. The audiovisual will be most effective if the trainer introduces it with information about its content and purpose and suggests that trainees observe it from specific perspectives that will be explored in a follow-up discussion.

### Role Playing

Skill training can be approached by the use of a number of different teaching methods. Role playing is especially helpful in improving communication skills and developing a variety of approaches. For example, trainees may be presented with the following situation:

> Mrs. Jamison is an 83-year-old woman living in the unit where you are working. She is very confused at times and becomes quite agitated when the staff attempt to get her to take a bath, saying that she has just had one. Yesterday she became so angry that she struck the staff member who had approached her about bathing.
>
> Consider different ways in which you could approach Mrs. Jamison that might reduce her resistance and agitation.

Some trainees are very uncomfortable with role playing. If they have opportunities to discuss the approaches or solutions to problems in pairs or in small groups, they share responsibility for reaching decisions and often are much less fearful of taking roles. It is helpful if the trainer comments on the fact that approaches are seldom perfect, but that the exercise will give both the role players and the observers opportunities to consider how the resident might be feeling when being approached by the staff. This often leads to suggestions of other methods that might be more effective. The trainer can also point out that role playing gives participants opportunities to test out and practice communication styles in a safe environment so that they will be better prepared to handle situations on the job.

The purpose of role playing is not only to increase communication skills but also to illustrate that many different approaches are possible. It can also lead to a discussion of the need for alternatives to the use of coercion and force.

## Experiential Exercises

Exercises can be designed to give trainees the experience, awareness, and skills needed to help residents continue to function maximally. Following is an example of a specific exercise dealing with
task breakdown:

> Mr. Jackson is one of the more severely impaired persons living in our
> dementia care unit. You will be working closely with him, and one of
> your responsibilities is to help him brush his teeth. Mr. Jackson is not
> always able to identify items that are lying before him. One of the first
> things you will need to do is to clear all of the items from the countertop
> except for his toothbrush and his toothpaste.
>
> Now jot down the steps that are involved in brushing one's teeth. What
> steps do you think Mr. Jackson will be able to manage? What steps will
> you need to do to enable Mr. Jackson to proceed?
>
> When he is finished, how can you help him recognize that he has done
> a good job?

In pairs or in trios, trainees can be given opportunities to discuss
the situation and consider the steps involved in completing the task.
This simple exercise can help them become aware of the need to
analyze even routine tasks, consider each person's capacity to function, and recognize the importance of the staff's communication with
the residents when they are working together.

## Empathic Exercises

Empathic exercises are designed to help the staff gain a better
understanding of impaired residents and a recognition of how their
own attitudes and ways of communicating may affect residents'
behaviors, moods, and feelings.

The staff may be strongly biased against and actually fearful of
residents who are combative. They can clearly indicate to residents
their hostility and anger, and this may only provoke further aggressive
behavior. The exercise illustrated in Figures 7.3 and 7.4 was designed
to help the staff gain a perception of a resident that extended beyond
the difficult behavior he or she might be exhibiting. The following
two case studies illustrate the effectiveness of the exercise in working
with both alert persons and those with dementia.

> *Case study 1.* Mr. Edison was a resident of a dementia care unit that had
> been established recently. He had been a major focus of one of the early
> staff training sessions as staff described their fears of his combativeness

and their unsuccessful attempts to work with him. One staff person showed bruises on her arm where he had struck her when she had attempted to get him to take a bath.

The problems were acknowledged by the trainer, but staff members were then asked to identify Mr. Edison's strengths and needs. A very different person emerged as they talked about his having a sense of humor when he was not angry, his close relationship with his family, his kindness at times when he saw someone in need of help, and his gentlemanly ways. He had a need for attention and perhaps some lighthearted activities.

The staff immediately began to spend more time with him in relaxed and undemanding ways. They occasionally involved him in games of "Uno," which he enjoyed and could still play. He became more relaxed, and he obviously enjoyed the staff. While his combativeness still resurfaced occasionally, the staff viewed Mr. Edison with such affection and acceptance that they were quick to cite their successes with him rather than the difficult situations.

*Case study 2.* Mrs. Baxter had lived in Bushnell, a home for elderly people, for seven years. She was a widow without children. She had had a cardiovascular accident (CVA) and spent most of her time in a wheelchair. In an interview with a staff person shortly after she moved to the home she talked of the good marriage she had had, the marvelous and interesting life she and her husband had enjoyed, and the grief over the loss of her husband that was still so much a part of her being.

In a training session with the staff of Bushnell, she was identified as one of the persons with whom the staff were having the most difficulty coping. The following comments were used to describe the "difficult behaviors" the staff had encountered: you have to watch everything you say; she is sarcastic; her mood swings are unpredictable; she is verbally abusive and very defensive; she is bitter, resentful, angry, and manipulative; she wants you and pushes you away at the same time; if you say "Good morning, it's a lovely day," she is likely to say "Phooey."

A discussion of her strengths elicited the following observations: she has a sense of humor that she does not show often; she is neat about her personal appearance; she is independent and self-determined; she is very proud; she likes children; she can talk on many subjects; she likes animals; she is helpful to the people at her table; she loves sports.

The staff described her needs as follows: she needs attention but will not admit it; she needs companionship; she needs a better self-image; she needs to have some control. This listing of needs led to a discussion of what could be done to improve her self-image—what role she might take that would help her recognize her worth and realize that others valued what she had to offer.

Bushnell had a weekly newsletter that primarily reported on upcoming or past events, but it also served as an excellent mechanism—through interviews with residents or personal histories—to acquaint everyone with the dimensions and history of the people who lived there. Some of the columns were prepared by residents. Shortly before the training session a new column on local sports written by one of the staff members had been introduced.

During the discussion of a possible role for Mrs. Baxter, Mrs. Tanner, the staff person who had written the sports column, suggested inviting Mrs. Baxter to write a weekly sports column. Mrs. Tanner visited Mrs. Baxter immediately after the training session, and although not greeted enthusiastically, she was not turned down. At first Mrs. Tanner made notes of any thoughts Mrs. Baxter had for the column, but soon Mrs. Baxter was writing her own. She accepted an invitation to visit and report upon a contest at a local figure-skating club—one of her first trips away from the home in several years. Her columns on skating, hockey, and football were written with droll humor and an obvious knowledge of the sports.

The staff noted that she was leaving her room much more frequently and joining others in their gathering places, and her hearty laughter could often be heard as she joked with residents and staff members. She told one of the staff that the residents were calling her by the name of the city's local radio sportscaster. She chuckled over this.

Such success, as illustrated with Mr. Edison and Mrs. Baxter, has impact upon the staff as well as residents. For the staff there is the sense of achievement and feelings of growth and a realization that they have the capacities to solve very difficult problems and improve the quality of life for the residents.

### Cartoons

Effective training needs to help the staff gain an awareness and understanding of the fact that many practices that become common-place in treatment settings are nontherapeutic and can create an environment that fosters sickness and dependency. Several methods already discussed can help trainees become more objective about their work situation and more cognizant of routines that should be changed.

Cartoons are excellent tools for examining practices. They have served for centuries to lampoon persons and their foibles. Cartoons are not always funny; they may represent a gallows humor that has disturbing or even tragic overtones.

Cartoons can be used to trigger discussions on a specific issue. One of the most effective uses of cartoons, however, is to ask participants in pairs or small groups to draw cartoons to illustrate incidents or practices that they feel are nontherapeutic for residents.

**Figure 7.5.** Cartoons drawn by staff in training sessions

To draw a cartoon one needs only the ability to draw stick figures. They are fun to sketch, and a well-drawn cartoon can result in instant comprehension of a situation. They allow participants to share positive and negative attitudes in an open and nonthreatening way, and they provide a method for bringing to the surface feelings about situations that might otherwise remain unsaid. Grouping is important in this exercise. Aides will usually be more comfortable working in groups with other aides than with their supervisors.

This exercise enables participants to accept criticism of practices that occur in long-term care settings, because the trainees are the ones who are identifying them and describing them vividly in the cartoons. This is a much more palatable method of examining nontherapeutic practices than having the trainer enumerate them in lecture form. Aides may not be able to change all of the practices identified in the cartoons, but the exercise helps increase their awareness of them. Figure 7.5 shows examples of cartoons drawn by staff persons in training sessions.

## Conclusion

Staff training is one of the most crucial factors in establishing therapeutic units for persons with Alzheimer's disease and other dementias. The special needs and characteristics of dementia victims make it necessary to select training content and methods that are designed to prepare staff members to assume roles and develop skills often considered nonessential in the traditional nursing home. To respond to the psychosocial needs of cognitively impaired persons, it is essential that the staff receive training that will increase their communication skills and their understanding of the disease and of the devastation the older person may be experiencing. It is the direct service staff who have the day-to-day contact with residents and who, if well-trained, have the potential for creating a good quality of life for impaired persons.

## References

Barney, J. L., C. Jansen, and J. K. Murdock. 1981. *Nursing aide training program for Michigan nursing homes.* Ann Arbor: Institute of Gerontology, University of Michigan.

Calkins, M. P. 1988. *Designing for dementia: Planning environments for the elderly and the confused.* Owings Mills, Md.: National Health Publishing.

Cohen, D., and C. Eisdorfer. 1986. *The loss of self: A family resource for the care of Alzheimer's disease and related disorders.* New York: W. W. Norton.

Coons, D. H. 1987a. Designing a residential care unit for persons with dementia. Washington, D.C.: Congressional Office of Technology Assessment, Contract #633-1950.0.

Coons, D. H. 1987b. Training staff to work in special care units. *American Journal of Alzheimer's Care and Research,* 2(5):6–12.

Coons, D. H. 1990. Residential care for persons with dementia: A link in the continuum of care. In *Dementia care: Patient, family, and community,* edited by N. L. Mace. Baltimore: Johns Hopkins University Press.

Coons, D. H., and L. Metzelaar. In press. *A trainer's manual for preparing staff to work in special Alzheimer's units.* Ann Arbor: University of Michigan.

Coons, D. H., A. Robinson, B. Spencer, and L. Green. 1987. *Designing the physical environment for persons with dementia.* A 20-minute slide/tape or videotape. Photomotion Producers. Distributed by Terra Nova Films, Chicago.

Cummings, J. L., and D. F. Benson. 1983. *Dementia: A clinical approach.* Boston: Butterworths.

Friedman, A., and A. Robinson. 1986. *Wesley Hall: A special life.* A 29-minute film or videotape. Innerimage Productions. Distributed by Terra Nova Films, Chicago.

Gwyther, L. P. 1985. *Care of Alzheimer's patients: A manual for nursing home staff.* Washington, D.C.: American Health Care Association and Alzheimer's Disease and Related Disorders Association.

Mace, N. L. 1987. Principles of activities for persons with dementia. *Physical and Occupational Therapy in Geriatrics,* 5(3):13–27.

Mace, N. L., and P. V. Rabins. 1981. *The thirty-six-hour day.* Baltimore: Johns Hopkins University Press.

Metzelaar, L., and D. H. Coons. 1986. Visits: An opportunity for sharing. In *A better life: Helping family members, volunteers, and staff improve the quality of life of nursing home residents suffering from Alzheimer's disease and related disorders.* edited by D. H. Coons, L. Metzelaar, A. Robinson, and B. Spencer, 47–91. Columbus, Ohio: Source for Nursing Home Literature.

Pastalan, L. 1976. *Age-related vision and hearing changes: An empathic approach.* Slide/tape training package. Ann Arbor: Institute of Gerontology, University of Michigan. Distributed by Terra Nova Films, Chicago.

Robinson, A., B. Spencer, S. Weaverdyck, and S. Gardner. 1987. *Helping people with dementia in activities of daily living.* A 22-minute slide/tape or videotape. Photomotion Producers. Distributed by Terra Nova Films, Chicago.

Robinson, A., B. Spencer, and L. White. 1988. *Understanding difficult behaviors: Some practical suggestions for coping with Alzheimer's disease and related illnesses.* Ypsilanti: Geriatric Education Center of Michigan, Eastern Michigan University.

Whyte, T., and T. Booth. 1989. Personal correspondence. Fir Park Village, Port Alberni, British Columbia.

Zgola, J. M. 1987. *Doing things.* Baltimore: Johns Hopkins University Press.

# CHAPTER 8

# Reducing Staff Burnout in the Dementia Care Unit

ANNE ROBINSON, M.A.,
AND BETH SPENCER, M.A., M.S.W.

Rose Marie White has worked 12 years as a nurse's aid at Country Lawn, a skilled nursing facility, longer than any other employee. She is thirty-one years old. For the last two years, she has been working in a dementia care unit that has 20 cognitively impaired residents. She is an excellent worker and has a great deal of patience in communicating with people who have language problems. She is well liked by the residents, the families, and other staff.

Until the last six months, Rose Marie was enjoying her job, but she has become increasingly discouraged. Recently, two other staff persons who were assigned to her shift have left and only one has been replaced. Working short staffed or with weekend pool staff who are unfamiliar with the daily routine and the special needs of each resident has begun to take its toll. Each shift seems endless and exhausting. Rose Marie feels that she is giving constantly while getting little in return and that her efforts are not appreciated or recognized.

The last three weeks have been particularly frustrating for Rose Marie. One of the men on the unit has become agitated and angry, striking staff members and other residents several times. Rose Marie is terribly worried about why he is doing this and is also concerned about the safety of other residents. She has approached the unit coordinator several times with her observations and concerns. No suggestions have been offered, however, of possible ways to cope with this problem. Quite perceptively, Rose Marie admits that she has begun to distance herself emotionally from several residents on the unit who have been difficult, even though she feels this is not right. The staff of the unit want Rose Marie to stay, but they are concerned that she is beginning to "burn out."

Rose Marie is worn down by the demands of caregiving; her frustrations and discouragement are exacerbated because she is not receiving any ongoing support or guidance from supervisory staff. She believes that without this support, the quality of care for the residents on the dementia unit will be jeopardized.

There is growing recognition that working with people with dementia in long-term care facilities is exceedingly fatiguing and stressful, both physically and emotionally. This may be the cause, in part, of the high rate of staff burnout and turnover in nursing homes (Hoffman et al. 1987; Kane and Kane 1982). Alzheimer's disease and related dementing disorders account for approximately one-half of the admissions to nursing homes in the United States (U.S. Congress, Office of Technology Assessment 1987). People with dementia are frequently institutionalized during the later stages of the illness when their cognitive and functional impairments are quite severe. The memory loss and other cognitive deficits may seem strange or frightening to the staff. They may feel the residents are ungrateful, when in fact they are incapable of understanding the efforts being made on their behalf. The staff are often poorly trained to cope with some of the emotional and behavioral problems that can accompany dementing disorders.

Although attention has been devoted to the problems of family caregivers, few studies have documented ways to alleviate low morale and burnout among paid caregivers. Research on family caregiving has repeatedly shown that caregiving is a very difficult process, one that can affect the caregiver's physical and emotional health and feelings of self-esteem and burden (Zarit et al. 1985, 1986; Rabins et al. 1982). Staff caregivers of residents with dementia are subject to many of the same stresses as family caregivers. Lack of knowledge about dementing illnesses can cause misunderstandings and resentments. Repeated experiences with behavioral problems without feeling able to manage them effectively contribute to the emotional and physical exhaustion of the staff as well.

This chapter will briefly discuss some of the literature on staff burnout and describe a number of strategies that can be used to help alleviate stress and prevent burnout in staff persons working in nursing homes with cognitively impaired persons.

## Strategies for Preventing Burnout

Very little substantive research has been done on the problems of staff burnout and stress in nursing homes. Heine (1986) describes the negative impact that job stress can have on the nursing home, the staff, and the way in which staff members provide care. Research conducted on the problem of job turnover in nursing homes indicates that 40–75 percent of nurse's aides leave their job within the first year (Stryker 1981). It has been suggested that the causes of staff turnover may in large part be related to the lack of proper job orientation, inadequate training, and the management style of the nursing home administrator (Bales 1975; Stryker 1982).

Waxman et al. (1984), in their study of seven Philadelphia-area nursing homes, found that in homes where "staff turnover was high, nurse's aides perceived the environment as being highly ordered, organized, and structured with explicit rules and procedures. When turnover was lower, the home was perceived as being administratively more loosely organized and less rigidly controlled" (p. 508).

Extrapolating from these rather broad research findings and from the experiences of dementia unit administrators, some specific suggestions for the dementia unit are offered below.

### Administrative Support

Positive and enthusiastic support of the dementia unit must come from the administration of the nursing home. This is particularly important because programing, staff roles, and interaction with residents differ greatly from practice in more traditional long-term care settings. Strong administrative backing for the program conveys to all the staff in the nursing home that the unit is a high priority. Both the board of directors and administrative staff need to communicate clearly their commitment to making the unit successful.

If the unit is just opening, having key administrative staff meet with small groups of staff from all departments is one way of orienting and involving everyone at the outset. Staff should be apprised of the philosophy of the unit, the program and its goals, and the need for interdepartmental cooperation.

As the program develops, there will inevitably be conflicts and strains among departments where the status quo is being disturbed. Changes in the routine in one area will create rumblings in another. These changes may involve redefining service responsibilities between departments such as nursing, dietary, and housekeeping. To help the staff in the dementia unit cope with some of the initial resistance to change, there should be a high level of interest and involvement by administrative staff in the day-to-day struggles of the program. Supervisory staff can act as buffers or advocates in supporting the interests of the unit with other groups in the nursing home who may be expressing some resistance and hostility toward the program.

Several programs have reported some of the problems they have encountered when there has been a lack of administrative interest (New York State Department of Health 1987). One coordinator said that because the criteria for admission to the unit were no longer being respected, the program had become a "dumping ground" for residents in the nursing home who were management problems for the staff. Staff members on this unit felt powerless and wanted supervisory staff to support the criteria that had been defined.

Ohta and Ohta (1988) in their critique of special Alzheimer's units reported that some had been established essentially to remove difficult patients from other parts of the facility so that they would no longer be problems to the staff and other residents. The units were not viewed as a means of upgrading the quality of life for those with dementia. Staff persons assigned to units like these cannot help but feel that they too have been transferred to the least desirable area of the facility.

### The Management Style of the Coordinator

The coordinator's role on the unit is a critical one. His or her interactions with the staff determine the emotional tone of the unit. If communications with the staff are authoritarian and demanding, staff members are often left feeling that their opinions and observations are not valued. In addition, an authoritarian style of working with the staff will often be reflected in the staff's interactions with residents.

Recent estimates suggest that 80–90 percent of the care in nursing homes is provided by nurse's aides (U.S. Congress, Office of Technology Assessment 1987). In traditional nursing homes they are told what to do, with very little, if any, opportunity to provide input regarding care and programing decisions. If the staff are consulted about decisions related to resident care or job expectations, they will usually feel better about their work and there will be a more relaxed, accepting emotional climate on the unit. Joint decision making, where appropriate, can help staff members feel much more in control of their jobs and their lives.

It is the coordinator's responsibility to model behavior that is appropriate and acceptable. Staff members will often be watching to see how the coordinator handles difficult behaviors or situations that arise with residents.

The difficulties that staff face in working with persons with dementia can create situations in which failure seems to predominate. The criteria that define quality in the traditional nursing home are often not applicable in a dementia unit. Schedules are not easily followed, tasks may not be completed on time, residents in the area may at times seem out of control. The staff need to be helped to understand that a major goal is to help residents enjoy life, and success is measured by the accomplishment of necessary tasks with the least amount of stress on residents. But staff members frequently need help in identifying what they are doing well.

It is important for all staff members on a dementia unit to be formally evaluated at least once a year. The evaluation should include a discussion of those aspects of the job the person is doing well, along with identifying areas for improvement. In addition to formal evaluations, it is important for the coordinator to provide constructive feedback to the staff on an ongoing basis. Administrators may feel they are losing control or becoming lax if they are not rigidly checking up on the staff and tightening the reins. Feedback, however, too often simply describes the shortcomings and errors of the staff. Below are examples of two ways of giving feedback to a staff member:

> If I hear you talk to Mr. James like that again, I will write you up. You know better than that.

> I noticed that Mr. James became very upset when you asked him to take a bath. Why not sit down with him for a while until he becomes comfortable with you? I saw you approach Mr. Frost the other day in such a pleasant way, and he responded immediately. It will probably take a while for Mr. James to respond, but give him time. Try chatting with him a while, then let me know how things go. I think he gets very frustrated when he can't do things, and needs gentleness and lots of time.

The second approach gives the staff person an alternative and, at the same time, recognizes something positive that he or she has done. Again, modeling of desired behaviors is a crucial task of the coordinator.

### The Permanent Assignment of Staff

Rotating staff on and off the dementia unit versus permanently assigning staff to specific shifts is controversial. Some programs have reported problems with burnout when the staff are permanently assigned to the unit. This often happens when a program has not made an aggressive commitment to looking at ways to reduce the stress staff may be experiencing.

Frequent rotation of staff members makes it difficult to provide a familiar and consistent environment, which is one of the requirements for a specialized dementia care program (Weaverdyck and

Coons 1988). The confusion and disorientation of residents are only increased by having to get accustomed to the ways of many different staff members. It also makes it exceedingly difficult, if not impossible, for staff members to get to know individual residents, their daily habits and routines. At best, staff-resident relationships are superficial.

Edelson and Lyons (1985) found that specific, permanent staff assignments lead to closer and more meaningful relationships with residents, in most instances producing clearly improved staff morale. The staff generally feel a greater sense of personal responsibility, autonomy, and control when they are assigned to a specific group of residents.

In units where the staff are frequently rotated, it is very difficult to build a tight, cohesive team of staff members who are committed to working together to identify and solve problems. The sense of camaraderie and identity that develops with being a member of a regular work group is reduced when the staffing is inconsistent.

The opportunity for work reassignment on a temporary or permanent basis, however, should be an option for those staff members who may become exhausted by the emotional demands of working on a dementia unit. Giving a staff member the option to work temporarily in another wing of the facility allows the person to reflect on what he or she wants to be doing. As was previously mentioned, caring for people with dementing disorders can be difficult, and not everyone has the skills or the patience to work in this setting.

One final comment regarding assignment of staff members. A policy should be developed that discourages pulling the staff from the dementia unit to fill in for nursing shortages in other areas of the nursing home. When staff members are required elsewhere, it is not unusual for the administration to take them from the area where residents do not complain or will not remember. This practice not only burdens the staff working on the unit, but it can have disastrous effects on the residents. Hurried rather than relaxed staff persons only increase the level of residents' anxiety and can be a precipitating factor for difficult behaviors. The administration needs to be fully aware of these problems when they are handling sick leave and vacation time.

## *Time away from Work*

Sometimes it is helpful to schedule social events for the staff. Occasional potlucks, barbecues, and the like can help foster team building and camaraderie. The opportunity to become acquainted with each other outside the work setting can help build supportive relationships among the staff. Some units have found periodic staff retreats a helpful way of building morale and airing concerns; these retreats can often combine social functions with staff meetings.

It is very important for staff members to have adequate time away from work. The coordinator of the dementia unit should limit the number of hours a staff person works to no more than eight or nine, except in cases of emergency. There are some staff members who seem to take pride in working 10- or 12-hour shifts, and of course, some facilities contribute to this by continually working short staffed and encouraging overtime. In addition, administrators often get into the habit of relying on the same staff members for emergencies or being on call.

The long-term consequences of this kind of involvement can be deleterious for both staff persons and residents. Inevitably, the staff become tired and short-tempered. Eventually they will most likely quit or move off the unit—in other words, they will experience burnout. In a situation where the staff member seeks long or double shifts, it may be helpful to find out what motivates this behavior. Is it because he or she has nothing else to do? Is the person making the unit a home away from home? Is it for the extra money? One recent study (Tellis-Nayak and Tellis-Nayak 1989) looked at how nurse's aides' cultural background and home life affected the way in which they delivered care to nursing home residents.

A related recommendation is that the staff be encouraged to take their vacation time. It is helpful to be flexible in honoring requests for time off, even when such requests are made on short notice. Some staff members like to accumulate their vacation time, viewing it as a kind of status symbol for the long hours worked. This behavior should be discouraged as it can only lead to burnout.

### Creating an Environment for the Staff That Encourages Innovation

For many direct care staff working in nursing homes, the routines involved in caring for confused, dependent residents can be difficult and tedious. The repetitive tasks of bathing, dressing, toileting, changing beds, and feeding day after day can become quite monotonous. Once these routines have been mastered, there are often few challenges in the nursing home environment for the staff. Research by Hackman and Oldham (1975) suggested that when work lacks challenge and stimulation, the staff person's involvement and motivation suffer, and burnout is more likely to occur.

Thus, in the dementia unit it is important for the coordinator to create a dynamic environment, one that encourages the staff to grow and to learn new skills in caring for cognitively impaired people. The challenge is to create an atmosphere in which the staff are motivated or inspired to give the very best care possible. To maintain this high level of energy and enthusiasm in the staff requires a great deal of skill on the part of the coordinator, whose primary focus should be on supporting and training the staff and on modeling behavior. If the staff feel they are being supported and encouraged, they will be more committed to looking at innovative care techniques. Obviously, the leadership style of the coordinator, as discussed earlier, is critically important in developing a supportive environment.

The coordinator should consider ways to tap some of the special talents the staff already bring to the job and to build on or refine those skills. For example, although staff members may have some excellent programing ideas they may not know how to modify activities to residents' skill levels.

One creative nurse's aide had several interests that became popular activities on a dementia unit. In one instance she brought in a racetrack with remote-controlled race cars. Several residents were able, with help from the staff, to learn to work the controls and delighted in racing the cars. Some participated by picking up cars that fell off and putting them back on the track. Still others enjoyed simply watching the activity and being part of the group.

Often staff members enjoy gardening, cooking, or woodworking activities, for example, but need a great deal of help learning how to involve cognitively impaired residents in those activities. Without training in task modification, a cooking project may be so unsuccessful that the staff member feels frustrated and believes that the residents are incapable of participating in any activities. The coordinator could use weekly staff meetings to focus on some of the techniques involved in modifying activities or tasks to different levels of impairment, as well as on different approaches to use in engaging residents in activities.

It is important for staff members to feel they play a central role in the unit. When the staff have been instrumental in developing and implementing activity programs, they gain a sense of ownership and pride in the unit. It is also helpful for supervisory staff to encourage the nurse's aides to be responsible for certain tasks on their shift and to be able to make decisions related to how and when they will carry out those tasks. Having areas of responsibility and being able to make decisions can greatly enhance staff morale and feelings about work.

To have a dynamic unit, the staff must be encouraged to take risks, to try new approaches and programs. This will happen only if the coordinator models this type of risk-taking behavior and if the staff are convinced that they will not be punished for failure.

Mistakes should be viewed as opportunities to learn more about a particular problem or situation. It is helpful to point out to the staff that when mistakes do not occur it may be because innovation is not occurring. At the same time, the staff need to be reassured that their jobs will not be in jeopardy if their ideas are unsuccessful. In facilities where there is a controlling, authoritarian style of management, staff members are often very hesitant about testing out ideas for fear of being reprimanded or even dismissed. When a program allows direct care staff to be innovative and provides the staff with opportunities to learn new skills, the job remains stimulating and burnout, to a large extent, can be prevented.

### Staff Development

Many of the underlying causes of job stress and burnout can be resolved through staff development programs. When new staff members are hired, very often little attention is given to orienting them to the philosophy of the facility. This frequently occurs when homes have chronic staff turnover problems. A well-designed orientation program can be an effective way of helping the new staff become acquainted with the dementia unit and its goals. This can be a good time to let new staff persons know that they are valuable members of the team, and that their opinions, observations, and ideas about the program and the residents will be valued and respected.

One particularly effective approach to orientation is the "buddy system." Instead of being immediately assigned to residents, new staff members attend training sessions and work alongside experienced staff members. Gradually, the new staff members begin to assume more responsibility working with several residents themselves, while being observed by their staff "buddies." Eventually the new staff members assume total responsibility for work on their shift. This kind of careful orientation of new staff persons can eliminate many of the concerns a new person may have about feeling incompetent in interactions with confused older people. Also, it is an excellent way of recognizing the skills and abilities of the experienced staff involved in the orientation. In addition, their modeling of communication techniques and approaches can help reinforce the kind of relationship that is valued between the staff and the residents on the unit.

An orientation program can also help new staff members develop realistic goals in working with cognitively impaired people. It can be very upsetting to become attached to people who continue to deteriorate despite your best efforts. New staff members may have difficulty recognizing that instead of helping a person with dementia to regain a particular skill, the ultimate goal is to help that person feel valued and fulfilled. This goal may be achieved by sharing refreshments together, holding hands with the person, or simply laughing or smiling together. Again, the coordinator will have to set the stage, making it acceptable, and in fact desirable, for the staff and residents to spend time in social interactions.

It is important for the staff at the outset to recognize momentary, short-lived pleasure as a legitimate therapeutic goal (Weaverdyck and Coons 1988). New staff members may be upset by the realization that residents with dementia may not remember pleasurable activities or conversations for very long. Helping the staff develop realistic expectations and goals may alleviate some of the frustration staff experience as people become more impaired.

As part of the orientation process, one program developed an orientation booklet for new or interested staff to read (New York State Department of Health 1987). In addition to a description of some of the rewards and challenges in working on the unit, it realistically described some typical examples of the frustrations and difficulties of the job. Written materials with practical suggestions can also be helpful because staff can refer back to them repeatedly when they are experiencing difficulties.

Another way of dealing with some of the stresses that occur on the dementia unit is to form a monthly support group for the staff. Support groups have become quite popular in mental health settings as an intervention for a wide variety of problems (Cherniss 1987). Maslach (1976) first proposed the support group as a remedy for burnout; she found that human service providers seemed to cope with stress better when they had opportunities to discuss their feelings about the job in a supportive group setting.

Support groups can be a very effective method for some staff members to share their feelings and frustrations about work and to realize that others have similar feelings and experiences.

A dementia unit in one nursing home used one of its monthly support group meetings for the staff to discuss grief and the ways in which staff were coping with the recent death of a resident. After an emotional discussion about the enormous loss and sadness that the staff were feeling, a decision was made to hang a photograph with a brief description of the resident in the hallway, where staff members and other residents could see it. This led to the creation of a memorial garden in the courtyard, where flowering shrubs would be planted in honor of deceased residents.

To a large extent, the success of a support group is dependent on the skill of the facilitator and his or her ability to create an accepting atmosphere and handle group dynamics. Support groups are different from therapy groups; the focus should be on work-related concerns. Similarly, care must be taken to ensure that the group meetings do not become "gripe sessions" in which the staff complain about administrators or administrative decisions. Scully (1983) suggested that "one way to avoid this pitfall is to emphasize problem-solving. In other words, the group should help its members to examine questions such as, Why is this situation a problem? What are the feelings associated with this situation? What are the factors that contribute to the situation? What can be done? What are the consequences of various interventions?" (cited in Cherniss 1987, p. 167).

Some staff members may not feel comfortable in this type of group, and no one should be compelled to attend. Some programs have made arrangements for a consulting psychologist or mental health worker to be available for staff members who prefer to talk to someone privately.

Some coordinators of dementia units have found it helpful to meet monthly with supervisory staff from other dementia programs in their geographic area. This can be an effective way of sharing some of the problems, concerns, and frustrations that can accompany new and innovative projects.

### Training, Staff Meetings, and Problem-solving Sessions

Another way of supporting the staff is to provide them with regular in-service training sessions. Short, weekly, informal staff meetings (e.g., 45–60 minutes) can be used for this purpose. Some staff meetings must inevitably be devoted to administrative procedures or issues, but others might be training or problem-solving sessions.

In keeping with the idea of shared decision making, it is important to encourage staff input into the development of agendas for staff meetings. For example, some units post a tentative agenda and ask the staff to add topics of concern. This helps ensure that their concerns and needs are being addressed.

Meeting times should be rotated to accommodate staff members from different shifts. Staff meetings are most helpful and successful when they are multidisciplinary, involving all staff members who regularly interact with the residents: housekeepers, nurses, nurse's aides, social workers, occupational therapists, and recreational therapists, for example.

The unpredictable personality and behavioral changes that occur in dementing disorders can be very frightening and overwhelming. Frequently the staff do not know how to respond in these situations; they feel helpless, anxious, and even threatened. Their understanding of Alzheimer's disease and other dementias often is minimal, and management strategies become limited to physical restraints and medications.

In-service training should focus on teaching the staff about the unique characteristics of the disease and problem-solving strategies that can help them become better equipped to cope. In a simple and practical way, the staff need to understand how the problems of dementia are different from some of the other disorders that affect residents in the rest of the nursing home.

In addition, training should focus on specific techniques and approaches that the staff can use in managing some of the difficult behaviors. It is important for the staff to understand why some of these behaviors may be occurring and to recognize that these behaviors are not deliberate. They also need to be given a repertoire of intervention strategies that can be used in responding to difficult situations. There are several practical books written for long-term care staff that can be used as reference guides when discussing difficult behaviors during staff meetings (Gwyther 1985; Robinson et al. 1988).

Once the staff have learned some of the skills involved in communicating with someone with dementia, their interactions with the residents on the unit will probably be more successful. The staff will feel more assured knowing they have the skills to draw upon when faced with a difficult situation. In-service training and problem-solving sessions can be an effective way of increasing the skills and abilities of the staff; equally important, these sessions are likely to increase their job satisfaction.

Teaching problem-solving skills and using them regularly in staff meetings and training sessions is one of the most effective tools for helping staff members cope with stress. Problem-solving techniques can be applied successfully to deal with difficult staff relations, interdepartmental problems, and dilemmas related to activities and to difficult behaviors of residents in the dementia unit. Below is an outline of one problem-solving approach that has been used effectively with staff members in long-term care settings.

*Definition of the problem.* The first step in problem solving is to identify the specific problem that needs to be addressed. Defining the problem specifically and narrowly is sometimes a difficult process. When applying this to a difficult behavior, for example, staff members should ask the following types of questions: When does the behavior occur? Where? With whom? In what way is the behavior a problem to the staff or other residents? Zarit and colleagues (1985) suggested keeping a daily record or log as a way of helping the staff clearly describe the problem.

*Goals.* The next step in the problem-solving process is to define clear goals for addressing the problem. These might include both long- and short-term goals, depending on the problem. For example, suppose the unit is having trouble gaining cooperation from the dietary department to implement a flexible breakfast schedule. The long-term goal might be a flexible schedule that makes breakfast available between 7:00 a.m. and 9:30 a.m. The short-term goals could include meeting with the dietary department, drawing up a statement about why this is an important part of the program of the dementia unit, and so on. Goals must be specific and realistic to be useful.

*Causes.* The next step in the process is to identify possible causes or reasons why the problem is occurring. If the problem is a difficult behavior, the staff might consider these questions: Are there some specific factors that seem to trigger the behavior? What are some possible causes for this behavior? (See Chap. 12.) For example, if a resident is having trouble eating, is it because there is too much food on the plate? Is he or she having a problem using the silverware? Noise? Impatient staff? Fatigue? Does the dining room look too institutional? Having staff brainstorm possible reasons why the behavior is occurring and writing them on a board or newsprint can be helpful.

*Strategies.* Once the staff have identified possible causes for the problem, the next step is to develop a list of possible strategies for responding to the problem. In developing a list of strategies it is important to share those strategies that have worked to date, as well as those that have not. For example, in a situation where a resident is resistant to bathing, one staff member may have been successful by giving the resident a choice of bath or shower, a technique that is important for other staff to know. Zarit and colleagues (1985) pointed out the importance of "not prejudging the solution . . . rather caregivers should be encouraged to be as uninhibited as possible in proposing solutions" (p. 102).

It should be emphasized to staff that problem solving is a process of trial and error. There are not always simple solutions. Sometimes staff relations or frustrations or interdepartmental problems can be resolved satisfactorily and relatively easily using a problem-solving approach. Difficulties with residents with dementia are often more difficult, and one solution generally does not solve the problem. More often a solution depends on a combination of different strategies. At the end of the problem-solving session, staff members should leave with agreed-upon strategies, and sometimes assignments, to try out during the week.

*Evaluation.* The final step is to carry out the plan and to evaluate its effectiveness. With difficult behaviors, this will involve careful documentation describing which interventions worked and which did not work. Many units have developed documentation forms, such as that in Figure 8.1. When dealing with other kinds of problems, carrying out the plan and evaluating it may take different forms.

## Applying the Strategies

Suppose Rose Marie White, the staff member described at the beginning of this chapter, brings her frustrations to a staff meeting. There are a number of potential problems here. One is the resident who has become quite angry and hostile toward the staff and other residents. A problem-solving approach could be used in thinking about possible reasons for his behavior. Staff members could brainstorm strategies and develop a plan of action for responding to his behavior. Staff members would report back the following week on the effectiveness of their strategies. As part of the plan, staff members might decide that the resident requires a medical examination, including a review of his medications. The coordinator or nurse would report back on those results.

Another serious problem related to Rose Marie's situation is the short staffing. This problem could be identified in the staff meeting, but it would most likely then become an administrative issue. A thoughtful administrator would keep staff members abreast of the efforts to recruit and train new staff members.

However, there may be times when it is necessary to use pool staff from an agency. Staff members on the unit could very effectively apply a problem-solving approach to the issue of working with pool staff. Possible strategies might include the unit coordinator requesting

Name of resident: _____          Date: _____

Long-term goal(s): _____

_____

_____

Short-term goal(s): _____

_____

_____

Strategy Tried          Time of Day        Staff Name          Results

_____

_____

_____

_____

_____

_____

Additional comments: _____

_____

_____

**Figure 8.1.**  A sample documentation form for evaluating difficult behaviors

consistency in the assignment of the pool staff from the agency, the development of a short orientation program for the pool staff, or reallocation of staff assignments and tasks when pool staff are working.

A supervisor or coordinator who was seriously concerned about Rose Marie's frustrations would spend some time individually meeting with her. A number of relevant issues have been discussed in this chapter: the possibility of involving her in the training of new staff, of changing her shift, or of rotating her out of the unit for a while; the importance of helping her evaluate how much she is working and whether she has accumulated vacation time that she should take;

and the possibility of involving her in a staff support group or linking her to mental health services if that is advisable.

There is no question that working on a dementia unit is a very difficult and often stressful job. It is a challenge for administrative and supervisory staff to develop a program that supports, respects, and values both residents and staff members at all levels. Providing the staff with some control over their worklife, involving them in decision making whenever possible, and teaching them problem-solving techniques can help create the humane environment that all people require in their work settings.

## References

Bales, J. 1975. Nursing centers take action to reduce employee turnover. *Cross Reference*, 5:7–8.

Cherniss, C. 1987. Staff burnout in dealing with the elderly: How to help the helper. In *Disturbed Behavior in the Elderly*, edited by A. G. Awad, H. Durost, H. R. Meier, and W. O. McCormick, 161–181. New York: Pergamon Press.

Coons, D. H. 1987. Training staff to work in special care units. *American Journal of Alzheimer's Care and Research*, 2(5):6–12.

Edelson, J. S., and W. H. Lyons. 1985 *Institutional care of the mentally impaired elderly*. New York: Van Nostrand Reinhold.

Gwyther, L. P. 1985. *Care of Alzheimer's patients: A manual for nursing home staff*. Washington D.C.: American Health Care Association and Alzheimer's Disease and Related Disorders Association.

Hackman, J. R., and G. R. Oldham. 1975. Development of the job diagnostic survey. *Journal of Applied Psychology*, 60:159–170.

Heine, C. A. 1986. Burnout among nursing home personnel. *Journal of Gerontological Nursing*, 12(3):14–18.

Hoffman, S., C. Platt, and K. Barry. 1987. Managing the difficult dementia patient: The impact on untrained nursing home staff. *American Journal of Alzheimer's Care and Research*, 2(4):26–31.

Kane, R. L., and R. A. Kane, editors, 1982. *Values and long-term care*. Lexington, Mass.: Lexington Books.

Maslach, C. 1976. Burned-out. *Human Behavior*, 5(9):16–22.

New York State Department of Health. 1987. Innovations in the care of the memory impaired elderly. Conference proceedings.

Ohta, R. J., and B. M. Ohta. 1988. Special units for Alzheimer's disease patients: A critical look. *Gerontologist*, 28(6):803–808.

Rabins, P. V., N. L. Mace, and J. Lucas. 1982. The impact of dementia on the family. *Journal of the American Medical Association*, 248(3):333–335.

Robinson, A., B. Spencer, and L. White. 1988 *Understanding difficult behaviors: Some practical suggestions for coping with Alzheimer's disease and related illnesses*.

Ypsilanti: Geriatric Education Center of Michigan, Eastern Michigan University.

Ronch, J. L. 1987. Specialized Alzheimer's units in nursing homes: Pros and cons. *American Journal of Alzheimer's Care and Research*, 2(4):10–19.

Scully, R. 1983. The work-setting-support group: A means of preventing burnout. In *Stress and burnout in the human service profession*, edited by B. A. Farber, 188–197. New York: Pergamon Press.

Stryker, R. 1981. *How to reduce employee turnover in nursing homes*. Springfield, Ill.: Charles C Thomas.

Stryker, R. 1982. The effect of managerial intervention on high personnel turnover in nursing homes. *Journal of Long-term Care Administration*, 10(4):21–33.

Tellis-Nayak, V., and M. Tellis-Nayak. 1989. Quality of care and the burden of two cultures when the world of the nurse's aide enters the world of the nursing home. *Gerontologist*, 29(3):307–313.

U.S. Congress, Office of Technology Assessment. 1987. *Losing a million minds: Confronting the tragedy of Alzheimer's disease and other dementias*. OTA-BA-323. Washington D.C.: U.S. Government Printing Office.

Waxman, H. M., E. A. Carner, and G. Berkenstock. 1984. Job turnover and job satisfaction among nursing home aides. *Gerontologist*, 24(5):503–509.

Weaverdyck, S. E., and D. H. Coons. 1988. Designing a dementia residential care unit: Addressing cognitive changes with the Wesley Hall model. In *Housing the very old*, edited by G. M. Gutman and N. K. Blackie, 63–85. Burnaby, British Columbia: Simon Fraser University Press.

Zarit, S. H., N. K. Orr, and J. M. Zarit. 1985 *The hidden victims of Alzheimer's disease*. New York: New York University Press.

Zarit, S. H., P. A. Todd, and J. M. Zarit. 1986. Subjective burden of husbands and wives as caregivers: A longitudinal study. *Gerontologist*, 26(3):260–266.

# Chapter 9

# Activities and Staff Approaches: The Impact on Behaviors

DOROTHY H. COONS

Persons with dementia exhibit many behaviors with which caretakers have difficulty coping. Some people may become explosive and combative as they attempt to struggle with changes and situations they can no longer comprehend. Some may wander incessantly, possibly in efforts to locate someone or something, or as a result of boredom or agitation. Incontinence may occur more frequently as impairment increases. Refusal to bathe, eat, or get out of bed may also occur as persons become more impaired. Staff members in dementia care units are constantly searching for ways to reduce the frequency of these behaviors. While there are many potential causes and a variety of possible interventions, this chapter will discuss the impact of an effective program of activities and various staff approaches upon behaviors.

## A Program of Activities

An environment in which nothing occurs except the bare essentials of existence fosters feelings of hopelessness, humiliation, boredom, and anger. Intact persons in such an environment may be able to articulate their feelings even though they may be powerless to bring about change. Cognitively impaired persons often can express their frustrations and anger only through behaviors that are identified as management problems.

One of the most effective ways to reduce the frequency and intensity of problem behaviors in persons in the middle stages of Alzheimer's disease is to develop a dynamic program of activities carefully selected to provide a sense of normality and feelings of

161

familiarity and satisfaction. While the therapeutic milieu, with its many components, attempts to design an environment similar to that in one's home, it has the potential of deliberately creating a prosthetic environment often impossible in the actual home situation. The prosthetic environment is defined here as one that deliberately incorporates features that can serve to compensate for the residents' cognitive impairments and sensory losses. The trained staff, the carefully selected program of activities, and the specially designed physical environment together can enable residents to continue to function in everyday activities by making constant adaptations to the fluctuating and changing capacities of the impaired persons. These ongoing evaluations and adjustments are often difficult, if not impossible, to implement by families caring for relatives at home.

### Maintaining Continuity with the Past

The therapeutic environment emulates a home in that it offers residents opportunities to continue in the normal social roles of homemaker, friend or social being, and family member—roles that encourage instrumental and "well" behaviors. These roles carry with them specific behavioral expectations that are usually understood by intact persons even though they may not comply with the expectations. The person in the role of homemaker is expected to assume the tasks essential for maintaining the home. In the role of friend the person is expected to communicate, share, or support (Coons 1989). The availability of social roles for cognitively impaired persons creates a lucid environment that offers tasks and social situations in a familiar context. The roles are available, but they are optional at all times. They are therapeutic for cognitively impaired persons only when there is an absence of stress or demands. The residents are able to assume these roles and respond to their expectations within the limits of their abilities because they are appealing and familiar.

Ritual and traditional practices play a vital role in helping elderly persons maintain a sense of continuity with the past (Shield 1988). The rituals can also help create a sense of community within a treatment setting and cohesiveness that does not exist in the medicalized institution.

In her tapestry of human experiences, Myerhoff (1978) described the importance of family, ethnic, and religious rituals in the lives of the elderly. Providing opportunities for residents to reminisce can help recapture some of the traditions that were important in the lives of their families and can provide staff with information that will enable them to individualize, rather than institutionalize, activities. When families visit, they can be encouraged to continue practices that were pleasing and memorable for the older family member. Special holidays that were celebrated by the family year after year with the same traditions and rituals are often the most difficult times for both families and their older relatives in nursing homes.

> For the Fullertons, visiting Mr. Fullerton's mother at Christmastime in the nursing home where she lived was a dreaded experience. The elderly Mrs. Fullerton remembered her son and his family, but she was no longer able to talk to them. The family visit consisted of a few awkward comments by family members, the giving of a gift to Mrs. Fullerton that they opened for her, and then a quick and uncomfortable parting.

> Mrs. Clark also lived in a nursing home, and she too was so severely impaired that she could no longer converse when her son and his wife, their children, and grandchildren came to visit. Christmas had always been a happy and exciting time in the Clark family. One of the traditions had been that decorating the Christmas tree was an activity shared by everyone amid the playing of Christmas music and popping popcorn.
>   When the Clark family visited the elderly Mrs. Clark at Christmas, they came prepared to have a wonderful time. They brought a small Christmas tree and a box of decorations that had been accumulated over the years. They also brought a tape recorder with Christmas tapes, a corn popper, and a variety of small gifts for everyone. Mrs. Clark's gifts were wrapped in gaily colored paper and tied with yarn bows without knots, so that she could open them with very little assistance. The tree was decorated with everyone's help including Mrs. Clark's, and the music and laughter and the aroma of newly popped corn lured several of the other residents to Mrs. Clark's room. The visit extended over several hours, and it was a joyous and fun-filled occasion. The recapturing of old and cherished traditions enabled all of the Clarks to enjoy the special event and retain a sense of family unity.

### Scope of Activities

The term *program of activities*, is defined here in the broadest sense to include all events that occur in the resident's day. These activities consist not only of special events but of the activities of daily living, household tasks in which residents can be involved, social interaction, humorous and lighthearted activities, and a variety of tasks that can be introduced (such as folding flyers or stuffing envelopes) to enable residents to serve as volunteers. These all can create a rich environment that provides meaning and purpose and a sense of achievement for residents (Zgola 1987).

If the program is to be therapeutic, all parts need to be managed in a supportive and "wellness-fostering" manner. The activities of daily living, for example, need to be viewed by staff not as routines or ordeals to be accomplished as quickly as possible, but as occasions for sharing with residents and helping them to continue in tasks or parts of tasks they are still able to manage alone or with help. All activities can provide occasions for social interactions and opportunities for the staff to help residents to continue to be involved and to develop a sense of belonging.

Activities effectively implemented can have impact on behaviors in a variety of ways. Residents' preoccupation with the tasks of the moment can help distract them from their problems, and the success they experience from their involvement seems to give them a sense of fulfillment and achievement. Well-planned and structured activities can facilitate social interactions between impaired persons in undemanding ways. The focus is on the task or activity at the moment, and the communication is often a natural reaction to what is happening. When residents are encouraged to participate in familiar and comfortable activities, some can proceed with minimal instruction and preparation. They may even be able to initiate some activities if materials and equipment are readily available, if they see others participating, and if the staff demonstrate that their efforts are acceptable and appreciated. Interesting and pleasant activities also help relieve boredom, one of the potential causes of some of the difficult behaviors.

During the Wesley Hall project, the staff on all shifts kept a daily log. They recorded special events, any problems they were having, their successes in working with residents, and specific ways in which residents were involved. The log became a method of sharing information and ideas and, at times, a catharsis when the staff was experiencing stressful and difficult situations. The following excerpts from the log written by one of the staff on the day shift illustrate the variety of tasks in which residents in the middle stages of Alzheimer's disease can be involved.

I approached Mr. Cooper about taking a bath. He became angry and struck out at me and yet he didn't seem to want me to leave. I waited and tried talking quietly to him, and after a while he calmed down and removed his clothes and let me help him with his bath. Then he shaved and by that time he was smiling. He walked down with me to the kitchen, and he mixed, baked, and frosted some brownies. He cracked three eggs after I showed him how. He stirred up the brownie mix and seemed quite pleased with himself. When he was finished, Mary [the housekeeper] playfully tossed a ball to him, and he demonstrated some tricky pitches—behind his back and under his leg—and laughed a lot.

The log continued, describing how others were involved.

Almost everyone was busy for a while today. Mr. Griffin mopped the men's bathroom, and Mrs. Radway mopped the dining room with some help from Mary. Mrs. Radway, Mrs. Jeffries, and Mrs. French each helped set her own table for dinner. After they finished eating, Mrs. Radway, Mrs. French, and Mrs. Devon helped clear the tables. Mr. Griffin helped scrape the dishes, and then, after I got the dishwater set up, Mrs. Butterfield washed and Mrs. Mackie dried. It has been a very good day, and everyone seemed in a relaxed and friendly mood.

Involvement to this extent comes about gradually as residents become comfortable with the environment and as the staff make it clear, by giving praise and by acknowledging even the smallest contribution, that they value residents' efforts. At the same time it is essential that the staff determine the amount and type of help each resident needs to complete a task. For Mrs. Jeffries to set the table, a staff person needed to point out the location of each placemat, the napkins, and so on, taking her through the total process of setting the table step by step.

A number of activities can be introduced spontaneously to help reduce stress and tension. Sing-alongs, ball tossing, and exercise programs can involve residents to the extent they want to respond, but even spectators can be helped to relax if the mood and activities are fun and entertaining. These activities can be especially effective after the evening meal, when restlessness and agitation often seem to reach a peak.

At times too much stimulation or confusion can cause residents to react angrily. Tasks or activities can be suggested deliberately or the person can be taken to another area in an effort to change the behavior.

Mr. Cowan occasionally became quite agitated when several other residents sat near him and attempted to carry on a conversation. He would jump up from his chair, stomp his foot, and begin to swear. The staff learned that one of the most effective interventions was to walk over to him and say quietly, "Mr. Cowan, I need your help very much. Will you help me push the food cart down to the kitchen?" (Or, "Will you go down to the lobby with me to pick up the newspaper?") Such appeals for his help seemed to please him, and by the time he returned to the unit he was usually relaxed and in a good mood.

For a period of time, Mrs. Reinhart wanted to spend much of her time in bed, getting up only occasionally to go to the bathroom or to come to the dining room for meals. The staff knew that she usually enjoyed the game of ball tossing when a group of residents gathered in the living room. They found that she could often be lured from her bed when a staff person went to her door and said, "Mrs. Reinhart, we are having a ball game in the living room and we need your good pitching arm."

At another time Mrs. Reinhart lay on her bed resisting all of the staff's efforts to get her to come to breakfast. A staff person went to her door and tossed in a rubber ball. Mrs. Reinhart immediately got out of bed to retrieve it and went to the living room for a short game of ball toss and then to breakfast.

If the staff who are on the night shift have a variety of one-to-one activities available, they can do much to reduce nighttime wandering and agitation. When a resident seems restless and too disturbed to sleep, the staff person can suggest that they prepare a snack together, or set the table for breakfast, or play a game together. The activity accompanied by lighthearted conversation can help the resident gradually relax and eventually return to bed with a sense of security and companionship.

When a program of activities encompasses the tasks and pleasures of normal living, there are many opportunities for resident involvement, resulting in a reduction in the frequency with which difficult behaviors occur. It becomes a method of helping residents avoid difficult behaviors rather than the staff's attempting to manage them when they occur.

## Staff Approaches

Staff persons can become effective in averting difficult behaviors, or at least reducing their intensity, by developing a variety of approaches and becoming sensitive to the changing moods of residents and the potential causes of the behaviors. No single approach is consistently successful, and the staff in dementia care units need to be constantly aware of the impact their responses, requests, or styles of communication have on residents and to make immediate adjustments when the person becomes angry or agitated. This may be difficult and stressful but, at the same time, it can be satisfying and rewarding when staff members are able to help impaired persons become more relaxed and responsive (Burnside 1976).

Staff members need to be sensitive to residents' needs or problems so that they can respond appropriately. They also need to learn about the residents' earlier habits and standards of behavior so that they can identify the possible cause of a behavior and change the practice, the physical environment, or the staff's approach to avoid the problem (see Chaps. 12 and 13). For example, the lack of privacy in some institutional settings may be one of the major causes of aggressive behaviors and combativeness. Most of the elderly currently living in treatment settings grew up in a period when modesty and privacy were considered essential. The cognitively impaired person may be unable to describe the embarrassment and shame of being forced to bathe or use the toilet with others in the vicinity, but the person's agitation can convey quickly to a sensitive staff member the wish for privacy (Edelson and Lyons 1985).

> Mrs. Oliver was in the bathtub being helped by Jean, an aide. The tub room was separated from the toilet area by a swinging half door that was hung about a foot from the floor. Suddenly Mrs. Oliver began striking Jean, and pointing to the floor beyond the door. When she yelled, "Out, out!" Jean realized that beneath the door she could see several residents walking around in the toilet area. A towel hung over the lower part of the door gave her the privacy she needed, and she was able to continue with her bath.

Environmental factors require frequent scrutiny, but it is also essential to assess systematically and regularly the possible medical causes of behaviors. Residents may be experiencing pain or discomfort that they cannot identify or describe, and the resulting behaviors may seem to have no clear relationship with the problem the person appears to be having. Improper dosages of medication may also trigger difficult behaviors (see Chaps. 12 and 14).

> Mrs. Jansen was a gentle woman whom the staff quickly became fond of when she moved into the unit. One morning she became quite combative. Her speech was limited to an occasional word or phrase, and she was unable to explain what was causing her anger. Examination revealed that she had a fecal impaction that was obviously causing her much discomfort. This was quickly corrected, and Mrs. Jansen returned to being her warm and pleasant self.

Because many persons with dementia are unable to express, even in a few words, what may be causing their behavior, the staff may be at a loss to identify what is triggering it. If the staff are taught to observe where, when, and under what conditions specific behaviors occur, they may find that a pattern emerges that will help them identify the cause. This, in turn, will enable the staff to make appropriate adjustments to help residents avoid specific behaviors (Robinson et al. 1988; Gwyther 1985).

### Diversion

If staff members intervene by providing a diversion or a distraction before a resident becomes extremely agitated, they can often help the person avoid strong reactions.

> Mrs. Overbrook rushed from her room in her nightgown yelling at Freda, the nearest staff person, "You never help me! I hate you! I hate you!" Freda said quietly, "I'm glad to see you Mrs. Overbrook. Let's take a look in your closet and see which of your pretty dresses you would like to wear today." She walked with Mrs. Overbrook to her room, and gradually Mrs. Overbrook relaxed as Freda helped her select a dress and proceed with dressing.

> Mrs. McKee paced restlessly up and down the hall, moaning and at times crying. Jean, an aide, fell in step with her and arm in arm they walked together as Jean talked about what a nice visit Mrs. McKee had had with her son the day before. Mrs. McKee could not remember the visit, but she listened attentively as Jean described how she and her son had spent the day together. After a while Mrs. McKee was willing to sit down with Jean to share a snack.

A number of items can be incorporated into the physical environment to provide interest and also serve as diversions when needed. Families can be asked to write notes on newsprint and post them on their relative's door as a reminder of a recent visit. Staff members can refer to the notes when residents complain that no one ever visits them. Framed prints or art pieces that are clear and easily identified or a large poster with residents' pictures can be a focus of attention and can serve to distract residents if they become agitated.

### Responding to the Emotional Tone

Many elderly people with severe cognitive impairment may no longer be able to put their feelings into words, but they may have the capacity to express their emotions clearly. *Emotional memory* is recall that provides the capacity to respond in ways that illustrate feelings and that are appropriate to those feelings. Emotional memory seems to be retained long after other memories are lost. Baruk (1954) expressed it with sensitivity, saying that in persons with severe dementia, "the consciousness of the heart . . . is frequently retained whereas the consciousness of the intellect is gone."

If staff members are sensitive to the emotions that are being expressed by older persons, they can help reassure or relieve the distress they may be feeling or respond to them in lighthearted ways when they seem to be feeling happy.

> Mrs. Scott had become so severely impaired that, with only an occasional exception, she expressed herself entirely by repeating the words, "We go here." Her emotional memory, however, was very much intact, and she was usually able to let others know how she was feeling.
>
> Her daughter arrived one day to see Mrs. Scott huddled in a chair in the dayroom of the nursing home in which she was living. Her daughter said, "Mother, you look exhausted. Do you want to lie down and rest for a while?" Mrs. Scott responded mournfully, "We go here! We go here! We go here! Oh God!" Her daughter quickly helped her to get into bed for a rest.
>
> On another occasion Mrs. Scott was attending a small birthday party that her daughter had arranged. When a staff person came into the room where the party was being held to wish Mrs. Scott a happy birthday, Mrs. Scott responded, smiling and almost giggling, "We go here, we go here, we go here!" The staff person said, "You are having a wonderful time, aren't you?"
>
> Gradually the staff learned, by heeding her body language and tone of voice, to interpret Mrs. Scott's moods and feelings as expressed with only three words, "We go here."

## A Lighthearted Approach

Joking and lighthearted banter sometimes help reduce tension. The style of humor can vary from gentle kidding to occasional clowning, absurdities to which even impaired persons may be able to respond. An informal, relaxed atmosphere encourages spontaneous and cheerful reactions that can ease tension and stress. It is important that the joking in no way belittle or ridicule the elderly person (See Chap. 10).

> Mrs. Zachary is quick to react with profanity and anger to any staff person's efforts. Jean, an aide, attempted to help her rise from her chair by reaching out for her hands. Mrs. Zachary immediately reacted by saying, "You ——— ———, you are trying to break my hands." Jean released her hands, knelt down in front of her and said playfully, "Wow, I must be strong! I always thought I was a weak one. Let's try again and you squeeze *my* hands this time." Mrs. Zachary reached for her hands and let

Jean pull her up. Mrs. Zachary laughed when Jean said, "You're the strong one! That was quite a hold you had on me."

## Touch

Touch is an important method of communication with impaired elderly persons. They may be able to comprehend a warm and spontaneous hug by a staff member better than words. Touch by a caring and affectionate staff person is probably one of the most therapeutic actions and can help combat the loneliness and sensory deprivation that the elderly experience. At the same time, touch can have a calming effect and can help reduce agitation and some of the difficulties behaviors. The staff need to be aware of and respect the fact, however, that not all people like to be touched (Burnside 1976).

## Explanation and Discussion

The style and degree of complexity of the staff's communication with cognitively impaired persons become increasingly important as deterioration occurs. Too frequently, the staff may assume that the person with dementia will not understand even simple explanations or instructions. At other times they may not recognize the communication problems a resident may be having and assume that the person is uncooperative when he or she does not respond. These assumptions lead to practices that fail to take advantage of the remaining capacities that may still be present in even very impaired persons.

Mrs. Zeller, a frail elderly patient in an acute care hospital, became quite disoriented after her admission. She was weak and in danger of falling if she attempted to get up from her bed alone. When the staff found her wandering around her room, they decided to use physical restraints as a precautionary measure. The restraints served the purpose of confining her to bed, but they also caused her to become increasingly agitated as she attempted to free herself.

Mrs. Dennison, a sensitive young nurse, observed Mrs. Zeller for several days, and was disturbed by the distress she seemed to be feeling and by her constant efforts to escape from the restraints. She spent time chatting with Mrs. Zeller in an attempt to develop a relationship with her and to gain an understanding of what she could comprehend.

Determined that the restraints should be removed, Mrs. Dennison sat with Mrs. Zeller one morning and began the conversation with, "Mrs. Zeller, this vest you have on upsets you very much, doesn't it? Do you know why they put the vest on?"

Mrs. Zeller said, "They think I'll fall."

Mrs. Dennison asked, "Do you think you might fall if you got up without help?"

Mrs. Zeller responded, "Yes, I probably would."

Mrs. Dennison continued, "I will take the vest off if you promise not to get up without calling for help. Are you willing to promise me?"

Mrs. Zeller nodded.

Mrs. Dennison then asked, "Do you know how to call for me?"

Mrs. Zeller said, "Yes, I push a button."

Mrs. Dennison smiled and said, "That's right. Try it now. What would you do if you wanted to call me?"

When Mrs. Zeller reached for the attachment on her bed that contained several buttons, Mrs. Dennison reminded her that it was always the red button that would let her know that Mrs. Zeller needed her.

Mrs. Zeller pushed the appropriate button and Mrs. Dennison assured here that she or whoever was on duty would come immediately when Mrs. Zeller pushed the button or called for them if she couldn't remember which button to push.

Mrs Dennison continued, "This is so important. We are so very fond of you and very concerned about you. Do you agree that we should put this vest back on if you try to get up without help?"

Mrs. Zeller nodded and reached out to pat Mrs. Dennison's hand and said, "I'll call you."

The intervention was a success. Mrs. Zeller could only occasionally locate and remember to push the call button. At other times she resorted to a yell of "Hey you!" to get the staff's attention, but she did not attempt to get out of bed without help. Even with her impaired memory, Mrs. Zeller was able to understand and retain the explanation and the instructions Mrs. Dennison had presented to her. Her agitation subsided, and she seemed relaxed and trusting in her relationship with the staff.

The approach illustrated here required that the staff have an understanding of how much the patient could comprehend and a commitment to take the time to establish a trusting relationship. It was also essential that the staff be willing to take risks while using every precaution to protect the individual from harm.

### Reassurance

The distress that many persons feel when they realize they are becoming cognitively impaired is expressed in many different ways. They may react in anger or sorrow, and if they are still able to communicate verbally, they may describe their feelings of hopelessness.

Mrs. George was sitting with Linda, an aide, sharing in the task of folding towels. Suddenly Mrs. George stopped working and, pointing to her head, said "Something is wrong up here. If I don't get help, what will I do?"

Linda did not deny the fact that Mrs. George had problems. Instead she acknowledged how she must be feeling and attempted to reassure her. Linda's response was, "I know how worried you must be. I want you to know that I will be here to help and take care of you, and so will Freda and Jane. You are very special to us." Linda's response did not entirely satisfy Mrs. George, but she relaxed and began working again, and Linda was soon able to joke with her about the mound of towels they had managed to fold.

An acknowledgment of the legitimacy of feelings can sometimes reduce the intensity of a person's reactions.

Mrs. Esher frequently became angry and combative when a staff person suggested a bath. Occasionally she accepted the idea if the staff member made the following or similar comments:

"I know you are angry, Mrs. Esher. I don't blame you. It's a lot of work to take a bath. Let's walk down the hall together and see if you feel in the mood when we get to the bathroom."

### Giving Choices

Giving residents choices when they resist certain activities can help them feel they have at least some control over their own lives. This approach also diverts attention away from the activity itself to the task of selecting one of the options. Following are several examples.

To Mrs. Esher, who resists taking baths, a staff person might say, "Mrs. Esher, would you rather take your bath this morning before you get dressed or after lunch?" Or the staff could suggest, "Mrs. Esher, after you have your bath let's have a snack together. Would you rather have a piece of pie or some fruit juice?"

To Mrs. Sullivan, who seems reluctant to join the music group, a staff person might suggest an alternative. "Mrs. Sullivan, would you like to sit over here away from the group so that you can see and hear what is going on and enjoy the music?" At a later time a staff person might approach her and say, "If you want to join the group, I will help you find a chair."

### Individualizing or Avoiding Schedules

Residents may have periods during the day when they are more receptive or when their energy levels seem to reach a peak. They may also have times of the day when they are disturbed; for example, the time after the evening meal may be an especially difficult period for some impaired persons. It becomes essential to recognize individual differences and to plan accordingly.

Stress in the early morning hours is greatly reduced if residents can select the time when they will have breakfast and get dressed. Times may vary from day to day, but the avoidance of a fixed schedule enables residents to follow their own lifestyles or their moods of the moment.

Individualized toileting schedules are essential for persons who have problems with incontinence. This requires a period of observation to determine how frequently each person needs to urinate, and times may vary greatly.

Set bath schedules, which often can be followed only if the staff use coercion, can cause much anger and resistance from residents and frustration and stress for staff members. Baths as well as breakfast time need to take into account residents' moods and capacities to respond at the moment. Such individualization of routines requires much staff flexibility and knowledge and constant awareness of residents' individual preferences.

## Conclusion

Ultimate goals in dementia care units are to provide a lifestyle that enables persons with dementia to continue to function, to enjoy what they are doing, and to live with dignity. To enable this to occur, there needs to be a constant examination and evaluation of the program of activities, of the physical environment, and of the approaches used by the staff to determine the impact they are having on residents. The program of activities and the variety of staff approaches described in this chapter will not occur without effective training and the strong support of the coordinator or the administrator. With this support, a dynamic and effective unit can be created that offers a program of daily activities that are interspersed, oftentimes spontaneously, with entertaining and amusing events or occurrences. What develops is a life for residents that is fun and involving and a work situation for the staff that fosters constant growth and creativity.

## References

Baruk, H. 1954. Some fundamental principles of neuropsychiatry of the elderly. In *Old age in the modern world*. Report of the Third Congress of the International Association of Gerontology. London: E. and S. Livingstone.

Burnside, I. M., editor. 1976. *Nursing and the aged*. New York: McGraw-Hill.

Coons, D. H. 1989. The therapeutic milieu: Social-psychological aspects of treatment. In *Clinical aspects of aging*, 3rd ed., edited by W. Reichel, 154–162. Baltimore: Williams and Wilkins.

Edelson, J. S., and W. H. Lyons. 1985 *Institutional care of the mentally impaired elderly*. New York: Van Nostrand Reinhold.

Gwyther, L. P. 1985. *Care of Alzheimer's patients: A manual for nursing home staff*. Washington, D.C.: American Health Care Association and Alzheimer's Disease and Related Disorders Association.

Myerhoff, B. 1978. *Number our days*. New York: Simon and Schuster.

Robinson, A., B. Spencer, and L. White. 1988. *Understanding difficult behaviors: Some practical suggestions for coping with Alzheimer's disease and related illnesses*. Ypsilanti: Geriatric Education Center of Michigan, Eastern Michigan University.

Shield, R. R. 1988. *Uneasy endings*. Ithaca, N.Y.: Cornell University Press.

Zgola, J. M. 1987. *Doing things*. Baltimore: Johns Hopkins University Press.

# Chapter 10

# Humor and Lighthearted Activities

## LILA GREEN

*A merry heart doeth good like a medicine;*
*but a broken spirit drieth the bones.*
(Proverbs 17:22).

Throughout history, humor and laughter have been believed to be both curative and cathartic. Depictions of mirth, jokes, and slapstick can be found among the wall paintings and hieroglyphics of ancient Egypt, and biblical references to humor offer even earlier documentation. Only recently, however, have health care professionals started to show academic interest in the therapeutic functions of humor for people who are physically or mentally impaired.

This chapter considers the effects of humor and lighthearted activities on elderly people who live in dementia care units. It presents the point of view that persons with dementia can be emotionally responsive and positively influenced by the use of humor in their everyday environment. The chapter also explores the impact of humor on professional caregivers, describing ways in which it can affect work performance, creativity, and motivation.

A major stimulus for the interest in the therapeutic effects of humor stemmed from the publication of *Anatomy of an Illness as Perceived by the Patient* (Cousins 1979). The author, Norman Cousins, is sometimes called the father of the "Ho Ho Holistic humor therapy movement." This book recounts Cousins's successful fight against a crippling, life-threatening form of arthritis called ankylosing spondylitis. In researching his illness, Cousins discovered that imbalances in the endocrine system could be caused by negative emotions. He decided to counteract his disease with positive feelings—with humor. It worked. Although his chance of complete recovery was said to be 1 in 500, he beat the odds—a feat he credits largely to the use of humor therapy. Although some physicians scoffed at his claims, citing that many had recovered from the illness without such methods, other doctors began to consider the potential impact of humor on recovery from illness. The publication of his experience sparked an explosion in research and writing about humor in health and healing.

Interest in the effects of humor on the elderly and on persons with Alzheimer's disease is a natural offshoot of the growing fascination with humor and health care that has sprung from Cousins's seminal work. Caregivers have discovered that many elderly people with dementia who are unable to remember the names of spouses or children are frequently able to sing an amusing old song from beginning to end or to make humorous remarks and clearly get enormous pleasure from it. The audience's appreciation and laughter in response to this effort usually lead to a lighthearted and relaxed feeling among all participants.

> A granddaughter told of her experiences with her severely impaired grandfather, whom she described as "the most fun of anyone in the family." He could be exceedingly exasperating, at times unmanageable, yet a few minutes later he would burst into song or act the clown in spontaneous and unexpected ways. These impromptu performances were constant reminders of the delightful person he had been before his illness, and helped her and others in the family cope with the stressful episodes that were occurring more and more frequently (Honel 1988).

The emotional memory of shared laughter seems to remain for a long time for people with dementia, even for some who are in the latter stages of the disease. The lyrics to the song "The Way We Were" (Hamlisch, Bergman, and Bergman, 1973) express it well: "Memories may be beautiful and yet . . . it's the laughter we will remember whenever we remember the way we were."

Although a specific humorous event may be quickly forgotten, the emotional memory of the experience lingers; good feelings and a sense of relaxation can cast a brighter color upon the rest of the person's day.

> On a particularly gloomy day, two small children came to visit a special unit. Their mother had brought with her several brightly colored balloons. Soon after their arrival the children and the residents who were gathered in the living room began a game of balloon tossing that drew much excitement and laughter from the children and smiles and chuckles from the older people. The effects of the pleasant experience continued long after the children were gone, and, with the bantering and playfulness of staff, residents were able to maintain the cheerful mood for a good part of the day (see Figure 10.1).

**Figure 10.1.** The cheerful mood when children visit

Humor is an elusive quality that is difficult to define. Webster's *New World Dictionary* gives one definition of *humor* as that which causes pleasant feelings or enjoyment, causing reactions of smiling, laughing, or feelings of amusement. Humor can be demonstrated verbally, with jokes, anecdotes, stories, puns, sarcasm, satire—or nonverbally, with smiles, funny faces, cartoons, clowning, or mime. Humor can be planned or spontaneous. Humor permits us to laugh at ourselves—at our imperfections—and humor can be nurturing and nourishing.

Even though different things amuse different people and make them laugh, humor usually has one or more of four basic character-istics—surprise, exaggeration, reversal, or relief of tension. Jokes frequently have an element of surprise. There seems to be one logical ending and then a new element to the story—the illogical and unexpected conclusion—brings laughter. Exaggerating things out of proportion, either unusually large or unusually small, can help things appear funny. Reversals too allow us to perceive situations from different angles—frequently offering fresh insights in a lighthearted and playful manner. Some forms of lighthearted tension and its release may produce a laugh or a smile.

> A resident in a dementia care unit came out of her room one morning with her blouse on backwards. When an aide noticed this and commented about it, the resident's spontaneous reply was, "That's all right, I don't know whether I'm coming or going." This exchange was greeted with much laughter and hugging between the two parties involved (Greensaft 1988).

## Potential Values of Humor

### Physical Well-being

In *The Laughter Prescription*, Peter and Dana (1982) stated that "laughter exercises the lungs and stimulates the circulatory system." The whole cardiovascular system benefits from robust laughter, because the deep respiration that accompanies it momentarily increases the oxygen in the blood. This can be of particular benefit to persons who have been inactive because of long-term or seriously debilitating illness. Norman Cousins likened the physical effects of a belly laugh to "inner jogging" because the physical mechanisms involved in laughing are similar to the desirable effects achieved by aerobic exercise, such as increased heart rate and stimulation of the abdominal wall muscles. Other physiological benefits of laughter include increased alertness and a temporarily higher threshold of pain due to an increase in the level of endorphins, or pain-killing chemicals produced by the brain (Dubos 1979). Laughter also helps people gain control over pain because it reduces overall tension and may help change a person's expectations from pessimism to optimism. Fry (1986) stated that "humor, mirth, and laughter have some impact on most, if not all, of the major human physiological systems," positively affecting muscle stimulation, muscle relaxation, clinical respiratory values, catecholamines, and alertness stimulation.

One controlled experiment of particular relevance to the persons living in institutional settings explored the effects of humor on perceived pain and affect in elderly residents of a long-term care facility. Subjects were chosen from those who suffered from chronic pain and frequently requested pain medication. They were divided into two groups, one to be shown humorous movies three times weekly for six weeks and the other to be shown nonhumorous movies. The pre- and post-scan of their charts revealed that there was a decrease in PRN medications for all persons in the humor group. The records of the nonhumorous movies group were not as decisive: medications decreased from some but not for others. The research instrument used to measure changes in affect revealed that those viewing the humorous movies had significantly higher affect scores than did those viewing the nonhumorous movies. The researchers concluded that pain perception in older people in such facilities is often aggravated by the hours of idleness forced upon them. They have more time to think about their physical condition and may become preoccupied with pain. Humor was shown to provide significant benefits to these aged clients. The researchers suggested that the physical effects of laughter combined with the psychological effects of alleviation of boredom were very beneficial (Adams and McGuire 1986).

Cheerfulness and lightheartedness are usually not characteristics of institutional settings, however. Nahemow (1986) deplored the absence of humor and vitality in many long-term care facilities. She pointed out that in such milieus there is no potential for growth. The elderly can become lethargic and less competent, not necessarily because of their impairments but as a result of the static and depressing environment in which they live.

### Mental Well-being

In addition to helping improve physiological functioning, humor and playful aspects of the self have been identified as a means of coping with stress and anxiety, of reducing depression, and of dispelling anger. Humor, flexibility, and spontaneity help greatly in relating to others (Adams and McGuire 1986). An amusing story, a cheerful act, or a playful activity can energize and aid both the initiator and the recipient of the humor and help reduce stress in the process. For this reason, humor is one of the most important coping mechanisms available to human beings—a biological phenomenon that, like crying, is shared with no other species on earth.

As the sources of stress change at various points in the life cycle, the target of humor may change. McGhee (1986) suggested that the elderly may be more concerned than young persons about poverty and loneliness. They may be worried about changes in physical appearance or the possibility of cognitive impairment. Their jokes may relate to these concerns as a way of helping them accept change and as a means of reducing the anxiety they may cause.

Everyone is subject to mental tension, strain, and pressure in today's fast-moving society. Working and living in a unit for elderly people with Alzheimer's disease can add to the amount of stress and strain to which both residents and caregivers are subjected. The first manifestation of stress is often heightened muscle tension. The body language of stress includes tight lips, frowning, raised shoulders, clenched fists. All of these are easily perceived by others and may adversely influence day-to-day interactions between the staff and the residents. Humor, laughter, smiling, and a light touch produce the opposite physiological responses to stress.

### Social Well-being

In one of his monologues, Victor Borge quipped that laughter is the shortest distance between two people. Humor can facilitate communication and strengthen relationships. We are attracted to people who smile or laugh, and we laugh more easily in groups. Laughter between a caregiver and a resident with Alzheimer's disease can help eliminate we-they or well-sick dichotomies. When someone is afflicted with a disease, caregivers frequently allow the illness to crowd out social interactions. They may forget that patients are people and are more than just their disease. A few smiles, chuckles, or laughs between the mentally impaired person and another bring those involved closer together and emphasize that they still have something in common. Health professionals always take a medical history, and often a psychosocial history of patients. There would also be value in taking a "humor and pleasures history." This history would be an informal way of looking at the whole person. By talking with people and their families it would be possible to find out who or what amuses them and what has always given them special pleasure. Is the resident someone who has always enjoyed laughing or initiating humor? What role did humor have in the family while that person was growing up? Was laughter encouraged or discouraged? Does the resident have a favorite funny story? Favorite performers or enter-tainers? Did the person have special interests that were absorbing and exciting? How did the person like to spend time when not working? All of this information can help caregivers know their "audience" and should be included in care plans for staff members in residential settings.

No one is ever too old, too young, or too sick to enjoy the benefits of humor, laughter, and playfulness.

Several residents were seated around a table helping an aide fold towels. The staff person suggested that it would be fun to whistle the tune, "Whistle While You Work." She started the tune and several residents joined in. One resident, however, listened intently for a few moments and then interrupted the whistling with the observation that someone was out of tune. This remark brought much laughter and many playful remarks, and several new attempts were made to upgrade the quality of the performance.

This episode illustrates the value of humor in reducing tension and in breaking the barriers between residents and caregivers.

The stimulatory effects of humor and lighthearted activities lead to greater alertness. Many examples of positive behavioral changes can be cited. Smiles from withdrawn residents, foot tapping to music from some previously unresponsive participants, and heightened awareness of the events of everyday life are indicators of significant effectiveness of a planned humor program (Ewers et al. 1983).

It is crucial for caregivers to remember that elderly persons with dementia are adults—not children. While the disease may restrict their ability to do many things, even severely impaired adults can be extremely sensitive to their surroundings and the approaches initiated by families or caregivers. Keeping conversations light and activities playful does not mean that the tone should be childish or patronizing. Activities, styles of communication, and the physical environment should all be age-appropriate. For example, mobiles, sometimes used to add whimsy and interest to the environment, are inappropriate if they are designed for babies and feature nursery-rhyme characters. In contrast, a simple handmade mobile with large pictures of grand-children, favorite pets, or garden scenes can provide lively interest without being demeaning.

"Sick humor" on the part of staff members that is directed toward residents can be demeaning and devastating. Appropriate and ther-apeutic humor shared between a staff person and a resident evokes a sense of empathy and mutual respect and reflects the feelings of pleasure that both experience in the opportunity to have fun together.

## Lighthearted and Pleasant Activities

Humor can positively touch the lives of the mentally impaired elderly by piercing language comprehension barriers. Even though some residents can no longer remember words and articulate thoughts to express themselves, they still may maintain a deep sense of pleasure and affection that can be expressed at appropriate times. There are many ways to inject humor into situations with impaired persons without relying on their comprehension of verbal humor. A flexible, relaxed, and accepting environment and a program of pleasant and lighthearted activities can offer many planned and spontaneous opportunities for laughter—shared laughter—to take place. Caregivers need to be aware, however, that people who have difficulties with concrete thinking are often unable to understand puns and verbal jokes and may feel uncomfortable when they are used.

A variety of lighthearted activities planned as a part of each day or introduced spontaneously can help lighten moods and create an interesting and absorbing life for impaired persons. Each activity should be evaluated, and residents should be observed carefully to ensure that they are responding positively to the activities of the moment, and adjustments need to be made when they are not.

*Music.* Music and singing are pleasant activities that can be introduced spontaneously to create a mood. Impromptu songfests with songs of a light and cheerful nature can help create a warm and sharing feeling. Staff members' awareness of the pleasure and relaxation generated by music and singing can lead them to plan and initiate singing and musical interactions to reduce tension and agitation. Listening to music of the 1930s and 1940s can often stimulate happy sentimental memories for many residents.

*Old film classics.* Silent film comedies are usually understood and appreciated by elderly residents, often eliciting happy reminiscences. Keystone Kops, Marx Brothers, Charlie Chaplin, Abbott and Costello, or Laurel and Hardy may be suitable selections. Musicals such as Fred Astaire and Ginger Rogers films or comedy classic videos such as "Candid Camera" frequently generate lighthearted feelings.

*Slide shows.* Slides are a most flexible medium. Photographic slides of residents and staff taken at parties, picnics, or social events are usually greeted with smiles, laughs, and cheerful banter. The group experience and flexibility that slides provide make this type of programing especially useful. Any slide show can be viewed in its entirety with taped narration, or a narrator can set the pace. When slides are shown in a darkened room, distractions may be lessened. The large, high-quality stationary image allows for maximal recognition and association. It should be noted, however, that some residents may find slide shows boring if they do not see well or are unable to follow the monologue. They may also be frightened by darkened rooms.

*Pets.* People with dementia need to feel loved and accepted, and pets, especially puppies and kittens, offer unconditional love, affection, and a spirit of playfulness that is hard to achieve from any other source. For some institutionalized persons, pets may be the only living things they feel they can trust. A pet can be a stress reliever and thus aid in lowering tension and blood pressure. Numerous anecdotal reports suggest that mentally impaired elderly persons become more alert when they are near a pet.

Watching birds at outdoor or window-ledge feeders offers bright splashes of color and movement that can be cheering. The songs of indoor birds in cages provide sprightly sound in long-term care settings. The grace and serenity of fish swimming in aquariums can be a pleasant sight to help enliven the physical environment.

*Children.* The natural ebullience and frequent giggling and laughter of small children can dramatically brighten the atmosphere of institutional settings. Children are usually nonjudgmental of, though often curious about, older persons and their mental deficits. A carefully planned activity with a young child such as decorating cookies or cupcakes can elicit many laughs and smiles, usually leading to feelings of pleasure and well-being for the older persons. Holding and rocking babies is calming for both participants. Looking at picture books or tossing a soft ball together may offer amusement. Children can be invited from nearby nursery schools or day-care centers, or families and staff can be encouraged to bring children to visit.

*Preparing food.* When residents in dementia care units are involved in the preparation of snacks, they can enjoy the resulting olfactory stimuli and the feelings of competence, usefulness, and familiarity with old skills. The pleasant aromas of muffins baking, popcorn popping, coffee percolating, or soup simmering can lead to satisfied and happy feelings and may help people recall events in their earlier lives when food was of special importance.

*Dance.* When verbal communication is difficult, dance movement may provide an alternative means of relating to others. Many elderly people in institutional settings have to deal with the loss of physical touch and closeness. In dance/movement activity, many body movements require hand holding and elbow tapping or some other form of touching, and this can provide physical warmth and comfort. Movement to rhythm can enhance feelings of contentment and well-being and help residents feel revitalized. Creative movement need not be as structured as formal organized exercise and may lead to playful interactions.

*Radio programs.* Elderly persons often appreciate and enjoy audiotapes of classic radio comedians such as Jack Benny, George Burns and Gracie Allen, Will Rogers, Groucho Marx, and other performers from radio's golden age of comedy. The sound of audiences laughing in addition to the stories, jokes, and songs on the programs promote a sense of lightness.

*Clowns and performers.* Persons with Alzheimer's disease are often very responsive to the nonverbal fun and humor of clowns, mimes, or jugglers. These performers are usually easily understood and can inject a merry touch to the social and emotional environment of any setting.

*Plants/gardens.* Working with plants can be an enriching experience and can give residents a great sense of achievement and pleasure. Looking at the growth of plants or at blossoms that their efforts have achieved may offer a feeling of pride and enhance self-esteem.

*Cheerful activities.* Activities need not be bland busywork. Simple but creative activities may provide a playful program.

> One very happy event that took place at Wesley Hall was called "An Evening of Modeling Hats." One aide had a large personal collection of hats, including baseball caps, straw sun hats, train conductors' hats, and elegant Victorian-era hats. She put her collection to use one evening by encouraging the residents to try on and model the hats. The residents and the staff were gathered in the living room of the unit. The aide initiated the activity by trying on a large, bright red hat and looking at herself in a hand-held mirror. She then turned around with a big smile and "modeled" the hat for the group of residents. This elicited spontaneous laughter from everyone. The evening progressed with both men and women trying on hats of all types, sizes, and shapes. They observed their reflections in the mirror and modeled their hats for the group. This activity resulted in much light discussion, reminiscing, and a sense of playfulness, but, most of all, much shared, spontaneous laughter.

All lighthearted activities should be carried out in a dignified manner befitting a group of older adults. Activities can be playful without being silly or degrading. The focus of activities should be upon the satisfaction the resident obtains from participation in a particular activity and not necessarily upon any specific accomplishment.

The introduction of activities that offer a spirit of lighthearted playfulness can help improve the quality of life in treatment settings and, in many instances, reduce the frequency of some of the difficult behaviors attributed to persons with Alzheimer's disease.

## The Role of Fun and Humor in the Work Situation

Except for the occasional birthday celebration or Christmas party, fun and humor are often missing from most job situations, including long-term care. Humor can help transform a boring or stressful work environment into an enjoyable and more productive one that improves work performance and encourages creativity. Employees who have fun at work are better satisfied with life in general and are usually far less depressed and anxious. Studies have shown that when employees have fun at their jobs, they have higher job satisfaction, they are less often late or absent, and employee turnover is less likely to occur (Abramis 1987).

Caring for elderly people with Alzheimer's disease may create a great deal of stress, resulting in low staff morale and high turnover. Many different lighthearted approaches can be used to improve staff morale in long-term care settings. Humor can help motivate by dissolving tension, defusing conflict, and relieving boredom. Humor can make a significant contribution to the effectiveness of a group. Among the many potential benefits of humor in group situations are more open, less defensive, and more effective communication, greater group cohesiveness, feelings of belonging, more problem solving, and more effective teamwork.

A humor history for the staff members would be a positive aspect to team building and would foster camaraderie. In learning about what a colleague considers to be funny, other staff members also get to see a dimension of that person that may not have been revealed to them before. To learn that someone else they work with shares their appreciation and enjoyment of a certain comedy show or cartoonist links them with that person in a new and mutually interesting way.

The staff can share humor in long-term care settings in a number of ways.

> One facility dramatically improved morale by dividing the staff lounge into two sections. One section was labeled "Good humor—jokes and funny stories told here!" and the other, "Griping, complaining, and gossiping." A sign on the wall of the humor area read "Why be serious about humor? Jest for the health of it." Since the lounge has been divided, no one ever goes to the "Griping" side and staff members report that they feel more refreshed and revitalized after their breaks. A supply of cartoon books, humorous magazines, and funny audiocassette tapes that are available for everyone to use during breaks adds to a more relaxed and convivial environment.

Staff members can be encouraged to start the workday with something that is positive or cheerful to share with the other staff members or residents. Arriving at work with a funny story instead of a complaint about the terrible traffic or parking will help brighten everyone's day.

A bulletin board, called a "Humor Board," can be created specifically for funny, amusing items only: cartoons, quips, quotes, clever signs, anecdotes, lighthearted items of all kinds (see Figure 10.2.) Different staff persons can be responsible for posting items on the board for a one-week period. Others have the opportunity to find out what each staff person considers humorous. This may soften the opinions staff members have about co-workers and help them feel warmer toward each other.

Conversations can be kept positive and upbeat and stretch the imagination. The following questions can help staff people get to know each other as individuals: What toys and games did you play with as a child? If you could have any view outside of your window, what would it be? What was the funniest thing that ever happened to you? If you could have anything at all for dinner tonight, what would be on the menu?

A baby picture contest is amusing and relaxing. It involves gathering pictures of the staff as babies or young children and having a contest to try to match the baby pictures with the correct adults.

Staff people should have opportunities to play together. Team games can be organized after work hours—softball games, bowling, or relays. They are fun for everyone and help build team spirit. Potluck picnics, pizza parties, or brunches are also good opportunities for staff to share pleasant events. Birthday celebrations for staff members can be made more meaningful and festive by inviting guests, or scheduling a clown, a magician, a mime, or a juggler to perform.

Rewards for job performance in the form of gift certificates, movie passes, restaurant vouchers, or other items can also help make work fun and give staff members feelings of being appreciated.

It is helpful for staff members to take their work seriously but to take themselves lightly, so that they can discover and appreciate the humor in everyday encounters. Even a little humor—just a light remark, not necessarily something very clever—can often relieve anxiety and stress.

## Conclusion

Humor has the potential for changing a drab, uninteresting, depressing environment into one that offers pleasure and fun. Humor, laughter, and a lighthearted approach in long-term care facilities

**Figure 10.2.** A humor board

and in units for elderly people with dementia are crucial in maintaining mental, physical, and social well-being. Humor helps to humanize institutional settings and to minimize individual deficits. It fosters a quality of life that offers some pleasure and happiness for all who work and live there. "A dementing illness does not suddenly end a person's capacity to experience love or joy, nor does it end her ability to laugh. . . Laughter might be called a gift to help our sanity in the face of trouble" (Mace and Rabins 1981, p. 163).

## References

Abramis D. 1987. *Fun at work: Does it matter?* Paper presented at the 95th Annual Convention of the American Psychological Association, New York.

Adams, E. R., and F. McGuire. 1986. Is laughter the best medicine? A study of the effects of humor on perceived pain and affect. *Activities, Adaptation, and Aging,* 6(3/4):157–175. Special issue.

Cousins, N. 1979. *Anatomy of an illness as perceived by the patient.* New York: W. W. Norton.

Dubos, R. 1979. Introduction. In *Anatomy of an illness as perceived by the patient, N. Cousins.* New York: W. W. Norton.

Ewers, M., S. Jacobson, V. Powers, and P. McConney, editors. 1983. *Humor: The tonic you can afford.* Los Angeles: Ethel Percy Andrus Gerontology Center.

Fry, W. F., Jr. 1986. Humor, physiology, and the aging process. In *Humor and aging,* edited by L. Nahemow, K. A. McClusky-Fawcett, and P. E. McGhee, 81–98. Orlando, Fla.: Academic Press.

Greensaft, M. 1988. Personal communication. Irvine, Calif.

Hamlisch, M. (music), A. Bergman, and M. Bergman (lyrics). 1973. The way we were. Los Angeles: Cole Gem EMI Music.

Honel, R. W. 1988. *Journey with grandpa.* Baltimore: Johns Hopkins University Press.

Mace, N. L., and P. V. Rabins. 1981. *The thirty-six-hour day.* Baltimore: Johns Hopkins University Press.

McGhee, P. E. 1986. Humor across the life span: Sources of developmental changes and individual differences. In *Humor and aging,* edited by L. Nahemow, K. A. McCluskey-Fawcett, and P. E. McGhee, 27–51. Orlando, Fla.: Academic Press.

Nahemow, L. 1986. Humor as a data base for the study of aging. In *Humor and aging,* edited by L. Nahemow, K. A. McCluskey-Fawcett, and P. E. McGhee, 3–26. Orlando, Fla.: Academic Press.

Peter, L., and B. Dana. 1982. *The laughter prescription.* New York: Ballantine Books.

# Chapter 11

# Partners in Care: The Role of Families in Dementia Care Units

## BETH SPENCER, M.A., M.S.W.

Every noon, and sometimes at dinner too, John Grant appears at the nursing home to feed his wife, Elsa. It is a time he treasures, a chance to share something pleasant with a longtime spouse who no longer knows his name. The nursing home has become an important part of John's world. He stops to chat with most of the residents and the staff and sometimes helps with small chores. He feels he plays an important part in Elsa's life and the life of the home.

Marie Spender's visits to her husband, Greg, are becoming less and less frequent. It is not that she has so many other things to do. Rather, she feels uncomfortable visiting the home, does not know what is expected of her, and feels that the staff resent her suggestions and concerns. Although she could no longer manage Greg's care at home, Marie feels terrible about the way their married life is ending.

Families are an important resource to the staff in long-term care settings, a resource that is sometimes overlooked. For many families, caregiving does not end at the nursing home door; most prefer to remain actively involved in the caregiving process out of love, guilt, and desire to ensure good care, or simply the habit of caregiving.

For the staff, families can be either a help or a hindrance: the challenge is to create an atmosphere that helps ensure positive family involvement. This chapter will explore some ways of doing that. The first part of the chapter will discuss some of the issues families bring with them, and how dementia care units and nursing homes can welcome and accommodate families. The second part will outline some specific activities that can be helpful to families.

## Creating a Welcoming Climate for Families

It has been demonstrated many times that most families institutionalize an elderly relative only as a last resort (York and Caslyn 1977;
Smith and Bengston 1979; Chenoweth and Spencer 1986). Yet many
nursing home staff persons continue to believe that residents have
been "dumped" by uncaring families. It is important for the staff of
a dementia unit or nursing home to understand and recognize the
significant burdens that most family caregivers have shouldered
before making the decision to institutionalize a relative with Alzheimer's disease or another dementing illness. Only through recognizing
and understanding the pain that families have endured will the staff
be able to create a truly comfortable, welcoming atmosphere for
them.

All of the research on caring for relatives with dementia has
documented that it is a very difficult process—a process that can
have serious effects on family caregivers' mental health, feelings of
self-esteem and burden, and social lives (George and Gwyther 1986;
Zarit et al. 1986; Chenoweth and Spencer 1986). By the time a
decision is made to institutionalize a relative with dementia, the
primary caregiver may have devoted years of his or her life to the
caregiving process. Often the caregiver's world has shrunk to the
home; his or her perspective has narrowed to an attempt to survive
the next day.

One study of caregiving relatives (Chenoweth and Spencer 1986)
found that the vast majority of caregivers who placed their relatives
in nursing homes (72 percent) were worn down by the demands of
24-hour care; they simply "couldn't take it anymore." A number of
these caregivers, most often elderly spouses, also became ill or had
accidents themselves, and were unable to continue to provide care
at home.

The decision to institutionalize a relative is often very painful for
families; there is not necessarily a feeling of relief afterward, even
though home care may have been extraordinarily difficult. Several
studies (George and Gwyther 1986; Zarit et al. 1986) found indications
that for some families the feelings of stress and burden do not end
with nursing home placement. It is important for the staff of dementia
care units and nursing homes to recognize that many families
continue to feel the stress of caregiving even though they may no
longer be responsible for day-to-day care.

When spouses or adult children have been caring for a relative
with dementia in the home for long periods of time, they are often
left exhausted, overwhelmed, and unsure about their decision to

institutionalize. Frequently they feel that no one else will be able to provide the kind of loving attention and caregiving that they have provided—and sometimes they are right. On the other hand, in many cases the person with dementia actually does better, or at least as well, in a congregate setting. Families sometimes need help in seeing the advantages and the ways in which their relative is benefiting or improving from the care in the dementia unit.

Many times families are unable to be as visible or involved as they might like to be or as the staff would like them to be. Sometimes family caregivers, particularly elderly spouses, are themselves ill and exhausted. Adult children may be torn between their love for a parent with dementia and other family or job responsibilities. Sometimes guilt keeps family members at a distance, something to which long-term care personnel need to be sensitive and ready to respond. Greenfield (1985) and Hershman (1983), among others, offered constructive suggestions for helping families cope with guilt.

Some family members have had a long history of difficult relations with the relative who now has dementia. This can cause a host of problems as the person becomes more confused and forgetful and the family is unable to resolve long-standing emotional issues. Often many of these old issues surface at the time of institutionalization or as the dementia progresses.

Some families find visiting confused and disoriented relatives especially difficult (York and Caslyn 1977; Smith and Bengston 1979; Hatch and Franken 1984) and need help with structuring more positive visits. Families occasionally choose a nursing home or dementia care unit because they believe their relative will get the best care there even though the unit may be at a distance from them; in doing so they may forfeit the ability to visit as often as they might like.

### Attitudes toward Dementia Units

If the person with dementia is moving from a retirement home or other part of an institution to a dementia unit, the move may not be terribly traumatic for the family. They may have already adjusted to the notion of institutionalization and come to terms with feelings of guilt or anxiety. On the other hand, the reputation of the dementia unit and an understanding of its goals are critical to a family's acceptance of the idea of placing their relative there. What they have heard about the unit from the staff and the residents in other parts of the institution can shape the way they feel about having their relative move to the unit. What the staff and the residents say about the unit will often be determined by attitudes created by the administration. Is it an environment where the staff enjoy working? Is it a prestigious place, or a last choice? Are the residents of the unit outcasts, or are they seen as people with special needs?

The reputation of the dementia unit can make an enormous difference in a family's acceptance of it. In well-regarded units with clearly conceived programs and goals, there are usually waiting lists and many families are eager to get their relatives admitted. As more and more dementia units are developed, families may be confused about what to look for. The national Alzheimer's Association has published a useful guide to assist families in selecting a dementia unit (Mace and Gwyther 1989).

Sometimes family members have not accepted their relative's illness, and their denial makes it difficult for them to understand the need for placement in a dementia care unit. In this case, the staff need to help families begin to recognize some of the problems their relatives are having and to understand how the dementia unit will help them compensate for these problems. One nonthreatening way of assisting families is to focus on very specific problems with activities of daily living—such as difficulty with dressing, bathing, or finding the way to the dining room—problems that may be easier for family members to accept than more abstract discussions of dementia, memory loss, or confusion. A good medical evaluation is always important for someone in the early stages of dementia, and this also can be a helpful way of convincing reluctant relatives that there is a problem.

At other times families may recognize the problem but are suspicious that the dementia unit is a dumping ground for the confused, a place of segregation without redeeming programs. Even if they recognize their relative's confusion and memory loss, many family members have trouble seeing their relative as someone who belongs in a unit with "all those senile people." They see their relative in the context of a long, loving history; they see the other residents as they appear now—confused, disoriented people without a past. Creating an environment that acknowledges and celebrates residents' pasts with pictures, posters, and histories can help both the staff and the families begin to see residents in the context of their whole lives.

When people with dementia are moving directly from home to the unit, the transition may be more difficult for both the resident and the family. Family members often are feeling very unsure and guilty about their decision to place their relative and need a great deal of reassurance that this is an appropriate move. The more that long-term care staff are able to involve families in decisions about the move and the care, and to enlist family help in the day-to-day life of the unit, the easier the transition will be for family members.

I have written about transition to the nursing home elsewhere (Spencer and Gilbert 1986), and most of the suggestions made there are pertinent also to the dementia unit. Emphasis in that chapter is on making the transition as smooth as possible for the person with dementia, and that is probably the most critical issue for family adjustment as well. If family members see their relative adjusting well, they are much more likely to feel comfortable about the move.

## Staff-Family Relationships

It is sometimes difficult for staff persons to remember that the nursing home or dementia unit is a new and alien world to the family. Many times family members have never before set foot in a long-term care facility, and they may be confused or intimidated by the new procedures and jargon.

Montgomery (1982, 1983), in her research on staff-family relationships and nursing home policies, found subtle differences in the ways nursing homes' policies created expectations for families. One home viewed families as "servants" who should be available to help with services to the residents and whose absence was viewed as neglect. A second home had no expectations or role for families, viewing them as outsiders or "visitors." In the third home, Montgomery found policies that viewed families as "clients," and the staff were encouraged and expected to spend time with families. As one might expect, the quality of relationships between the staff and the family members varied greatly from home to home, based on the unwritten policies, the climate, created for families.

It is up to the top administration of the home or unit to set the tone for family involvement. Are families to be viewed as servants, outsiders, or partners in care who may also have needs of their own that need attending? If staff members are expected to interact well with families, they must have overt permission and training to do so.

One of the most important facets of good staff-family relationships is the process of resolving complaints. If a climate can be established whereby families feel comfortable expressing their concerns and are aware of the proper channels for doing so, many conflicts can be avoided. This requires training of both the staff and families. The staff must be aware of family needs and perspectives, of how to address family concerns, of when to direct families to counseling; families need training in how to choose their issues and bring their concerns to the attention of appropriate staff persons in the most effective manner.

In a number of ways, units or homes can set a positive tone with families early in the relationship. If the unit is just opening, family meetings are an important way of orienting and involving families at the outset. Families should be apprised of the philosophy of the unit, the program and goals, and special training that the staff will be receiving. The enthusiasm and clarity of the staff will make all the difference in convincing families that they wish to place their relatives in the unit. If it is not a new unit, families still need all this information and should be met with individually.

Providing information in writing to families is very important, since they are often distracted and upset at the time of the move. Some of the information that may be most useful includes the following:

1. Philosophy and program goals of the dementia unit
2. Staff responsibilities (i.e., whom to talk to about what)
3. Visiting policies for relatives, clergy, and friends
4. Policies about personal possessions and furnishings for residents' rooms
5. Information about care conferences
6. Policies about chemical and physical restraints, "heroic" measures, feeding tubes, how sudden illness or deterioration will be handled
7. Special criteria for decisions to move residents out of the unit to another facility or part of the facility (families need to be aware of the possibility of relatives reaching a point where they are no longer appropriate for the unit)

A "family buddy system" may be a good way of helping to orient new families to the unit, by linking new families with a family that has been involved in the unit for some time. This can develop into an informal support network for families, something that is often needed but unavailable. Frequently there is no formal mechanism in long-term care settings for families to meet other families.

Keeping in touch with families is a very important part of running a successful dementia unit. There are a number of ways to do this. Even those families who are present every day can benefit from some of the more formal staff-family communications.

One important means of communication is the care conference. While many facilities routinely invite families to care conferences, many others do not. Most family members who have been part of care conferences, either routine ones or meetings held to discuss a particular problem that has arisen, are enthusiastic about their value. They feel that they are truly being consulted and informed and that the best decisions about care can be made when the staff and the families act in concert. Family members can often provide information about their relative's past life that is helpful to the staff, and they may have useful suggestions about ways of handling particular problems with their relative. It is important to explain to families ahead of time what a care conference is and why it is being called. Some families have mistakenly assumed that a conference means their relative is in trouble.

For families who are not able to visit often, occasional phone calls or letters from a staff person can be very reassuring. Most families live in dread of calls from nursing homes, because they hear only when their relative has become a problem or is critically ill. One way of changing this negative image of the nursing home or dementia unit is to make families feel more involved through phone calls or letters that simply inform them of some of their relative's activities and ups and downs. It can be very gratifying for families to hear about particular activities in which their relative has been involved, or ways in which the staff have solved a problem with the person.

Some dementia units have devised short, simple newsletters as a means of keeping in touch with families. These might highlight activities or programs on the unit, introduce and feature staff members, and discuss family involvement on the unit.

## Activities for Families

### Family Groups

An orientation meeting for families has already been mentioned as a good introduction to the dementia unit when it is first opening. There are many other ways in which family group meetings can be an effective way of improving the quality of life.

Some nursing homes have used family councils very effectively, and there are many ways in which a family council also could be helpful to a dementia unit. Family councils on a dementia unit could be involved in a variety of activities, from advisory to programmatic. They might help arrange educational sessions for families or staff members, assist with recruiting and using volunteers, plan recognition events for staff members, organize orientation sessions for new families, help plan programs and activities for residents of the unit, write a newsletter for families and volunteers, and present family concerns to the staff. Some families welcome the opportunity to have this type of active involvement in the unit or nursing home.

Family support groups are another type of group activity that is gaining recognition in long-term care settings (Helphand and Porter 1981). Many families not only find the decision to move a relative to a nursing home or dementia unit very painful but also continue to struggle emotionally with the decision, in addition to the pain of watching their relative decline. Support groups can be a very effective means for some families to share their feelings, learn from others' experiences, and realize they are not alone.

Not everyone feels comfortable in this type of group, and the success is often dependent on the skill of the group leader or facilitator (Schmall 1984). Although support groups are not therapy groups, they often require the leader and members to cope with powerful emotions, and with the normal problems that can arise in group situations. Some support groups for families of dementia victims are time-limited, usually focused for six or eight sessions on particular topics. Others continue indefinitely, with members coming and going as they feel the need. Depending on the size of the dementia unit and the interest of families, support groups can be very useful for families.

Some families need more help than is available through groups. There are many situations where families might benefit from the availability of counseling services, especially right after the move or when crises arise. Such services can be arranged on a contractual basis with outside mental health care workers, or they can be part of the responsibility of social work or other staff.

### Educational Sessions

Many people who would feel uncomfortable about attending council meetings or support groups will readily attend sessions that are billed as educational. Educational groups are sometimes the most effective means of creating a positive relationship with families, while providing them with the tools to improve the quality of their involvement with their relatives and with the dementia unit. Some possible topics for educational family sessions are as follows:

*Introduction to the staff.* This gives families an opportunity to meet the staff in the unit (and in the larger institution if appropriate). Many times families are unaware of the identities of key people in different departments: who is responsible for what, whom to turn to for help in solving different kinds of problems. This can give families an opportunity to meet housekeeping, maintenance, and dietary staff, for example, whom they may never otherwise meet. Perhaps most important is an opportunity for families to meet and speak with the direct care staff who care for their relatives, particularly on shifts when families are not normally present. Introduction to the staff might comprise several sessions.

*Normal aging changes.* Most family members can benefit from a session that outlines normal physical changes in the aging process, as they are often confused about what is dementia and what is normal aging. They may be unaware of changes in vision or hearing, for example, that can affect their relative's ability to function.

*Information about Alzheimer's disease and related illnesses.* While the staff should be well versed in the dementias, some families may be unfamiliar with this information. A health care professional discussing symptoms, diagnosis, and the progression of dementia can often elicit family concerns and questions that may not arise in other contexts.

*Emotional issues for families.* A discussion of some of the emotional issues for relatives of institutionalized dementia victims can be a very cathartic experience for families. The opportunity to have some of their anger, guilt, and sadness legitimized can be therapeutic as well as educational.

*Communication techniques.* One way of helping families with visiting problems is to train them in communication techniques to use with their relatives. Again, this is an area that the dementia unit staff should be trained in and that families may not be.

*Difficult behaviors.* For both the staff and families, the presence of difficult behaviors, such as wandering, incontinence, or agitation, can be devastating. Discussion of possible causes and interventions can be very reassuring. It may also help families learn to interact more successfully with their relatives.

*Medications.* Families often have many unanswered questions about medications, their uses and side effects. Many also fear that institutions will overmedicate their relatives. Having a physician, a nurse, or a pharmacist discuss common medications used in the treatment of dementia symptoms, as well as other common conditions, can be extremely reassuring.

*Depression.* Depression is a fairly common condition among dementia victims. It can be helpful for both the staff and families to have a psychiatric or other health care professional discuss how it manifests itself in people with dementia and how it is commonly treated.

*Daily routines on the unit.* Describing for the families a typical day on the unit can be a very helpful way to explain the unit's philosophy and for them to understand how their relative is functioning. It can also assist them in understanding why some times of day are better for visiting, and in planning how they would like to be involved in their relative's care.

*Discussion with activity staff.* It can be extremely helpful to have the activity staff describe the kinds of activities residents are involved in, how they manage to persuade people to participate, and how activities are tailored to the abilities of residents, and to present some of the positive experiences their relatives are having.

*Successful family visits.* One of the hardest things for many families is to visit a relative who is confused and has memory problems—particularly if they are not able to visit often. Family members frequently welcome help and suggestions for making visits easier.

*Ways to be involved.* A session that presents opportunities for family involvement in the unit can result in many benefits to both the staff and families. A family committee or council might grow from this, which could help formalize and expand roles for families on the special unit.

*Activities of daily living.* A practical, skill-building session for those families who wish to be involved in the direct care of their relative can be very useful. For example, this session might include information about how to assist with incontinence and bathing, and how to transfer people from chair to bath or from wheelchair to bed.

### Family History

One way of beginning to establish a good working relationship with the family is to ask for their help in putting together a good social/medical/family history of their relative. A simple biography of the person is a good beginning. Other useful information might include, for example, the person's past food preferences, daily routines, and previous coping strategies. This background information can be particularly helpful to the staff in working with the person, but it is often the kind of information that a person with dementia can no longer provide. The family is in a unique position to assist with this, and if this kind of history is provided orally to a staff person for the records, it can be a very useful and informative process.

Families might also be encouraged to provide biographical information about their relative in other ways. Labeled photographs can be an attractive and helpful decoration for both the residents and the staff. Some families may wish to make posters using old family photographs to trace and highlight their relatives' lives; short, simple paragraphs naming the people and describing the event in each photo can make this a useful tool for both the staff and residents. Such posters or photos can provide a focus for conversations between the staff and residents, may help residents retain information about themselves and their lives, and can help the staff begin to view residents as people with interesting past lives.

### Ongoing Family Involvement

If families wish to remain involved in the care and are physically and geographically able, the staff can help them become a "partner in care"—to carve out a role for themselves in the daily caregiving activities concerning their relative.

Many families visit every day or several times a week, becoming well acquainted with the staff and the routines. Reactions to this vary enormously—some facilities welcome the help and appreciate the family involvement; with others, the staff complain about family interference and generally make them feel unwelcome, often in subtle ways.

Helping with meals is one of the common and obvious ways for families to be involved. Many people in the middle stages of dementia can still feed themselves, but they may need encouragement or assistance in becoming organized. If mealtimes are made a social, "family-style" affair, families can help in many ways. Simply sitting at the table chatting or serving people can be an enormous help to staff persons, but many family members will need encouragement from the staff to do this. Often they are afraid of interfering with routines, and the staff may be reinforcing this fear. To achieve relaxed, pleasant meals, families (and volunteers) should be encouraged to be present at mealtimes, to participate in meals if possible, or to bring their own and join in. This relaxed, welcoming approach to meals is not the normal institutional style, but it can be a great asset when trying to create a homelike atmosphere for people with dementia. However, it may take some discussion with families and volunteers to establish a routine that is helpful rather than disruptive.

Other families often are (or would like to be) involved in bathing or dressing their relatives. Again, these are areas where families can be very helpful to the staff, if they are welcomed and encouraged. Since bathing is often a time of great stress for people with dementia, the presence of a family member may be soothing. Families should also be able to provide useful information on former bathing habits— whether the person preferred baths or showers, the time of day the person usually bathed, and other bath routines that may help relieve some of the anxiety.

To make maximal use of families in these situations and to make it a pleasant experience for them, it is important for the staff to meet with families and discuss communication and intervention strategies, as they would at staff meetings (Rubin and Shuttlesworth 1983). Families should be shown where supplies are kept and given explicit permission to use them. Staff persons must be aware, however, that not all families can or wish to be involved in personal care activities; this should be a choice, not an expectation. There should be a wide range of options for family involvement in the home or in the unit.

One dementia unit made a concerted effort to recruit and involve families in a variety of ways, particularly programing (Hansen et al. 1988). Evaluations of the program revealed that family volunteers felt their programming activities were therapeutic to the residents and helpful to the staff, and they were pleased to have special roles in the unit. The staff expressed new respect for the family volunteers, whom they saw as coping better than others with their relatives' impairment. The staff found weekend programing especially helpful.

### Helping Families with Visiting

For most of us, visiting is associated with talking—but when dementia victims can no longer speak clearly or have difficulty understanding, families are often at a loss as to how to have successful visits. In addition to not being able to communicate, dementia victims are sometimes agitated, distracted, or withdrawn. All of these problems can make visits very uncomfortable for families.

Some years ago, while a nursing home resident, Frances Avery Faunce (1969) wrote a book about nursing home visiting. The following story from her book illustrates one of the most important suggestions for family visiting.

One rainy Saturday afternoon in the nursing home, I was in a pensive mood. I had been lucky. For many weeks my visitors had been frequent and friendly—my very lifeline. But this rainy afternoon I couldn't be hopeful. . . . Then, through our window, I saw the flash of a big familiar white car. Here were my faithful deacon and his wife. . . . In Ellen's hand I could see a brown paper bag. They had remembered. They would! I felt more like a child than a woman of seventy-seven years. I thrilled at their remembering—their caring that much about what might have seemed like a little thing for they were a busy couple. . . .

For Bill and Ellen had brought the one thing I craved on that humid afternoon—a carton of plain coffee ice cream. What was more, they had brought a carton for "Nana"[her roommate] too, having learned earlier that this was also her favorite flavor. As an extra touch, Ellen had thought to bring two silver spoons from her home, such as our nursing home couldn't afford, and so much nicer than plastic store spoons. All so simple? Yet that "party" rested us, cheered us, amused us—all four of us, I believe. Over and over I am impressed by the big lift that a seemingly small gesture can give to the morale of a lonely patient. (pp. 23–25)

Though Frances Faunce did not have dementia, the story illustrates an important point. What made this visit successful was the thoughtful (though simple) planning undertaken by her friends. The silver spoons added a dimension of specialness to the visit that obviously made an impact.

For families who are struggling with visiting a relative with dementia, one of the most helpful things they can do is to plan their visits carefully, a process that is foreign to many people. Often a successful visit can be planned by bringing something to focus their relative's attention. These might be photographs or photograph albums, picture books, pets, children, or refreshments of some kind. The burden of trying to communicate orally can be minimized and the focus can be on the activity, child, or pet, releasing both resident and family from the pressure to make conversation.

Tasks that are shared between family members and a relative can be especially satisfying if the tasks are carefully selected and necessary preparations precede the visit. Refreshments prepared together can be as simple as frosting store-bought cookies or as complex as making fruit salad. Simple craft items to be used as gifts can enable an older relative to continue to feel a part of family birthdays or other special events. Other shared activities can include playing games, working puzzles, taking care of indoor plants, or walking or exercising together. They can provide a focus for visits when conversation is difficult (Metzelaar and Coons 1986).

In addition to planning, families often benefit from some training in how better to communicate with nonverbal or partially verbal people, problem-solving techniques, and how to plan simple tasks for people with dementia. One such program (Shulman and Mandel 1988) found that 80 percent of the families in the communication training course felt that their visits to impaired relatives had improved.

## Conclusion: One Daughter's Experience

The following illustrates one case in which a family member was able to implement some of the ideas discussed here, and to feel better about her relationship with her mother.

In the past Alison Brown visited her mother every week. The visits left Alison frustrated and miserable. They had never had an easy relationship, and now it was much more difficult. Mrs. Ross could no longer speak a coherent sentence. Sometimes she just sat listlessly, looking at her hands folded in her lap and ignoring Alison's presence. Other times she seemed glad to see Alison but no longer remembered her name or the relationship. Alison's visits grew shorter and less frequent as they became more difficult.

After a while Alison became part of a family group that was working on developing strategies for better visits with relatives with dementia. The group spoke about ways of communicating with aphasic relatives, activities that could be done together, and how to gear activities to the remaining skills of residents. On her weekly visits, Alison began bringing old family photographs, which she and her mother looked at together and commented on. While Mrs. Ross could not usually remember names or places, she seemed to enjoy looking at them and hearing Alison describe them. Alison felt an immense sense of relief that she had something concrete to converse about with her mother.

Eventually Alison began a small reading group, consisting of her mother and three other dementia residents. She brings very short and amusing stories, simple poems, and picture books. Those who can still read take a turn, others nod their heads, smile, or just listen. Although the four women never remember that it is time for the group, they seem to enjoy it once they are together. After they read they drink juice and eat cookies, and over time a comfortable feeling and some simple conversations have developed.

Now Alison feels that she is not only helping the staff by holding this group but is also interacting with her mother in a positive way for the first time in a long time.

## References

Chenoweth, B., and B. Spencer. 1986. Dementia: The experience of family caregivers. *Gerontologist*, 26(3):267–272.

Faunce, F. A. 1969. *The nursing home visitor: A handbook written from the inside.* Nashville: Abington Press.

George, L. K., and L. P. Gwyther. 1986. Caregiver well-being: A multidimensional examination of family caregivers of demented adults. *Gerontologist*, 26(3):253–259.

Greefield, W. 1985. Disruption and reintegration: Dealing with familial response to nursing home placement. *Journal of Gerontological Social Work*, 8(1/2):15–21.

Hansen, S. S., M. A. Patterson, and R. W. Wilson. 1988. Family involvement on a dementia unit: The resident enrichment and activity program. *Gerontologist*, 28(4):508–510.

Hatch, R. C., and M. L. Franken. 1984. Concerns of children with parents in nursing homes. *Journal of Gerontological Social Work*, 7(3):19–30.

Helphand, M., and C. M. Porter. 1981. The family group within the nursing home: Maintaining family ties of long-term care residents. *Journal of Gerontological Social Work*, 4(1):51–62.

Hershman, P. 1983. *Reducing family guilt about nursing home placement.* Health Communication Issues, Newsletter of the International Communications Association, 9.

Mace, N. L., and L. P. Gwyther. 1989. *Selecting a nursing home with a dedicated dementia care unit.* Chicago: Alzheimer's Disease and Related Disorders Association.

Metzelaar, L., and D. H. Coons. 1986. Visits: An opportunity for sharing. In *A better life: Helping family members, volunteers, and staff improve the quality of life of nursing home residents suffering from Alzheimer's disease and related disorders*, edited by D. H. Coons, L. Metzelaar, A. Robinson, and B. Spencer, 47–91. Columbus, Ohio: Source for Nursing Home Literature.

Montgomery, R. 1982. Impact of institutional care policies on family integration. *Gerontologist*, 22(1):54–58.

Montgomery, R. 1983. Staff-family relations and institutional care policies. *Journal of Gerontological Social Work*, 6(1):25–38.

Rubin, A., and G. E. Shuttlesworth. 1983. Engaging families as support resources in nursing home care: Ambiguity in the subdivision of tasks. *Gerontologist*, 23(6):632–636.

Schmall, V. L. 1984. What makes a support group good? It doesn't just happen. *Generations*, 9(2):64–67.

Shulman, M. D., and E. Mandel. 1988. Communication training of relatives and friends of institutional elderly persons. *Gerontologist*, 28(6):797–799.

Smith, K. F., and V. L. Bengston. 1979. Positive consequences of institutionalization: Solidarity between elderly parents and their middle-aged children. *Gerontologist*, 19(5):438–448.

Spencer, B., and M. H. Gilbert. 1986. Transition to the nursing home. In *A better life: Helping family members, volunteers, and staff improve the quality of life of nursing home residents suffering from Alzheimer's disease and related disorders*, edited by D. H. Coons, L. Metzelaar, A. Robinson, and B. Spencer, 13–33. Columbus, Ohio: Source for Nursing Home Literature.

York, J. L., and R. J. Caslyn. 1977. Family involvement in nursing homes. *Gerontologist*, 17(6):500–505.

Zarit, S. H., P. A. Todd, and J. M. Zarit. 1986. Subjective burden of husbands and wives as caregivers: A longitudinal study. *Gerontologist*, 26(3):260–266.

## Suggested Resources for Educational Sessions

Cohen, D., and C. Eisdorfer. 1986. *The loss of self: A family resource for the care of Alzheimer's disease and related disorders*. New York: W. W. Norton.

Coons, D. H., L. Metzelaar, A. Robinson, and B. Spencer, editors. 1986. *A better life: Helping family members, volunteers, and staff improve the quality of life of nursing home residents suffering from Alzheimer's disease and related disorders*. Columbus, Ohio: Source for Nursing Home Literature.

Mace, N. L. 1987. Principles of activities for persons with dementia. *Physical and Occupational Therapy in Geriatrics*, 5(3):13–27.

Robinson, A., B. Spencer, and L. White. 1988. *Understanding difficult behaviors: Some practical suggestions for coping with Alzheimer's disease and related illnesses*. Ypsilanti: Geriatric Education Center of Michigan, Eastern Michigan University.

Thompson, W. 1987. *Aging is a family affair: A guide to quality visiting, long-term care facilities and you*. Toronto: NC Press.

Zgola, J. M. 1987. *Doing things*. Baltimore: Johns Hopkins University Press.

# Chapter 12

# Assessment As a Basis
# for Intervention

## SHELLY E. WEAVERDYCK, Ph.D.

Assessment is a systematic method of observing and describing a phenomenon. Each discipline or profession has its own methods and its own focus of assessment, as well as its own tools (e.g., Kane and Kane 1981; Burnside 1988).

In this chapter, assessment by caregivers as a basis for the planning of intervention in dementia will be discussed and an assessment protocol outlined. The intervention may have as its goal the reduction or elimination of a particular behavior or an increase in an individual's level of functioning. Various contributing factors will be addressed in the assessment protocol and discussion, including the cognitive functioning of the individual who is being assessed. Seven intervention strategies that allow for assessment while the caregiver is helping a person are also suggested at the end of the chapter.

There are two basic questions to ask in an assessment: *What is happening* (What is the identified behavior or actual level of functioning?), and *Why is this happening* (What are the possible causes of this behavior or level of functioning?). The answers to these two questions form a basis for answering a third: *What are we going to do about it* (What is the appropriate intervention?). This third question is addressed in Chapter 13. In this chapter, these three questions are asked in the context of four factors: the environment, the caregiver, the task, and the person. When a caregiver encounters a particularly undesirable behavior or wants to initiate a task or activity with an individual who has dementia, the assessment of these four factors will suggest possible interventions or options.

It is important to ask why a behavior or a particular level of functioning occurs. Many times a caregiver assumes that the dementia simply causes the behavior or impaired functioning, and to some extent this is true. Clearly, there would be no reason to intervene or to assess if there were not some dementia, presumably resulting from an untreatable brain pathology, underlying the behavior or impaired functioning. The dementia or brain pathology may not be the only contributing factor, however; behavior and performance are heavily influenced by fatigue, motivation, physical disability independent of the dementia, and environmental factors. (We all have had occasion to witness a reduction of a behavior, for example, simply by removal of the individual to a different environment.)

It is important to note that there may be a variety of reasons for a particular behavior, such as wandering (Hussian and Davis 1985; Snyder et al. 1978). Treating or intervening in the wandering behavior without addressing the underlying cause of the wandering on each particular occasion will likely prove to be only occasionally effective and often frustrating and counterproductive. One individual may wander on different occasions for different reasons: on one occasion she may be searching for her dead husband, on another occasion she may be trying to go home, and on still another occasion she may simply feel restless or need to use the bathroom. Similarly, different people may wander for different reasons. The wanderer frequently may not know or be able to articulate the motive for wandering (if there is one), nor is the goal or cause of the wandering often readily apparent to the caregiver on any given occasion. An assessment can aid the caregiver in determining the cause of the wandering or at least the factors that seem to trigger it. The caregiver may then intervene effectively by addressing the source or possible causes instead of simply the symptom.

The assessment is similarly effective in identifying a single causative factor that appears to precipitate a variety of behaviors. For example, anxiety over a dead spouse may result in wandering by one person, searching and rummaging by another person, and hollering for or shadowing a caregiver by still another person. This same variety of behaviors may be caused by a single source in just one individual. Addressing the underlying anxiety rather than simply the symptomatic behavior may be the most effective method of intervention.

In this chapter the four influencing factors (the environment, caregiver, task, and person) will be identified and discussed by asking the two basic questions (What is happening? Why is it happening?). The conceptual framework of the protocol will be outlined and illustrative questions the caregiver can consider will be suggested.

When a caregiver is asking a resident with dementia to do something (e.g., to brush his or her teeth, to help bake a cake, or to

**Table 12.1.**
**Some Factors to Assess in Dementia When Planning Interventions**

| | |
|---|---|
| Environment | Physical |
| | Social |
| | Emotional |
| | Cognitive |
| Caregiver | Characteristics |
| | Interactions |
| Task | Emotional appeal |
| | Physical demands |
| | Cognitive complexity |
| | Social context |
| Person | History |
| | Medical and physical status |
| | Emotional status |
| | Cognitive status |
| |   Sensory functions |
| |   Perception and comprehension |
| |     recognizing objects; judging distances and spatial relationships; understanding speech and written words; understanding gestures and pictures; recognizing colors, shapes, sizes |
| |   Executive functions |
| |     recognizing own abilities, disabilities, needs, desires; memory; logic; ordering; planning; abstraction; choosing among options; problem solving; shifting from one idea or activity to another; getting started |
| |   Expressive functions |
| |     ability to do something when asked; ability to find words to speak and to write |
| |   Motoric functions |

*Source:* Adapted from Weaverdyck 1987 and Weaverdyck 1990.

roll over in bed) or is trying to distract a person from engaging in an undesirable behavior, the caregiver should ask himself or herself questions similar to those listed below. The assessment process is not always easy. Sometimes the answers to these questions are difficult to discern and may require the assistance of a person with expertise in this area. In most cases, however, when caregivers ask themselves or other caregivers these questions, some possible answers readily emerge that yield ideas for specific interventions. The four factors and their components are listed in Table 12.1. (For a more detailed description of the issues addressed in this chapter, see Weaverdyck 1987 and Weaverdyck 1990.)

## The Environment

The environments that influence a person's behavior and level of functioning include the physical, social, emotional, and cognitive. This chapter will focus primarily on the physical environment, which includes, for example, the physical objects surrounding the individual, the actual building, the sounds heard there, and so on. All that the individual hears, sees, feels, tastes, and smells constitute the physical environment.

In identifying and documenting *what* is happening, the caregiver should note exactly what is occurring in the physical environment at the moment. The more details that are identified, the more likely the caregiver will be able, by documenting several similar incidents, to discern patterns that suggest possible environmental triggers of behaviors or causes of impairments.

Some of the environmental factors to note include the time, the specific place (room, part of the room), or the number of people in the environment and their impact on what the individual is experiencing (e.g., can the individual hear someone making a noise, see someone sleeping, sense that someone is unhappy or in need of help?). The nature and appropriateness of cues in the environment should be noted.

People with dementia may become increasingly reactive to their environment rather than acting upon it. They rely on cues around them instead of on their own thought processes to tell them what to do (Weaverdyck 1987; Weaverdyck and Coons 1988; Lawton 1986).

Because of memory problems and an impaired ability to evaluate or screen out contradictory cues, people with dementia are probably particularly vulnerable to distracting or unintentional cues. For example, the author was recently conducting a group cognitive assessment using adult-like assessment blocks (Bloomer 1987) with a small group of dementia residents in a long-term care facility. The group was sitting around a small table in a room that was also used as a dining room. The group behavior was very appropriate until a staff person came into the room and began putting bibs on each of the residents in anticipation of an upcoming meal. Immediately, most of the residents began putting the blocks into their mouths as though to eat them! Clearly, they did not disassociate the cues of the bibs for eating from the cues of the blocks and previous activity for assessment. They apparently did not recognize that the bib was intended for a future activity, not a present activity. Such an example of unintended responses to contradictory environmental cues illustrates the sensitivity of people with dementia to unintentional cuing by caregivers.

Questions a caregiver might consider include these: Is the environment reassuring, interesting, and safe to the individual? If the environment is crowded, cluttered, noisy, or too sterile and devoid of appropriate cues, it may feel frightening and confusing to the person. Cues in this context mean any information available to the person, regardless of its type or source. These range from signs on the walls, to colors strategically placed, to sounds that indicate what is behind closed doors, to verbal instructions from another person. Are there enough cues in the environment to tell the person what to do? Are the cues obvious and understandable, or are they confusing and contradictory?

Are there environmental cues that tell a resident to behave one way (e.g., to behave as a patient in a medical facility) while internal cues tell him or her to behave another way (physically the person with dementia may feel quite normal and healthy and therefore not like a sick patient). When the person responds to internal cues saying that he or she is healthy and normal and that it is time to go home, there may be social cues urging still another kind of behavior. For example, when the person tries to go home, a caregiver may say, "This is your home now." The traditional nursing home does not look at all like a home, much less like the home this person has lived in for most of his or her life. The information the person is receiving is contradictory and confusing. The external cues do not match the person's own internal cues, and the cues in the environment are not consistent with each other.

Are the cues consistent across sensory modalities? Is the caregiver asking the person to prepare for a shower (an auditory cue) while holding a breakfast tray (a visual cue)? The breakfast tray may be a more powerful cue to the person than the verbal request. Are the cues plentiful and appropriate, and do they address as many senses as possible? For example, it is sometimes helpful to show a person a dress while asking her to come to her room to get dressed.

Are the cues familiar to the person with dementia? Does the toothpaste look like toothpaste to the person, or is it in a container that looks quite foreign? Are the cues in familiar and expected places? Is the room appropriate to the task the caregiver wants the person to attempt? For example, is the grooming taking place in the individual's bedroom, or out in a dayroom or hallway that does not provide a familiar and typical context for grooming? Mirrors in the bedroom and over bathroom sinks may be recognized and used more appropriately than mirrors in hallways. Are the signs on doors and drawers intelligible to the person (e.g., some people need large print or pictures)?

Questions about the social environment include the following: Are the person and setting prepared for the task beforehand? Is anyone else or everyone else doing the same task? A person may find it confusing to be asked to do a task no one else is doing. Is another person talking loudly and drowning out the request? Understanding of the behavior of others may be a powerful cue. Is there privacy for an activity that the person sees as·private (e.g., going to the shower room appropriately covered)?

Questions about the emotional environment include these: What is the emotional tone of the situation and the setting? Is it relaxed, jocular, rushed, angry, nervous, tense? Emotional tone is frequently created by people's moods and the general environmental ambience. Such emotional tenor can be a powerful influence on behavior.

## The Caregiver

A resident's behavior and level of functioning may be influenced by the characteristics of the caregiver as well as by the quality of the relationship and interactions between the caregiver and the resident.

The caregiver should ask, Does this resident like me? Do we have a personality clash? Do I like this resident? How well have we gotten along in the past? Does he or she know/remember me? Trust me? Answers to these questions may suggest to the caregiver a particular approach. It may be that someone else should help the resident that day, although some programs discourage the staff's "trading" residents.

The caregiver should also ask, How do I feel right now? Am I rushed, angry, tired, impatient? Do I want to do this task with the resident? How invested am I in intervening right now and in this way? Often a resident can sense the feelings of a caregiver regardless of what the caregiver says or does. Frequently, it is this feeling level to which the resident responds, rather than to the caregiver's words or actions. The caregiver should also note the expectations he or she has of the resident. Are they appropriate to the resident's level of functioning or extent of cognitive or emotional impairment? Does the caregiver know the resident's particular abilities and disabilities, strengths and needs?

The interaction between a resident and a caregiver may determine the success with which a resident accomplishes a task or refrains from a particular behavior. The quality of the interaction affects the resident's emotional response to a request as well as his or her ability to understand and to respond physically. It is important to take into account the changes in sensory functions that frequently accompany aging, as well as the cognitive changes resulting from the dementia. Dementia can compound normal sensory changes and may exacerbate the inability to understand, since the resident is less able to compensate for sensory changes.

In monitoring one's interactions, a caregiver should ask, Does this person see and hear me? Can this person understand me? Am I surprising or frightening this person? Did I warn this person that I was coming and prepare him or her for what I was about to say? Are my suggestions or instructions short, simple, and clear? Is my voice pitched low to enhance the person's ability to hear me? (A person with a hearing problem frequently has difficulty hearing high frequencies.) Am I talking too loudly? (A well-meaning but loud voice may falsely suggest to the resident that the caregiver is angry or anxious.) Do my words match the expressions on my face, and match my "gut" feelings? Am I being dictatorial or condescending rather than respectful? Am I communicating reassurance and warmth, both verbally and nonverbally? Am I talking in a calm voice, with a slow but normal cadence so the resident can use inflection to help interpret my meaning?

## The Task

In assessing the task, the caregiver should examine the emotional dimensions of the task as well as the demands it makes on a person's cognitive, physical, emotional, and social abilities. The task is the activity in which an individual is engaged or in which a caregiver wishes to engage the resident. Sometimes the task is an undesirable behavior (e.g., attempting to leave the area). In such a case, the caregiver examines the meaning, value, or purpose of the behavior to the resident as well as to other involved persons.

The emotional dimensions might be addressed by the following questions: Is this a task most people like to do (e.g., eating something sweet versus changing clothes)? Is there an inherent appeal to the task? Does the person want to do it? Does the person like this type of activity? If the task is unappealing, it may need to be altered to be more pleasant. The examination of the demands a task makes on a person's cognitive, physical, emotional, and social abilities may require some sophistication and perhaps professional expertise.

Identification of the body parts that are used to complete a task

**Table 12.2.**
**Task-Complexity Model for Task Modification**

| Task Features | Task Steps | Task Objects | Body Parts Used |
|---|---|---|---|
| Number |  |  |  |
| Variety |  |  |  |
| Abstractness |  |  |  |
| Novelty[a] |  |  |  |

*Source:* Adapted from Weaverdyck 1987 and Weaverdyck 1990.
*Notes:* This model can be used as a method for assessing and simplifying a task for someone with dementia. Each square can be filled in with a rating of "low," "moderate," or "high," to indicate the extent to which the task feature affects each task component. Generally, tasks with many "high" and "moderate" ratings are very complex and difficult for someone with dementia. Modifying the task by reducing the "high" and "moderate" ratings to "low" may simplify the task and therefore enable a person with dementia to perform the task successfully.
[a] "Novelty" means the extent to which each component is unfamiliar to the person.

can help illuminate some of the physical demands. Clearly, a task that demands walking is inappropriate for someone who is not ambulatory, or a task that requires fine motor coordination or strength in the fingers is not appropriate for someone with severely arthritic hands. A task that requires a substantial amount of verbal communication will be inappropriate for someone who is severely aphasic. A group activity may not be appropriate for someone who prefers to be alone.

The task-complexity model presented in Table 12.2 identifies those characteristics of a task that may make it particularly difficult for someone with dementia. This model requires that a task be broken into *identifiable steps or subtasks*. It requires identification of the *objects or materials to be manipulated* in the task, and it requires the identification of the *parts of the body* a resident must use to execute the task. Each of these three components is evaluated for number, variety, abstractness, and novelty. The higher the rating, the more difficult the task may be for someone with dementia. For example, if the objects to be manipulated are highly abstract (such as words or pictures rather than actual three-dimensional objects), or if many parts of the body are to be used, the task may be too difficult unless the other features such as variety and novelty are minimal. Dressing requires the use of many parts of the body, but it is highly familiar (if a familiar routine, familiar context, and familiar clothes are used) and concrete, and so many people with dementia are able to dress themselves, at least partially, well into the course of their dementia.

By using the task-complexity model, a caregiver can determine whether or not the task is too complex for the resident. The caregiver can also modify the task by reducing the novelty, variety, abstractness, or number of steps, objects, or body parts used. Eating can be simplified, for example, by reducing the number or variety of food items on the plate, or by providing only a spoon, or by making the dining room and table appear similar to those of the resident's own past. Tailoring a task's length and complexity to a resident's needs and competencies may be all that is needed to allow the resident to accomplish the task independently and successfully. Similarly, when a resident is engaged in a behavior that a caregiver wishes to change or reduce, the caregiver can use the task-complexity model to identify a similar behavior or task with which to replace it. An examination of undesirable behavior should include an evaluation of the behavior that is as objective as possible before any attempts are made to alter it. The caregiver can foster this objectivity by asking some questions: What sort of satisfaction or gratification (either conscious or unconscious) does this resident seem to derive from this behavior? What might be the resident's goals in performing this behavior? Who, if anyone, is this behavior actually harming or bothering? Would it be more helpful simply to remove the person who is bothered by the behavior, rather than addressing the behavior or the person performing it? Are there benefits to the resident resulting from this behavior that may outweigh the disadvantages to caregivers (e.g., wandering can improve a resident's circulation or chances of remaining ambulatory, even if it means wandering into other people's private spaces)?

## The Person

The person is the most complex and difficult to assess of the four influencing factors. Generally, the aspects of a person that should be assessed include the person's history, medical and physical status, emotional (affective) status, and cognitive status. Each of these will be briefly discussed.

History includes a person's social, psychological, intellectual, and medical and physical histories. It also includes past habits, daily routines, and information from both before and after the onset of the dementia. It would identify preferences or habits. Has the individual been a "night" person or a "morning" person? How much sleep did the person usually get or need? When was his or her most productive time of day? What are the person's color or food preferences? What routine has the person always used when grooming or getting dressed? Sometimes it is very helpful to have a family member demonstrate the routines for grooming and self-care or activities of daily living the family has used so that familiar routines can be continued.

Ongoing assessment of the individual's medical status is essential. This includes the duration and type of dementia, other medical or physical disorders, and medications that may be exacerbating dementia symptoms (see Chap. 14).

A resident's physical condition should also be regularly monitored. Many times a person's response to a request is slowed down because of the body's inability to move quickly. Sometimes the response is so slow that the resident, because of impaired memory, has forgotten the request by the time the body is ready to respond. The caregiver can prolong independence by adjusting expectations, rearranging the environment, or using various helping strategies to accommodate the physical impairment.

Vision and hearing should also be assessed regularly to ensure that the resident is seeing and hearing instructions and cues from the environment or from the caregiver. Sometimes a caregiver will attribute a lack of response to stubbornness when in fact the person simply did not hear or understand the request. With the added dementia, the person may be unable to use logic or memory or may become anxious and frightened, further reducing the chances of understanding. The resident's resistance may be avoided simply by a caregiver's conscious attention to the adaptation of the methods of communication.

Undesirable behavior may have a physical origin. In one facility, one individual became restless and began to wander whenever she needed to use the bathroom, even though she denied needing the bathroom at the time. Sometimes hunger or fatigue causes resistance or impaired functioning. A caregiver may succeed in reducing the behavior more effectively and less painfully by addressing potential physical discomforts.

Caregivers frequently find it difficult to address wandering and excessive hollering behaviors. Often, out of desperation or a lack of obvious alternatives, the intervention chosen is medication, or restraint in a geri-chair or wheelchair, or confinement to the resident's room (Hiatt 1985). In cases such as these, regular monitoring of the resident's physical condition is imperative. Medication can impair a person's sense of balance and increase the likelihood of falls (which then further motivates a caregiver to use a geri-chair as a restraint) as well as increase agitation or motor restlessness.

When an individual is confined to a wheelchair or geri-chair for long periods of time, muscles can atrophy and joints (particularly hips and shoulders) can become misaligned or affected in other ways because of the poor distribution of weight enforced by ill-fitting chairs. The body of an older person who is frail and at risk for pain, bone fractures, and skin breakdown simply cannot accommodate such prolonged pressure or abnormal positioning. Pains, abnormal tension, and deformities develop that can exacerbate restlessness, anxiety, and discomfort. Ultimately these practices may result in an increase in symptoms such as hollering and increase the risk of falling. The person frequently becomes nonambulatory and non–weight bearing, so that transferring and other caregiving becomes more difficult (and sometimes less frequent, resulting in an increase in incontinence, for example). Ultimately much more care will be required, and the care will be more strenuous, increasing the risk of injury to the caregiver. Interventions other than physical restraint in a geri-chair would be more effective and more humane, and ultimately easier for the caregiver.

A resident's emotional status will likely have a major impact on his or her behavior and level of functioning. In considering a resident's emotional status, a caregiver might ask, How does the resident feel right now? Is the resident engaged in a behavior I am trying to stop? Does the resident seem to want to engage in this behavior? The behavior may not be satisfying a resident's needs or desires. Helping the resident find a behavior that is more satisfying may be a key to reducing the undesirable behavior. If the caregiver is trying to introduce an alternative, does the resident seem to enjoy the suggested alternative behavior or task? What kind of mood is the resident in? Should the caregiver wait for a change of mood?

Is this person typically upbeat or depressed? Does the person seem to prefer a fast or slow pace? Does the person like to be kept busy, or is he or she content just to sit and relax? Does the person derive pleasure from highly social or more solitary activities? Tailoring activities and approaches to a person's preference may be crucial to their success.

Are there objects in the environment or perhaps dates that trigger certain emotional states in this resident? Do holidays tend to be sad times or happy times? Family or longtime friends may be the only source of answers to some of these questions.

Is there a pattern to the person's moods throughout the day (e.g., more relaxed and compliant in the morning and more anxious in the late afternoon or evening)? Does the person need to feel a sense of responsibility in order to be productive and happy, or prefer to be waited on and cared for? Does the person worry about the needs of others, or demand to be attended to immediately and order others about? Does the person need a sense of private space or territory over which he or she has authority? This seemed evident in one woman who, in a dining room in a facility, frequently shouted, "This is my house! Why are these people in my house? Get out of my house!"

When some of these emotional issues or preferences are identified (sometimes with the help of a professional or a family member), interventions can be considered that may immediately or ultimately improve the resident's behavior or level of functioning. It is helpful, for example, to follow a resident's preferred schedule for the day's activities, such as a specific order of eating breakfast, getting dressed, showering, reading or looking at the newspaper, socializing, and so on.

Dementia is essentially a cognitive disorder. As a progressive, currently irreversible disorder, it reflects the growing severity and spread of the brain pathology. It is necessary, therefore, to examine closely the specific cognitive functions that are affected by brain damage, and to identify those cognitive functions that are still intact and those that appear to be impaired. Sophisticated assessment requires the skill and experience of a neuropsychologist or cognition specialist. A caregiver can, however, be alert to various types of cognitive functioning and can learn to tailor the caregiving to accommodate an individual's abilities and disabilities. A caregiver can prolong independence and a sense of well-being by compensating for or assisting specific impaired cognitive functions, and by enhancing and relying on intact cognitive functions. Signs posted on doors that indicate what is behind them or that discourage a resident from entering, for example, can help compensate for impaired memory.

A person's cognitive functioning can be seen as a path along which information is processed through five types of functioning or phases: sensory, perception and comprehension, executive, expressive, and motoric.

The first is the sensory phase. Is the person physically receiving the information? That is, can the person see, hear, taste, feel, and smell at a sensory level? The normal sensory changes of age frequently affect this phase, as do waxy ears or incorrect glasses and hearing aids.

The second is the comprehension and perception phase. Does the person recognize or understand the information received through the senses? For example, does the resident recognize a toothbrush for what it is? Can the person read to the extent of understanding the letters and words?

The third phase, the executive level of processing, is the highest level of cognitive functioning (Lezak 1983). At this level, the brain organizes the information and uses functions such as memory, logic, ordering, planning, and abstraction to digest the information and to make it useful. This level of functioning is usually particularly impaired in dementia (Cohen and Eisdorfer 1986; Fuld 1983).

In the fourth phase of cognitive functioning, the expressive phase, the brain tells the body what to do based on the information it has received. Apraxia and aphasia are two disorders that can be localized at this phase. In the former, the brain cannot tell the body what to do at will or at a conscious level. For example, if simply told to put on a sweater, a person may not be able to do it. It the person wants to go home, however, and putting on a sweater is part of this larger task, he or she can put on the sweater quite easily. In expressive aphasia, the person is unable to produce the words he or she wants to say, but can sometimes say the words if they are a part of a larger phrase or even a song (Bayles et al. 1986).

In the final phase, the motoric phase, the body responds physically to the brain's instructions. However, sometimes the body responds motorically so slowly that upon finally getting to the door, for example, a person may have forgotten the reason for having walked there in the first place.

Assessment of cognitive functioning is extremely important to any dementia care/intervention program. Unfortunately, such assessment is frequently overlooked, perhaps because it is complex and may require the services of a specialist, or perhaps because it is simply forgotten as a possible cause of behavior or a change in general functioning (Teri and Lewinsohn 1986; Brink 1986). Undesirable behaviors, resistance, poor performance on a task, or a lack of an adequate response to a request may often be attributed to a lack of motivation or to orneriness on the part of a resident. Such behavior or impairment is probably more often due, however, to fluctuations in the person's cognitive functioning or to environmental conditions. Awareness of the importance of cognitive assessment, and of some of the types of cognitive functioning to which one should be alert, can help avoid such damaging and unproductive misperceptions on the part of the caregiver.

When assessing sensory functions, a caregiver should be alert to both verbal and nonverbal indications from the resident to determine if the resident in fact heard or saw the information. Monitoring the manner and techniques with which one interacts with a resident and the specific environmental conditions can contribute greatly to success. Background noise and a clutter of objects in the visual field can impair a resident's ability to hear and to see, for example. Getting the resident's attention before speaking is also helpful.

There are many possible impairments and competencies to note with regard to perception and comprehension. Can the resident read the signs that are intended as cues? Does the resident recognize an object for what it is? (A disorder related to object recognition is called visual or object agnosia, which is different from the inability to name an object.) Can the resident judge distances, knowing how far it actually is, say, when a caregiver tells him or her where the bathroom is? Can the resident see or put objects in order? When a caregiver points out landmarks in the hall, can the resident see where the landmarks are in relation to each other? A resident who has poor eye-hand coordination, or cannot see exactly where an item is, may be able to eat if the caregiver simply moves the person's hand to the food item. It might be that the resident does not perceive items to the right or left, and moving them into his or her intact visual field is necessary (Wolanin and Phillips 1981). A person's ability to concentrate or tendency to be distracted are also important to note.

Impairment in the executive functions can cause many difficulties. A caregiver should note how well a resident consciously knows his or her own abilities or disabilities. A resident may not be able to articulate or recognize internal needs (the need to eat or urinate, or the desire for some peace and quiet, for example). It is important to note the conditions under which a resident remembers information more easily, so that those conditions can be encouraged. It may be that a person needs very tangible cues rather than simply words. Holding up a comb while asking someone to go comb his or her hair may be necessary. When faced with a plate full of a variety of foods, a person may have a difficult time choosing among the options and so may choose none. Frequently, a person has trouble shifting focus from one task to the next and needs time to make the shift or to get started on an activity.

A person's inability to perform tasks or to respond verbally may reflect a problem at the expressive level of functioning. It may be that a resident can dress alone but does not know it, or can do it only without consciously attending to each step. Avoiding interruptions or introducing mild distraction with pleasant conversation may foster success in the latter case.

Establishing the optimal conditions for the performance of a skill is extremely important. It may be that consistency and routine are important. Frequently, a person can perform a task, but only if the setting, the order of steps, or the task materials are familiar. Identifying the environmental triggers that work for a particular person can be crucial to that person's independent functioning.

The importance of identifying the individual's physical motoric abilities has already been noted. The slowed physical reactions that frequently accompany normal aging can become particularly problematic in dementia, when a person's ability to retain a goal or memory is compromised. A caregiver may need to repeat instructions at intervals or help out by speeding the resident's movements or reducing distances. Prosthetic devices, such as thick-handled spoons, may be helpful for people with physically impaired hands and other body parts. It is also important to note whether one side of the body or one particular part of the body is weaker than the others.

## Strategies for Assessing While Helping

How can caregivers go about assessing or getting the information necessary to answer the types of questions presented in this chapter? A professional assessment can be helpful, particularly if caregivers can indicate to the professional the sort of information they hope to gain from the assessment.

The caregiver can also gain much information by alert observation and by fostering good assessment techniques as a part of the caregiving process. These techniques can be formal or informal. The caregiver can document observations and then study them for patterns across time. For example, a caregiver may begin to notice that each time a particular resident tried to get into the elevator to leave the floor over the past month, the behavior was preceded by an altercation between the two roommates in the next room. Or a caregiver may notice that a resident was particularly easygoing whenever a particular staff person was on duty.

The most important elements to proper assessment by a caregiver include astute observation, discreet helping, and knowing what types of information are needed.

In observing, it is important to give the resident time, a precious commodity in most caregiving settings. By giving the resident extra time to receive the information, to process it, and to act on it, a caregiver may see the resident perform functions he or she typically had not performed previously. It is important to watch while the resident is acting both consciously and unconsciously.

When caregivers know what to look for, they are able to glean much information from these observations. In general, a caregiver attempts to seek information that will provide various possible explanations for a resident's behavior or level of functioning and information regarding behavior occurrences, task performances, and the environmental conditions. Some ideas of what to look for in individual residents can emerge from discussion and questions raised at staff meetings and by studying the documentation on an individual. Note especially the situations in which the behavior or impairment is evident. The impairment may in fact be hiding an actual competence that is obscured by adverse environmental conditions. Note the conditions under which the impairments occur, the resident's pacing, the task steps that seem to give particular trouble, the coping strategies a resident uses when faced with obstacles. The caregiver should continually ask, Why is this resident behaving like this?

To gain information about a resident, a caregiver can use at least seven specific strategies while helping that resident (Weaverdyck 1987):

1. Waiting
2. Slowing down
3. Asking if the resident wants help
4. Prompting verbally or nonverbally
5. Encouraging the resident
6. Providing feedback to the resident
7. Doing all or part of the task for a resident

These strategies are listed in order from least intrusive to most intrusive. A key to assessment is letting the resident do as much for himself or herself as possible. The least intrusive strategies restrain the caregiver from interfering, so that observations of the resident's actual competencies and impairments can be more easily conducted. A caregiver may derive the maximal amount of information from the encounter by offering help in the order indicated. The helping strategies should be used and help should be offered, if necessary, at each step of the task. Use of the strategies should be tailored to the individual and to the particular situation.

First, the caregiver simply waits to see how the resident handles the situation or task step. Giving the resident time is important.

Similarly, slowing down will allow the caregiver time to observe more leisurely as well as accommodate the slowed processes of the resident. Asking if the resident wants help before simply providing the help can give the resident an opportunity to indicate (verbally or nonverbally) that what is needed is simply more time or more information regarding the task.

Prompting, rather than doing the task for the resident, is another way of giving help minimally and discreetly so as to interfere as little as possible in the resident's own demonstration of skills and preferences. A verbal prompt may be simply "Pull it up" or "Over here." An example of a nonverbal prompt would be positioning the resident's hand on the stocking, for instance, or just initiating a step.

An example of encouragement would be a caregiver saying, "You're doing great!" at strategic points.

Providing feedback includes giving the resident information regarding progress. This strategy particularly addresses the resident's potential inability to check his or her own progress by observing the environment or the results of a particular performance. An example would be a caregiver saying, "You're almost there" or "That's right."

Finally, a caregiver may need to do parts of a task or a task step for the resident. A caregiver can gain the most information about the resident's abilities (and perhaps most likely boost the resident's self-esteem) by doing as little of the task step as possible, and then only after the other helping strategies have been tried. It may become apparent to the caregiver, after studying the resident's performance over time, that the resident cannot perform steps that rely heavily on a particular cognitive function or set of cognitive functions, or on a certain physical skill.

## Conclusion

The use of assessment as a part of caregiving can greatly enhance the effectiveness of the caregiving provided. It makes the caregiver much more knowledgeable about the actual functioning level of the person with dementia, and also helps identify the sources or triggers of behaviors the caregiver finds undesirable. By elucidating the reasons for impairments or particular behaviors, the assessment can suggest ideas for methods of intervention.

A caregiver who is knowledgeable about a resident's specific abilities and disabilities or preferences can be more effective in getting useful information from a consulting professional. It will also be more helpful to the consulting professional when a caregiver can give very explicit descriptions of a resident's behavior and mental status.

Researchers who study the natural course of dementia must frequently rely on the observations of the direct caregivers who know the dementia victim best. The more skilled a caregiver is in observation and in nonintrusive helping techniques, the more detailed, thorough, and accurate this information can be, and therefore the more valuable the contribution to the study of dementia.

A caregiver who uses good assessment techniques is in a much better position to encourage appropriate behaviors and level of functioning. By carefully assessing each of the four factors—the environment, caregiver characteristics and interactions, the task, and the person with dementia—the caregiver will be able to specify the sources of difficulty and therefore be in a better position to see the potential of any given intervention strategy. Ideas for creative intervention will come much more easily to a caregiver who assesses. If a caregiver discerns a factor in the environment to be a primary source or trigger of undesirable behaviors, it will be possible to focus on just that factor, at least initially, to alleviate the behavior more quickly and to avoid other more difficult and potentially damaging methods of intervention (see Chap. 13).

Adapting the environment, altering expectations for a resident's behavior or performance, modifying methods of communication, simplifying a task by reducing one or more of the dimensions identified in the task-complexity model, and using the assessment helping strategies are some of the many ways in which assessment can have a direct impact on the planning and efficacy of interventions and on the general quality of care provided for people with dementia.

### References

Bayles, K., A. Kaszniak, and C. Tomoeda. 1986. *Communication and cognition in normal aging and dementia.* New York: Little, Brown.

Bloomer, H. H. 1987. *The Bloomer performance blocks.* Unpublished paper. Normal, Ill.

Brink, T., editor. 1986. *Clinical gerontology: A guide to assessment and intervention.* New York: Haworth Press.

Burnside, I. M., editor. 1988. *Nursing and the aged,* 3rd ed. New York: McGraw-Hill.

Cohen, D., and C. Eisdorfer. 1986. *The loss of self: A family resource for the care of Alzheimer's disease and related disorders.* New York: W. W. Norton.

Fuld, P. A. 1983. Psychometric differentiation of the dementias: An overview.

In *Alzheimer's disease: The standard reference*, edited by B. Reisberg, 201–210. New York: Free Press.

Hiatt, L. G. 1985. *Intervention and people who wander: Contradictions in practice.* Paper presented at the 38th Scientific Meeting of the Gerontological Society of America.

Hussian, R., and R. Davis. 1985. *Responsive care: Behavioral interventions with elderly persons.* Champaign, Ill.: Research Press.

Kane, R. A., and R. L. Kane. 1981. *Assessing the elderly: A practical guide to measurement.* Lexington, Mass.: Lexington Books.

Lawton, M. P. 1986. *Environment and aging*, 2nd ed. Monterey, Calif.: Brooks/Cole.

Lezak, M. 1983. *Neuropsychological assessment.* 2nd ed. New York: Oxford University Press.

Snyder, L. H., P Rupprecht, J. Pyrek, et al. 1978. Wandering. *Gerontologist*, 18(3):272–280.

Teri, L., and P. Lewinsohn, editors. 1986. *Geropsychological assessment and treatment: Selected topics.* New York: Springer.

Weaverdyck, S. E. 1987. *A cognitive intervention protocol: Its derivation from and application to a neuropsychological case study of Alzheimer's disease.* Dissertation. University of Michigan. Available from University Microfilms International, 300 N. Zeeb Road, Ann Arbor, Mich. 48106. Publication #8712237.

Weaverdyck, S. E. 1990. Neuropsychological assessment as a basis for intervention in dementia. In *Dementia care: Patient, family, and community*, edited by N. L. Mace. Baltimore: Johns Hopkins University Press.

Weaverdyck, S. E., and D. H. Coons. 1988. Designing a dementia residential care unit: Addressing cognitive changes with the Wesley Hall model. In *Housing the very old*, edited by G. M. Gutman and N. K. Blackie, 63–85. Burnaby, British Columbia: Simon Fraser University Press.

Wolanin, M. O., and L. R. F. Phillips. 1981, *Confusion: Prevention and care.* St. Louis, Mo.: C. V. Mosby.

## Chapter 13

# Intervention to Address Dementia As a Cognitive Disorder

SHELLY E. WEAVERDYCK, Ph.D.

This chapter will discuss some of the strategies and types of intervention appropriate for cognitively impaired persons with dementia and identify some conceptual issues to consider when developing an intervention plan. First, the fundamental features of dementia that make it different from other disorders typically encountered in long-term care settings will be noted. This will be followed by a discussion of the implications of these features with respect to intervention and some criteria for defining a dementia intervention program. Five types of intervention programing will then be identified. Finally, the four target areas identified in Chapter 12 as important areas of assessment will be noted and briefly illustrated as vehicles of intervention.

The interventions suggested here can be used in an effort to increase the level of functioning of a person with dementia, or to avert or respond to behaviors that the caregiver believes to be undesirable or unhealthy. These suggestions are not detailed, but are simply illustrative of the types of intervention that address the cognitive changes in dementia and that could be available in a dementia program or unit. (For more specific intervention suggestions see Weaverdyck 1987; Coons and Weaverdyck 1986; Robinson et al. 1988; Holden and Woods 1982; and Zgola 1987.)

### The Clinical Features of Dementia

There is little rigorous clinical research regarding the behavioral and cognitive course of dementia, particularly research of the kind that examines the order and rate of deterioration of the full range of

224

cognitive skills in the individual's own setting. A substantial amount of clinical observation, however, has been reported in the literature. Based on these clinical reports and research conducted to date (Cohen and Eisdorfer 1986; Fuld 1983) as well as my own clinical and research experience (Weaverdyck 1987), five characteristics are identified here that appear to be fundamental to dementia. Together, these make dementia, such as Alzheimer's disease, a disorder different from other disorders frequently encountered in nursing homes and other long-term care facilities. They form the basis for a set of criteria that determine the extent to which an intervention program is specially designed to address the dysfunctions common in dementia. They can also be used to determine whether a unit is justified in calling itself a dementia program. (For a more detailed discussion and application of both the features and criteria see Weaverdyck and Coons 1988).

The five fundamental characteristics of primary dementia (a dementia that is progressive and is the result of a, to date, untreatable brain pathology) are as follows:

1. Primary dementia is a cognitive disorder.
2. It is frequently difficult to ascertain the specific competencies and impairments the person with dementia is experiencing, and the extent to which these skills and deficits play a role in the person's daily functioning.
3. The deterioration is progressive.
4. There is an increased dependency upon the environment for information regarding appropriate behavior.
5. There is an increased reliance on overlearned skills, information, and contexts for behavior.

### A Cognitive Disorder

Dementia is primarily a cognitive disorder. Compared with the cognitive deterioration evident in dementia, the physical, medical, and emotional aspects of the dementia victim are essentially intact, at least until the advanced stages of the disorder (Corsellis 1976; U.S. Congress, Office of Technology Assessment 1987). As the person ages, physical or medical disorders may accompany, but are usually etiologically unrelated to, the dementia. It is generally not until the advanced stages that dementia victims require major medical intervention. This is not to say that medical monitoring is not extremely important; it is. Slight physical discomforts or medical conditions such as fever or constipation can exacerbate confusion in the person with dementia. But for the most part, the individual requires supervision of behaviors and daily functioning in the activities of daily living rather than, for example, gastrointestinal tubes.

Some of the implications of this cognitive deterioration are evident in the discussion of the other four features.

### Obscured Abilities and Disabilities

In a dementia disorder, people's physical and emotional aspects can be much less impaired than their cognitive functioning, causing them to appear to be nearly normal at times. For example, it is sometimes possible for a visitor to converse for several minutes with the cognitively impaired person before becoming aware that the person is not fully competent.

In dementia, more than in some disorders, it is often difficult to sort out the specific cognitive skills in the individual that are impaired from those that are intact. Because the damage to the brain is less localized than it is in some strokes, and because there is major damage to several brain structures whose functions interact in complex ways, the resulting impairments of cognitive skills and functions mediated by the various brain structures are particularly complex (Corkin et al. 1982). The task of sorting out the exact level of impairment of the various functions can seem overwhelming, particularly in the middle stages. Furthermore, many dementia victims in the middle and later stages are unable to perform on the tests conventionally used by neuropsychologists to assess cognitive functioning, and they are thus labeled untestable. They may not understand the instructions, may not be able to focus long enough to make the testing valid, or may not be able to produce the answers because the questions or demands are simply too difficult for them.

Many times a competency in one area may be hidden by impairment in another. For example, a person may have difficulty finding the bathroom after asking for directions, not because of a memory problem but perhaps because of never having recorded the information when it was given. The person may have difficulty recognizing the distance to the bathroom door, or recognizing the relationship of various landmarks to each other. Rather than attributing this inability to find the bathroom to a memory disorder or to disorientation, it would be more correct to identify it as a perceptual problem.

Because a person appears normal, it is easy to overestimate his or her level of functioning. By the same token, as a caregiver observes the overwhelming deterioration it becomes easy to underestimate a person's abilities, and hence tempting to do everything for that person.

Many times, a caregiver attributes a dementia victim's resistance or nonresponsiveness to motivation. "She can do it when she wants to" is a frequent comment. The resistance or lack of response is more likely due to an actual cognitive impairment, however, than to a desire to irk the caregiver. A "refusal" to walk, for example, may reflect a problem of apraxia (the inability of the brain to tell the body what to do), particularly if the person can walk with a larger goal in mind (e.g., going out the door) or when not focusing on the actual walking because it is part of a series of task steps.

Similarly, a person with dementia may be unable to compensate for the sensory changes that frequently accompany normal aging. Upon opening the clothes closet door, for example, a healthy older person usually needs to take some time to allow the eyes to adjust to the reduced level of lighting in the closet. The healthy older person knows, consciously or unconsciously, not to worry but just to wait a moment for the eyes to become adjusted. Such a person can also rely on memory and logic to determine what is in the closet and where. Someone with dementia may not be able to compensate for this very common sensory change, because memory and logic are likely impaired. The temporary "blindness" may cause anxiety or even panic, so the person may appear overwhelmed by the task of selecting clothes from the closet. Allowing extra time and reassurance and describing the contents of the closet in a simple manner can be very helpful in such a case. Even more helpful might be to change the environment (install brighter lights in the closet to match the level of lighting in the rest of the room) to accommodate the normal sensory changes. The problematic impairment most easily susceptible to intervention in this case is not the impaired memory or logic but the normal changes in the eye.

### A Progressive Disorder

The primary dementia disorder is progressive. At this point there is no known method for reversing the brain pathology underlying the dementia. Caregivers must adjust their goals to be more existential rather than aiming for permanent gains or improvement. Good feelings may at times be legitimate as a sole objective for an activity.

Working with persons whose overall functioning continues to decline regardless of the interventions introduced can be discouraging and a source of burnout. The caregiver needs to learn to see and appreciate small improvements as major victories.

The caregiver also needs to recognize the vast potential of environmental adaptation, task modification, and alterations in caregiver-resident interactions as methods of intervention. The individual's functioning in everyday tasks may be improved considerably by simply focusing on and adjusting the environment, task, or interactions employed. It is possible that the day-to-day fluctuations often apparent in the dementia victim's behavior and level of functioning result more from environmental conditions or the person's emotional state than from changes in the brain functioning underlying the dementia disorder. In such cases, intervention has enormous potential for success.

### Increased Environmental Dependency

As the dementia progresses, the person may become increasingly dependent upon the environment for cues on what to do and how to behave. The person may gradually become more reactive to external stimuli (or internal bodily stimuli) and less able to observe, analyze, and act on the situation at hand. When brought to a room for a church service, for example, and told that this is a church service, the person may know how to behave only if the room looks like a church, or if hymns are audible or a robed speaker is visible. Otherwise, the person may speak loudly or rise to leave at inappropriate times.

Because dementia impairs memory and logic (both deductive and inductive) as well as the ability to think abstractly, the environment must become evermore concrete and obvious in its cuing as the dementia becomes increasingly severe. Instead of signs saying "Exit Only in Emergency," for example, painting exit doors to camouflage them may be more effective in preventing people from wandering out doors.

A person may also have difficulty evaluating stimuli and monitoring internal feelings, needs, and wants, and thus be less able to resolve inconsistencies or problems. A person may not recognize the sensation of hunger, for example, but may begin to feel restless and to wander as mealtimes approach. The person may be unable to solve the problem by seeking food.

This increased reliance on environmental cues rather than cognitive awareness and problem-solving ability suggests also that cues should offer emotional appeal rather than purely "cognitive" information. Instead of simply posting a sign that says "den " with an arrow, for example, a caregiver may create a path to the den by placing various cues that attract a person emotionally rather than only cognitively. In this way a person more in the mood for a quiet, cozy den than for a lively, airy living room will, consciously or unconsciously, find the emotional cues attractive and will more likely follow the cues to the den. In order to respond effectively to the sign alone, the person would need to be able to recognize a current preference for a cozy den and the misfit between that preference and the mood of the living room, then remember that the den is cozy and understand the sign providing directions to it.

> Mrs. Shane is in a bright, busy living room, but at the moment she would prefer a quiet, parlor-type area where she can be away from the bustle. She does not know or consciously recognize this preference, so she does not get up to go find an area that better suits her mood. She happens to see, however, a luxurious potted plant with a dim lamp hanging near it. She is attracted emotionally to the plant and moves toward it. As she approaches the plant she sees beyond it another plant next to a chair, or perhaps a den area.
>
> A path had been designed to draw someone along by appealing to the emotional level—not by addressing the cognitive level through abstract and potentially meaningless signs bearing the word *den* and an arrow. Such a path can also encourage a person to turn corners and discover other spaces that may not be visible unless consciously sought. Mrs Shane was relying on the environment to take her to the den, rather than consciously seeking out the den on her own initiative.

The implications of this increased environmental dependency for intervention include rigorous environmental analysis to discern the messages the environment is conveying to the person with dementia. Because some elements in the environment may be more prominent than others, it will become increasingly important for the caregiver to be skilled at seeing and hearing the environment from the perspective of the person with dementia to avoid unintentional and inconsistent cues.

Inconsistent and unintentional cuing often occurs in long-term care facilities. For example, a staff person is retrieving breakfast trays and, while holding a tray, tells a resident that it will be time for a shower in just a few minutes. The breakfast tray may be a more meaningful cue than the verbal warning to anticipate a shower. Upon returning to help with the shower, the caregiver should not be surprised if the resident insists on eating breakfast rather than taking a shower.

### Increased Reliance on Overlearned Skills, Information, and Contexts

A person with dementia is usually better able to perform skills or tasks that are familiar than those that are new. A person can often get dressed well into the course of the disorder, if the routine is the lifelong, accustomed one. When new steps or unfamiliar settings are introduced to the dressing task, the person may have difficulties. The ability to adapt is clearly impaired.

Similarly, a person may remember and retain the ability to be socially correct by using common clichés. For example, someone may act and speak very competently socially when meeting a new person but may say the same thing to everyone upon the first meeting, with little variation. The ability to remember overlearned or automatic conversations and behaviors is more intact than the ability to assimilate new information and skills.

It is important to keep the setting for various tasks as familiar and congruent as possible with a person's past settings for the same tasks. A person may be able to eat better if the dining room setting is similar to what he or she has been used to. The person may be able to dress more easily when putting clothes on in an accustomed order. The person may be less resistent to bathing if asked to bathe at the same time and in the same manner he or she bathed throughout adult life. People with dementia can frequently perform quite complex tasks if the tasks are familiar; they simply may not believe or remember that they can perform those tasks (Moscovitch 1982; Schacter et al. 1983).

### Implications of Dementia Characteristics for Intervention

To be effective, a dementia program should meet the following four criteria (Weaverdyck 1987; Weaverdyck and Coons 1988): (1) flexibility and versatility; (2) a sophisticated psychosocial (i.e., nonmedical) approach in addition to competent medical attention; (3) regular assessment; and (4) familiarity and congruency.

### Flexibility and Versatility

Because the dementia disorder is progressive and dynamic as a result of the spreading brain pathology, planned interventions must be ever changing to meet the changing needs and functioning levels of the person with dementia. Flexibility and versatility are also important because of the idiosyncratic nature of the dementia's behavioral and cognitive course. The idiosyncrasies observed may simply reflect researchers' limited knowledge regarding multiple types of Alzheimer's disease, or the nature of the dementing disorder, or genuine differences in individual responses to the brain pathology and concomitant disorders. In any case, there does seem to be a great variation among dementia victims in terms of their cognitive functioning and the behaviors they exhibit.

Reactions to obvious and subtle environmental changes may also account for idiosyncrasies and fluctuations in functioning levels and behaviors. A dementia program must be able to address these individual differences and changes through genuine flexibility and variety.

### A Strong Psychosocial Component

A strong psychosocial component in addition to competent medical attention is particularly important in a dementia program. It was noted above that dementia care requires supervision of behavior and assistance in daily tasks more than sophisticated ongoing medical intervention. At the present time, the domain of dementia care falls somewhere in between that of the medical treatment offered in most nursing homes and the psychological or psychiatric treatment offered in most mental health facilities (U.S. Congress, Office of Technology Assessment 1987). Because of a possibly increased sensitivity to unrelated medical disorders, careful ongoing medical monitoring and care are extremely important but should not be the entire orientation.

Since dementia is a disorder of the brain whose symptoms are impaired cognitive functioning, intervention should address the effects of the cognitive and not simply the emotional or physical functioning. The assumption is that the depression and other mood swings often evident in dementia may have more to do with the person's inability (or reactions to that inability) to perform normal daily tasks than with a fundamental psychopathology. The emotional stresses that accompany normal aging may also be affecting the individual and should be considered when intervening.

### Ongoing Assessment

Because the person is changing, and because external factors such as the environment play such a major role in the person's functioning and behavior, ongoing assessment and documentation of cognitive functioning and the conditions that seem to foster certain behaviors and levels of functioning must be conducted. The assessment should include observation and analysis of the individual as well as of the environment, the task, and the caregivers.

### Familiarity and Congruency

The reliance of the impaired person on overlearned skills, information, and contexts, and the implications of this for intervention, have already been noted. To the extent that a caregiver can arrange for the person to be performing familiar tasks "automatically" rather than through conscious attention and effort, the person may be successful. Making the person's environment and interactions with the caregiver familiar and consistent with the past will probably also contribute to an increased level of functioning and a reduction in behaviors the caregiver believes to be undesirable.

One implication of this criterion is the therapeutic importance of fostering a setting that is as normal (i.e., as congruent with the person's past life) as possible. Suddenly putting an individual in a setting and routine that are foreign or that are typically reserved for "patients" and the physically sick will likely be confusing and contribute greatly to impaired functioning and undesirable behaviors.

## Intervention Contexts

The above four criteria for intervention programs specializing in dementia will be further elaborated on in a discussion of the following five components of a dementia program: (1) activities programing; (2) general environment; (3) caregiving staff; (4) activities of daily living; and (5) therapies or interventions specific to particular behaviors or levels of functioning. Ideally a dementia program would hone its effectiveness in each and all of the five components simultaneously, but in fact it will most likely specialize in only some of them. Especially for a dementia program that is just beginning, it may be more reasonable to specialize in only one or two at first and then gradually build up the focus and effectiveness in each of the other components.

### Activities Programing

Activities programing includes all the individual and social group activities available to a person with dementia, except the activities of daily living (such as grooming, bathing, toileting, and other self-care). The activities include those that are diversionary and recreational (such as singing and group or individual games), creative (such as arts and crafts), and household maintenance activities (such as baking, cleaning, and washing dishes). Also included would be any other activities that most people do throughout the day, including volunteer work or employment.

The programing aspects of the dementia program will be successful to the extent that they provide residents a variety of opportunities to perform normal activities in normal ways—that is, the extent to which they are similar to the person's own past habits and preferences and to those in which most people of that age engage in this society (Wolfensberger 1972). The emphasis is not only on the normal but also on variety, so that various individuals and various moods of any single individual can be accommodated.

There must be appropriate flexibility in scheduling. If someone is a night person, for example, and prefers to stay up late but then sleep late in the morning, breakfast should ideally be served when the person is ready for it rather than only when the kitchen staff are ready to serve it (Coons and Weaverdyck 1986). The caregiving staff should also be prepared to rearrange schedules when the planned timing of some activities seems inappropriate on any given day.

Spontaneity should be encouraged through staff training and skills and permission for spontaneity, and also through the easy accessibility of props and ideas in the environment. It is generally much easier to initiate and maintain a conversation when there are "conservation pieces" lying about the room. The person with dementia needs the concrete trigger, and the visitor or staff person needs the idea when running low on creativity.

Regardless of the particular activity, the nature and level of cognitive functioning on the part of the individual must be noted and accommodated. This requires regular assessment and subsequent adaptation of expectations. Clearly, activities programing is a major component of the dementia program and as such deserves substantial attention in terms of funding and personnel.

### The Environment

The environment includes the physical, social, emotional, and cognitive environments. Because of its major influence, the environment has the potential for being either a serious hindrance or a major help to the person with dementia (Lawton 1986; Hiatt 1986). The role of the environment in a dementia program is to stimulate, inform, cue at appropriate times, support, and compensate for the level of functioning idiosyncratic to each individual. It will also be successful to the extent that it has the flexibility to accommodate changes in each individual's needs, desires, and resources, especially as the individual comes increasingly to rely on it. It must also provide a variety of options or choices that are visible and comprehensible and that can effectively attract individuals with various moods and abilities.

One major challenge in using the environment as a context of intervention is to tailor it to match the needs of the individual, particularly in a group setting and particularly as each individual deteriorates at his or her own rate. A program may choose to accomplish this by providing a series of step-down units or by adapting the environment of one unit as its residents deteriorate.

One example of environmental adaptation to the deterioration of a cognitive function is the increased concreteness of cues. At first a caregiver may paint a resident's bedroom door a particular color to distinguish it from other doors. As the ability to abstract and to appreciate the meaning of symbolic representation deteriorates, the person may not recognize the significance of the color on the door, since color has no inherently meaningful relationship to the identification of the room behind the door. At that point, a caregiver may put a sign on the door verbally identifying it as the person's bedroom. When someone can no longer read or comprehend the meaning of written information, a picture of that person or of a bedroom may be posted on the door. When someone no longer recognizes two-dimensional photographs or pictures, a personally meaningful and appealing object may be put on the door, or the door may simply be held ajar so that the person can see his or her own bed and possessions in the room from the hallway.

The environment should provide living spaces that vary in the mood they foster in both private and public spaces, so that people can match the environment to shifts in their moods and preferences.

It is important to remember that the person with dementia will likely rely heavily upon the environment to determine how to behave; therefore, all cues should be consistent with each other and congruent with the person's past. If caregivers want a person with dementia to act normally, then the environment must communicate that desire in a way the person can understand. If a dementia program is where the person lives, then the environment (physical, social, and emotional) must be like that of a home. As long as the environment looks and is conducted like a hospital, the person will at some level get the message that he or she is a patient and is expected to act like a patient, that is, sick and incompetent.

### Caregivers

The caregiver provides an important context for intervention in a dementia program. The behavior, manner, attitude, personality, role, and methods of communication of the caregiver all play a major role in the confused person's behavior and level of functioning. It is important that the staff be trained to be flexible and have a variety of roles, a repertoire of approaches, and methods of communicating to accommodate the unpredictability and the variety of moods and situations occurring in the caregiving setting (see Chap. 9). The staff should be trained to recognize the types and levels of cognitive functioning that may affect a person's ability to understand cues and to perform tasks. They should be able to see a dementia victim not simply as a diseased state or a set of impairments but as a *person* who has many competencies and positive qualities as well. There should be sufficient support for staff that creativity and ingenuity can be encouraged.

To make the versatility possible, the caregiving team should be interdisciplinary. As noted above, the number of staff persons responsible for nonphysical or nonmedical care should be substantial. The staff should be at least minimally skilled in assessment techniques, so that they can adjust their interactions with residents and their expectations of resident behavior appropriately.

### Activities of Daily Living

The activities of daily living (ADL) should be one of the most frequently used contexts for both intervention and assessment. Instead of doing the grooming or bathing tasks for the person, the caregiver can assist the person in such tasks. Using the helping strategies and task-complexity model presented in Chapter 12, the caregiver can assess an individual's level and method of functioning, and then tailor tasks accordingly. The ADL should not be rushed through, but should be allowed to extend over a period of time long enough to allow genuine assessment and intervention to occur. While such time spent on ADL may reduce the time available for other diversionary or therapeutic activities, the interventions occurring during ADL may be particularly effective because of the inherent relevance and familiarity of the task. Caring for oneself with grooming has psychological significance (Weaverdyck 1987).

## Therapies

For a dementia program to be genuinely committed to intervention at a sophisticated level, it must ultimately develop therapeutic interventions that include informal as well as formal, perhaps specialized, professional consultation services. Therapies could include structured one-on-one or group skill-focused sessions in which a caregiver discerns conditions under which functioning is optimal. as well as aids in the person's recovery of skills that may appear to be lost. They may include counseling sessions for the person with dementia, or the development of intervention plans for a specific behavior. They may include meetings for caregivers in which the strengths and needs of a given resident are identified and plans of action drawn up. They may include specific techniques such as task breakdown, analysis, and modification.

Clearly, such therapies would rely on accurate and frequent assessment of the individual as well as of the environment, tasks, and caregivers' qualities and interactions with residents. Documentation is an important part of the dementia program and must be accommodated in terms of caregiving schedules and environmental settings. Documentation of individual functioning as well as of the context in which behaviors occur is critical to the success of an intervention program. Antecedent events, environmental conditions, the social situation, and various aspects of the individual's demeanor, behavior, and apparent level of cognitive functioning should be documented in each "incident" of an undesired behavior. Assessment and documentation are also important in developing interventions that address the cognitive functioning of the individual.

Some specialized therapies frequently used include behavior modification, validation therapy, and reality orientation. Validation therapy, in particular, can be very helpful in appropriate cases if used by sensitive, skilled, and specially trained caregiving staff (Feil 1982). Unfortunately, these "therapies" rarely address significantly the cognitive functioning of the individual. Since dementia is at base a cognitive disorder, to address only, or even primarily, the behavior or the emotional status of the individual with the dementia is to address only the symptoms rather than the underlying causes of the problem.

While reality orientation purports to address cognitive functioning, most programs teach only the verbal recall of certain facts. This particular aspect is monitored and encouraged, while the myriad other affected cognitive functions are usually ignored.

Behavior modification assumes that an undesirable behavior can be reduced by manipulating the reward system that encourages it. Hussian and Davis (1985) examined some of the possible motivational causes of various behaviors. What they did not do is examine the deficits in cognitive processes that likely underlay the behaviors. If a behavior results from a misinterpretation of an environmental cue, for example, or from a response to an inconsistent or unintended environmental cue, then the most effective remedy would probably lie in the modification of the environmental cues, not of the person or the behavior. The behavior will very likely disappear or be reduced if the environment is modified to accommodate the person's particular cognitive abilities and disabilities or the person's needs (McEvoy and Patterson 1986; Horton et al. 1982).

Probably the most serious shortcoming of behavior modification is that it can easily constitute a form of "psychological restraint," just as drugs can be a form of chemical restrain and geri-chairs a form of physical restraint. By simply addressing the symptom and not the underlying cause, caregivers may be wresting a great deal of control away from the individual. Clearly they are often not viewing the situation from the individual's point of view.

Behavior modification frequently attributes a habitual or an emotional motivational source to a behavior and overlooks the possible cognitive factors. An example would be the dilemma and solution one facility considered with regard to a resident who would eat only his dessert. The staff was considering a behavior modification program to encourage the resident to eat his entire meal. It may be true that the primary reason for this resident's eating only his dessert is because he likes and wants the dessert, but does not like or want anything else. On the other hand, there may be other explanations. Usually dessert is served by itself as a single item, while the main course includes several items on the plate. Many times in dementia, a person is overwhelmed by a variety of items in the immediate environment and can respond more easily when only one or two items are presented. It may also be that the problem is one of "visual neglect" (a neuropsychological disorder in which a person may physically see an object but does not recognize its presence unless attention is drawn to it) and consequently a limited visual field, so that a single item placed right in front of the person is easier to recognize and negotiate. Sometimes in dementia there is a problem with initiation. The person is unable to get started on a task or needs extra time to get started. Since the dessert is served last, it may be that the elapsed time for processing or initiation was finally enough to allow the person to begin to eat. Sometimes a caregiver keeps trying to encourage a resident to perform a simple task with no response, or a faulty one, then suddenly the resident can do it perfectly or nearly so. The resident needed a warm-up time or a practice time before it suddenly became possible to respond. Another possible explanation may simply be the color of the dessert. Desserts are frequently made to look more appealing than main-course food; the visually contrasting color intensities or outlines of the dessert may be just the extra help the resident needed to overcome some of his sensory changes. Then too, desserts are frequently softer and easier to eat than main-course foods. While it may not be clear to the caregiver which explanation is most plausible or that it is only one as opposed to several explanations in combination, clearly there is a good possibility that motivation or stubbornness is not the only or even primary reason. The staff had not even considered the various possible cognitive and environmental explanations for the behavior that would suggest interventions quite different from, and probably simpler than, behavior modification.

A similar problem exists when caregivers attempt to introduce active intervention using methods or assumptions that treat dementia more as mental retardation (amentia) than dementia. Dementia is very different from mental retardation or "developmental disabilities." With dementia, a person is deteriorating from a previously higher level of cognitive functioning; with amentia, a person has not previously been at a higher level of functioning. In amentia, a caregiver frequently takes the role of a teacher of new skills; in dementia, one does not generally *teach* new skills. The job of a caregiver of someone with dementia is to discern the conditions under which the person can recall and express the skill or perform the task. Very often the ability to do the task is intact; it is the ability of the brain to tell the body what to do or the ability to recognize that this is the appropriate time to do the task that is impaired. The differences between the two disorders can appear to be subtle, but in fact they call for very different approaches in terms of interventions, goals, and caregiver roles (Weaverdyck 1987).

### Assessment Factors As Avenues of Intervention

Chapter 12 identifies assessment questions to be asked regarding four target areas: the environment, the task, the caregiver, and the person. The assumption is that each target area may be playing a significant causal role in the behavior or level of functioning of the person with dementia. The final section of this chapter illustrates briefly how a caregiver can use the answers to those questions as a basis for the planning of general or individualized interventions. Each of the four target areas will be noted as potential avenues for intervention. When a caregiver is trying to prevent or to stop a particular behavior or to improve the level of functioning on a particular task, each of these four factors must be assessed, then used as a means of attaining the objective.

## The Environment

The environment (including the physical, social, emotional, and cognitive) should tell a person with dementia what to do at any given moment. There should be as many cues as possible, and they should be understandable to the person. The cues should stimulate as many of the senses as possible and should be as redundant as possible without cluttering the environment. Meaningless noise, confusion, clutter, and crowds should be kept to a minimum. With dementia one may have a hard time sorting meaningless cues and stimuli from those that are meaningful or important. Cues should not be confusing or inconsistent.

The general environment should feel reassuring, interesting, and safe to the person with dementia. The caregiver should constantly be alert to any evidence the dementia victim expresses of being nervous or uncertain.

In the physical environment, cues, such as signs appropriate to each person's level of comprehension, should be placed so that they are clearly visible. This may mean three-dimensional cues down a hallway so that they can be seen from any vantage point. The cues should also seem familiar to the person.

A person who is being asked to do a task should be warned about the task ahead of time and should see other people engaged in similar or obviously complementary tasks. If the task is a private task (such as combing one's hair), then it should be conducted in privacy.

The general tenor of the emotional environment should be relaxed and perhaps lighthearted, but always warm and reassuring. This emotional ambience can be created by the caregiver's expressions and pacing, the quiet organization of schedules, and a calm but stimulating physical environment.

There should be appropriate cognitive stimulation in the environment. If a person has always been a classical music lover or an art lover, there should be classical music and art available in the environment. Topics of conversation and activities should be age-appropriate and tailored to the individual. It is possible to have simple conversations (e.g., those that avoid the need to produce names or factual information) regarding fairly complex issues such as politics or methods of rearing and disciplining children.

### The Task

The task can be defined as any activity being performed on a resident's own initiative that may or may not be seen as desirable by the caregiver (e.g., leaving through an exit door). It can also be defined as any activity the caregiver is introducing that may or may not be seen as desirable by the resident (e.g., walking away from the door or brushing one's teeth). It is important to recognize the inherent appeal of the task to the person with the dementia. If it is one the person simply does not like to do (e.g., take a shower), then the caregiver may need to make the task more appealing. It is also important to evaluate the complexity of the task, and to modify the task if it is too difficult for the person (see Chap. XII).

### The Caregiver

Sensitivity to the caregiver's role and interactions with the resident is essential to the success of any intervention. The caregiver should get the person's full attention before speaking or making a request. Instruction should be short and simple. The caregiver should speak clearly and with a pitch low enough to accommodate the sensory changes of a given individual. Words and gestures should match facial expression and posture. Because of a possible sensitivity to the emotional tenor of an interaction, a person may respond to the actual emotions of the caregiver rather than to what the caregiver is saying or trying to communicate. Most important, the caregiver should convey a feeling of respect, warmth, and reassurance. One way the caregiver can do this is by explaining simply to the resident what he or she is doing or intends to do. Sometimes when a particular caregiver is unable to adapt to a resident's needs or preferences at the moment, a different caregiver may need to help the resident that day.

### The Person

Intervention with the person may prove to be the most difficult of the four target areas in which to intervene. Collecting as much information as possible regarding the person's history (social, psychological, and medical) is certainly important. If the caregiver is to attempt to retain past roles and familiar environments and routines, then it is important to acquire such information from the family. Ascertaining a person's use or preference for coping strategies in the past may help the caregiver encourage the use of similar coping strategies in the current crisis. Adjusting schedules to match the person's preferred routines may be an important intervention.

In general, the person should be treated with respect and appropriate affection. It is important to help the person with dementia save face as much as possible. One way in which the caregiver can do this is by helping avert situations in which someone's deficits or mistakes are exposed. The caregiver can also try to be honest and sympathetic without being condescending. Instead of correcting a person who announces the intention of leaving to keep an appointment, the caregiver may simply suggest they go together to check the calendar.

Helping the person relax and feel comfortable and secure will most likely improve the person's level of functioning and reduce behaviors that caregivers find undesirable. Caregivers can do this by speaking calmly and using appropriate touch to reassure and to guide. Caregivers can also emphasize what the person does well and can remind the person of the abilities he or she still retains. Keeping the individual occupied with meaningful activity is also a key to the reduction of anxiety.

The caregiver can attempt to ensure that as much as possible is done to encourage optimal functioning at each of the five phases of cognitive processing: sensory, perception/comprehension, executive, expressive, and motoric. Once the person has been thoroughly assessed for the ability to function at each of these phases, the caregiver will probably have a better idea exactly which interventions can be most helpful. Very often in dementia, the executive phase functions are most severely impaired and the sensory and motoric functions the least impaired (Fuld 1983).

Because of normal sensory changes, however, an older person with dementia may need special accommodation at the sensory phase. Accommodation of sensory impairments may include speaking clearly and directly to the person and avoiding soft consonants, ensuring that the person wears clean and appropriate glasses and a hearing aid, and has increased lighting. Using colored pictures rather than black and white, or concrete objects rather than pictures, may accommodate sensory as well as perceptual disorders.

To accommodate perceptual or comprehension disorders, a caregiver can emphasize high contrast in the color, size, and shape of cues and adjust the level of abstractness of the cues (e.g., avoiding words if the person cannot read). The caregiver can generally substitute or reinforce verbal cuing with nonverbal cuing, such as demonstration, gestures, showing objects, and adding multisensory information. Short sentences (e.g., "Please come") rather than long sentences (e.g., "Let's go to the dining room together") may be helpful when giving instructions to someone who is aphasic. Pointing to objects may assist a person with visual field inattention, and approaching a person's "best side" may help him or her understand or respond to the caregiver.

The deficits in higher cognitive functions, such as the executive functions, can be addressed by repeating instructions or goals often. Allowing the person time and several attempts may also make a dramatic difference in performance. Giving only one request or instruction at a time, stating requests directly ("Come with me" rather than "Perhaps you'd like to join us"), and providing context ("It's morning, please get up") will be helpful to some people. Many times injecting humor relaxes and stimulates a person. Jokes must be concrete for many people, however, and teasing or making a person the butt of jokes should be absolutely avoided.

Caregivers should avoid abstract activities that require someone to visualize steps and end products when that person has difficulty generating images or keeping them in mind. For example, standing in front of a mirror to see how one looks is useful only if the person has a mental standard with which to compare the mirror image. Providing structure so that the person does not need to "figure things out" may be critical for some people. Talking a person through a task is one way of providing such a structure. When someone asks a question over and over again, remember that for that person this may feel like the very first time the question has been asked.

Expressive dysfunctions can best be accommodated by allowing extra time and by reducing anxiety. When a person is having difficulty finding the word he or she wants to use, patiently waiting or eventually suggesting possible word choices will likely be most helpful. If someone cannot name an object or produce a word, the caregiver should not assume that the person does not recognize or know how to use the object. Similarly, a caregiver should not assume that someone cannot perform a particular task simply because the person cannot perform it upon command. The caregiver may need to give the person extra time or help the person shift from one activity to another or from one task step to the next. Group activities, depending upon the activity and individuals involved, should most often be quite small, perhaps four to six people.

Interventions that address the motoric or physical disabilities of the person with dementia may sometimes be crucial to successful performance on a task. Physical therapy should not be ruled out simply because of the presence of dementia. Reducing distances for persons with mobility problems and reducing demands on dexterity for persons with coordination problems, as well as allowing extra time for the physical execution of movements, are all very important interventions.

## Conclusion

This chapter has presented some suggestions and issues regarding active intervention in dementia versus simple custodial care or the use of only comfort-safety measures. Dementia is a cognitive disorder, and the cognitive aspects must be addressed if the intervention program is to be effective and humane.

Some clinical features of dementia have been identified, as well as criteria for the definition of appropriate intervention in dementia. Contexts for intervention have also been suggested as components of an effective dementia program, and the use of the environment, the task, the caregiver, and the person as bases for intervention planning has been illustrated.

There is still much to learn regarding the appropriateness of various intervention approaches in dementia. It is important, however, to avoid oversimplification in our quest for responses to difficult situations and behaviors, and to avoid the therapeutic nihilism that frequently plagues caregivers in long-term care settings. Much can be done to enhance the cognitively impaired individual's ability to function effectively and appropriately, and it is the responsibility of the intervention setting to undertake the job with energy, sophisticated expertise, and genuine commitment.

## References

Cohen, D., and C. Eisdorfer. 1986. *The loss of self: A family resource for the care of Alzheimer's disease and related disorders.* New York: W. W. Norton.

Coons, D. H., and S. Weaverdyck. 1986. Wesley Hall: A residential unit for persons with Alzheimer's disease and related disorders. In *Therapeutic interventions for persons with dementia*, edited by E. D. Taira, 29–54. New York: Haworth Press.

Corkin, S., K. Davis, J. Growdon, et al., editors. 1982. *Alzheimer's disease: A report of progress in research.* New York: Raven Press.

Corsellis, J. 1976. Aging and the dementias. In *Greenfield's neuropathology*, edited by W. Blackwood and J. Corsellis. London: Edward Arnold.

Feil, N. 1982. *Validation: The Feil method: How to help disoriented old-old.* Cleveland: Edward Feil Productions.

Fuld, P. A. 1983. Psychometric differentiation of the dementias: An overview. In *Alzheimer's disease: The standard reference*, edited by B. Reisberg, 201–210. New York: Free Press.

Hiatt, L. G. 1986. Environmental design and mentally impaired older people. In *Alzheimer's disease: Problems, prospects, and perspectives*, edited by H. J. Altman, 309–320. New York: Plenum Press.

Holden, U., and R. Woods. 1982. *Reality orientation: Psychological approaches to the confused elderly.* New York: Churchill Livingstone.

Horton, A., and contributors. 1982. *Mental health interventions for the aging.* Brooklyn: J. F. Bergin.

Hussian, R., and R. Davis. 1985. *Responsive care: Behavioral interventions with elderly persons.* Champaign, Ill.: Research Press.

Lawton, M. P. 1986. *Environment and aging*, 2nd ed. Monterey, Calif.: Brooks/ Cole.

McEvoy, C., and R. Patterson. 1986. Behavioral treatment of deficit skills in dementia patients. *Gerontologist*, 26(5):475–478.

Moscovitch, M. 1982. A neuropsychological approach to perception and memory in normal and pathological aging. In *Aging and cognitive processes*, edited by F. Craik and S. Trehub. New York: Plenum Press.

Robinson, A., B. Spencer, and L. White. 1988. *Understanding difficult behaviors: Some practical suggestions for coping with Alzheimer's disease and related illnesses.* Ypsilanti: Geriatric Education Center of Michigan, Eastern Michigan University.

Schacter, D., J. Harbluck, and R. Kirschbaum. 1983. *Laboratory simulation of memory disorders: Source amnesia.* Paper presented at the meeting of the International Neuropsychological Society, Mexico City.

U.S. Congress, Office of Technology Assessment. 1987. *Losing a million minds: Confronting the tragedy of Alzheimer's disease and other dementias.* OTA-BA-323. Washington, D.C.: U.S. Government Printing Office.

Weaverdyck, S. E. 1987. *A cognitive intervention protocol: Its derivation from and application to a neuropsychological case study of Alzheimer's disease.* Dissertation. University of Michigan. Available from University Microfilm International, 300 N. Zeeb Rd., Ann Arbor, Mich. 48106. Publication #8712237.

Weaverdyck, S. E. 1990. Neuropsychological assessment as a basis for intervention in dementia. In *Dementia care: Patient, family, and community*, edited by N. L. Mace. Baltimore: Johns Hopkins University Press.

Weaverdyck, S. E., and D. H. Coons. 1988. Designing a dementia residential care unit: Addressing cognitive changes with the Wesley Hall model. In *Housing the very old*, edited by G. M. Gutman, and N. K. Blackie, 63–85. Burnaby, British Columbia: Simon Fraser University Press.

Wolfensberger, W. 1972. *The principle of normalization in human services.* Toronto: National Institute on Mental Retardation.

Zgola, J. M. 1987. *Doing things.* Baltimore: Johns Hopkins University Press.

# Chapter 14

# The Role of the Physician in Dementia Care Units

JOSEPH J. GALLO, M.D.,
AND WILLIAM REICHEL, M.D.

Many nursing homes adopt the organization and conventions of the hospital (the so-called medical model). For example, nurses wear white uniforms, and life is strictly regimented for the convenience of the institution. In units for the care of Alzheimer's disease and other dementias, the focus moves away from emphasis on the "sick role" and stresses the creation of a "therapeutic milieu." Paradoxically, despite de-emphasis on the medical model of nursing home care, support and input from the medical staff are crucial to the success of the dementia care unit. This chapter discusses the roles of attending and consultant physicians in the dementia care unit and highlights essential aspects of patient assessment and management.

Alzheimer's patients are distinctly burdensome for caregivers. Physically robust patients with intellectual impairment who wander, are restless, have catastrophic reactions, require extensive help with activities of daily living such as bathing and dressing, and may be incontinent of urine exasperate even the most dedicated caregiver. Add to this the emotional burden of a parent who no longer recognizes family or who makes false accusations, and the profound impact dementia has on the family is clear. In contrast to the common myth that families abandon the elderly, families tend to go "above and beyond the call of duty" in providing care. Consequently, when caring for the patient with dementia exceeds the family's capacity, it is not surprising that family members react with guilt, fear, anger, shame, doubt, and sorrow.

Because disturbing and annoying behaviors are so commonly seen in Alzheimer's disease (AD), patients with the disorder are often difficult to manage in nursing home settings that also must accom-

245

modate elderly persons who have functional impairment yet are cognitively intact. Surroundings that are safe for the demented patient may be too confining for patients who are alert. On the other hand, a demanding, stimulating environment may be ideal to combat apathy and depression in cognitively intact residents, but at the same time may throw into sharp contrast the deficits in mentation and behavior displayed by Alzheimer's patients. The guiding notion of the dementia care unit, then, is to create an environment of caring without simultaneously insulating affected patients from the larger community of family, recreation, and medical care.

## Goals of Dementia Care Units

Dementia care units can create a positive environment for the affected patient. In a structured, controlled environment, residents could have more freedom to move about, reducing stress and the need for physical and pharmacologic restraints. Since medications and environment and not the severity of dementia are correlated to falls and fractures in patients with AD, injuries might be minimized in such units. Patients could be cared for by staff persons with a special expertise and desire to work with the problems of dementia. Residents who are cognitively intact could be cared for in other parts of the facility without the distraction of demented patients with behavioral problems. Support groups for the staff and families could be a focus for the unit, involving the family and the community in the care of the patient and facilitating discussion of ethical issues. Such units might serve as centers for training and research in the treatment of AD.

There is now some evidence to suggest these goals can be met by dementia care units. Improvement in mental and emotional status, enhanced ability of patients to perform the activities of daily living, reduction in the use of neuroleptic medication, increased socialization, increased involvement of family members in caregiving, and reduction in troublesome behaviors, such as agitation, have been reported in such units.

Whether these goals will continue to be met if dementia care units become more common is unknown. With higher staff-to-patient ratios and a greater proportion of registered nurses, care in specialized units is likely to be more costly. Resistance to participation in such units may come from family and patients, who may not wish to acknowledge the implications of the diagnosis of AD, as well as from the staff, who may be hard to recruit and retain for the day-to-day care of demented patients. There has also been a suggestion that workers' compensation claims are increased. In addition, specific procedures regarding admission and discharge criteria, particularly as the disease progresses and care becomes more difficult, have not been worked out.

## Physician Roles in Dementia Care Units

A nursing home is, first of all, a "home." Numerous writers have expressed reservations about the "medicalization" of the nursing home—that is, inappropriate application of an aggressive model of medical care, borrowed directly from the acute care hospital, which fails to take into account functional, ethical, and quality-of-life factors in medical decisions. Considering the history of poor physician involvement in nursing homes, the potential for improving the quality of medical care through increased physician presence in dementia care units is welcome. However, the focus shifts from cure to assessment and functional improvement.

### Working with Nurses, Social Workers, and Other Professionals

To accomplish this shift, the physician must view nurses and social workers on the unit as partners who contribute special expertise in the care of the patient. In most nursing homes, nurses not only provide ongoing care and periodic evaluation but also are generally the staff members most familiar with the patient's functional status and the degree of family involvement. Social workers are usually most adept at exploring family dynamics, assisting with financial arrangements, and acting as an advocate for the patient. These roles are not, as a rule, rigidly fixed. Other professionals such as dieticians, occupational therapists, physical therapists, and dentists will be essential members of a core assessment team to work closely with the nursing staff and to be available for continuing evaluation and treatment.

Regular patient care conferences attended by members of the primary team caring for the patient, including the physician, are essential to facilitate communication about specific needs of patients on the unit. When families are involved in such conferences, family members may more readily view themselves as allies of the staff, opening the door to closer cooperation and communication and providing an opportunity for mutual education and understanding.

The nature and frequency of and possible solutions to behavioral problems of demented patients, for example, are best defined and managed when the physician works in concert with the nursing and social work staff. Thus, the physician should be available, at least by phone, when problems arise for which the staff require advice. The use by the nursing staff of a unit "communications" notebook is sometimes helpful to be sure that specific matters that arise at odd hours are attended to and not forgotten. In units with an "open" medical staff, that is, open to physicians in the community, ensuring physician availability is of particular importance. Units with a restricted ("closed") medical staff may have easier access to medical and psychiatric consultation.

Encouraging the nursing staff to set patient care standards that provide alternatives to the use of restraints and medications through educational activities and the quality-assurance program is an important leadership role in the dementia care unit. Taking the time to prepare in-service training about AD and to attend patient care conferences sends a clear signal of physician interest and caring. Such activities are essential to maintain and improve the knowledge, skills, and interest of everyone involved in patient care and, indeed, might be a requirement of physicians who desire attending privileges in the unit. In addition to a penchant for working with demented elderly patients, willingness to cooperate with nursing, social work, and other professionals in problem solving would seem an essential quality of physicians who work in dementia care units.

### Working with Families

The physician should be able to work with families as well, keeping in mind the powerful emotions frequently evoked by the diagnosis of AD. When caregivers must deal with the gradual loss of a loved one to AD, their initial response may be denial (Teusink and Mahler 1984). The caregiver makes excuses for the patient's memory loss, and takes false comfort from the relative preservation of remote memory. Once the memory deficit is so great as to be undeniable, the caregiver unwittingly helps the patient compensate and becomes overinvolved with the patient's routine tasks. As deficits become more pervasive, the caregiver feels anger at the disease, the patient, and the staff. There may be guilt about how things were handled and about surreptitious wishes for the patient's death. Last, some acceptance may emerge that the loved one is no longer the same person. Not all caregivers go through this stereotyped sequence reminiscent of Kubler-Ross's stages of psychologic changes in terminal illness, but the analogy is useful to physicians who must deal with families (Teusink and Mahler 1984). Compassionate care of the family of an elderly person with AD demands that the physician provide information about diagnosis, course, and ethical issues regarding AD. Caregivers are often not given adequate information on what to expect even if the diagnosis of AD is established. Most caregivers bringing an affected elderly person to a geriatric evaluation clinic at the Iowa Methodist Medical Center wanted to know what the future course of the disease would be, what the cause of the patient's deterioration was, and whether everything had been done to find out if the etiology was treatable. The label dementia had been given to the patients referred to the clinic, yet 68 percent of the caregivers stated as the reason for the visit an inadequate explanation of how the diagnosis of AD was made or what to expect as a result.

Thus, patient and family education about the illness is an important function of the medical staff. Indeed, the only "family therapy" many families need to cope with AD is information about diagnosis and prognosis. The helpful classic book *The 36-Hour Day* is aptly titled and may be recommended to caregivers as a resource book (Mace and Rabins 1981).

A discussion with the patient and family of ethical issues regarding cardiopulmonary resuscitation and aggressive modes of providing nutrition can be useful to prepare care plans before acute situations arise. The nursing staff should be given the opportunity to participate in such discussions, because the nurses not only will be responsible for carrying out the plan but also may have developed a close relationship with the patient and the family and frequently are present at the time of death.

### Quality Assurance

Quality assurance (QA) in the nursing home, to review the medical care delivered there, has its own special problems and possibilities, but might be particularly important in dementia care units. QA criteria are based on standards of practice regarding structure (organization of medical care), process (procedures of medical care), and outcome (results of medical care), while the subsequent data analysis provides information on how well the criteria agreed upon are followed in actual practice. The trend in evaluating care in the long-term setting is to put relatively more emphasis on outcome criteria, such as measures of patient functioning, and less emphasis than in the past on structure criteria, such as building and fire code regulations.

To illustrate QA with a simple example, a standard of care agreed upon by the medical staff may be that each patient's chart have a problem list and orders that correspond. QA criteria would then call for a problem list and corresponding orders on every chart. Data analysis would seek to determine whether such criteria are being met. The results of the analysis would then be distributed to the staff for correction of deficiencies.

Review of psychotropic drug use is another example of a QA study that might be undertaken. Process criteria for such a study might include the presence in the chart of documentation of the indication for the prescription, evidence of monitoring for side effects such as orthostasis and neurologic abnormalities, use of appropriate dosages, and documentation of attempts at withdrawal if appropriate. Outcome criteria might include the demonstration of a decrease in identified target symptoms such as restlessness and an increase in other behaviors such as socialization. Other examples of QA studies include avoiding combinations of interacting medicine, management of incontinence, confusion, or other geriatric problems, and documentation of physician response to nursing, patient, and family concerns.

Quality assurance may be fertile ground for cooperation between medical and nursing staff, since the QA criteria regarding specific problems such as wandering or the use of restraints can be addressed from medical and nursing points of views.

### The Organization of the Medical Staff

Organization of the physician staff in the dementia care unit may take various forms depending on the unit's historical development and the resources of the home. The medical staff may be "open," which means physicians in the community will be invited to continue to attend their patients after admission to the unit. In other cases, the unit may be organized so that part-time staff physicians are available for consultation and oversight of activities on the unit. A network of consultants including a neurologist, psychiatrist, urologist, physical medicine and rehabilitation specialist, cardiologist, and nu-tritionist, with established communication lines through a team leader, is clearly a requirement. Ideally, consultants will meet with primary medical and nursing staff caring for the patient. Since involvement of the physician in the dementia care unit may be more intense than in a general community nursing home, special background or training may be desirable for the team leader and for physicians admitting to the unit.

Physicians involved in the care of patients in dementia care units, whether internists or family physicians, should be able to provide ongoing continuous medical care with appropriate consultation when necessary. Specific rules regarding the use of consultants on the unit are not possible, because appropriate use of consultants depends on the availability of specialists, the interest and capabilities of the medical staff, local custom, and the resources available to the nursing home; however, geriatric psychiatry or neurologic consultation might be mandatory before or immediately following admission to the unit. For example, the unit may routinely have all patients evaluated by a geriatric psychiatrist or geriatric nurse practitioner at admission. Such consultation would help corroborate the diagnosis and quantify cognitive deficits. Otherwise, consultations may be reserved for patients who have atypical clinical features, such as aphasia out of proportion to memory deficit, or who have an atypical course, such as rapid progression or progression that is not in keeping with the expected sequence of deterioration of functions for AD.

Schwartz (1982) characterized the physician who provides good-quality care for nursing home residents as a "gerontophile," one who enjoys dealing with the elderly in established long-term relationships. Such a physician is ever willing to learn from patients as well as form professional relationships with other nursing home staff. Physicians working in a dementia care unit must also consider worthwhile the effort required to deal with dementia and the challenges it poses, and should derive satisfaction from the small, slow, and often distant gains that are possible.

## The Diagnosis of Alzheimer's Dementia

Initial assessment of the patient accepted for the unit should include a review of available records and a family interview to determine the extent of the dementia evaluation before admission. Despite disillusionment with the concept of "reversible" dementia (Clarfield 1988), a reasonable search for reversible concurrent illnesses and to exclude possibly treatable causes of dementia would seem warranted.

Dementia implies a global intellectual deficit that is defined in the third revised edition of the *Diagnostic and Statistical Manual of Mental Disorders* (DSM-III-R) as sufficiently severe to result in social dysfunction. Memory loss is frequently paramount, especially in patients with AD; but in keeping with the idea that the deficit is global, decreased abstraction ability, poor judgment, personality changes, difficulty in the comprehension and use of language, or impairment in other higher integrative functions must also be present. Thus, the definition of *dementia* highlights the importance of mental status testing. Sometimes the term *organic brain syndrome* is used as if it were a specific diagnosis; however, the term should be avoided, since there are actually many organic brain syndromes of which dementia is but one.

Alzheimer's disease is a specific dementia syndrome characterized by the insidious progression of intellectual impairment, typically affecting memory early in the course of the disorder. Definitive diagnosis of AD would require brain biopsy or autopsy, but clinical criteria suggested by McKhann and associates (1984) permit classification into "probable" and "possible" AD. For the diagnosis of "probable" AD, dementia must be established by clinical examination (facilitated by the Folstein Mini-Mental State examination or similar examination, as discussed below). In addition, progressive deficits are found on examination in two or more areas of cognition (language, memory, judgment, calculations, and abstractions), there is no disturbance of consciousness (to distinguish from delirium), the patient is usually over age 65, and there is no secondary systemic disorder to account for the findings. Furthermore, the diagnosis is supported by progressive deterioration in activities of daily living and evidence of cerebral atrophy on computed tomography (CT) scan. When the course of the dementia is suggestive of AD but does not quite fit the criteria, the diagnosis is said to be "possible" (McKhann et al. 1984).

It must be emphasized that the diagnosis of AD is currently a clinical diagnosis. Cerebral atrophy on cranial CT scan is not sufficient for diagnosis of Alzheimer's disease, because some elderly persons without intellectual impairment have cerebral atrophy. Serial CT scans, however, show worsening atrophy over time in patients with AD, and, furthermore, the rate of ventricular enlargement is correlated to the rate of cognitive decline (Friedland 1988). Newer imaging techniques, such as single photon emission computed tomography (SPECT), may make it possible to diagnose AD more definitively even at an early stage.

The Inventory of Diagnostic Clinical Features of Dementia of the Alzheimer Type is a scale that may assist the clinician in the diagnosis of AD (Cummings and Benson 1986). The maximal score of 20 is attained by patients with uncomplicated dementia of the Alzheimer's type. Higher scores (14 or greater) reflect greater consistency with the diagnosis of AD; lower scores suggest another diagnosis. The inventory assigns greater weight to loss of intellectual functions than to motor abnormalities, reflecting the generally normal results of motor examination of patients with AD with simultaneous early impairment of language and memory. Demented patients who present with signs or symptoms of a movement disorder suggest a diagnosis other than AD.

Vascular dementias, particularly multi-infarct dementia, form the other major category of dementia in the elderly. There may be evidence of a halting progressive dementia with associated hypertension or strokes. The neurologic examination may reveal spastic limbs, brisk reflexes, plantar extensor responses, and abnormal gait. Personality is relatively preserved. The CT scan reveals evidence of infarcts in only half of patients suspected of having multi-infarct dementia, although nuclear resonance imaging may be more sensitive. Some investigators have shown that, when blood pressure in hypertensive patients with multi-infarct dementia was lowered below an optimal range, the patients exhibited further cognitive decline. On the other hand, patients with multi-infarct dementia who stopped smoking actually improved (Meyer et al. 1986).

The Hachinski Ischemic Score may help distinguish multi-infarct dementia from other types of dementia. Items include abrupt onset, fluctuating course, relative preservation of personality, emotional lability, history of hypertension or strokes, focal neurologic symptoms or signs, and evidence of atherosclerosis (Hachinski et al. 1975). The scale may be most useful to rule out vascular dementia in the patient with a low score (Liston and LaRue 1983).

Senile dementia of the Binswanger type (SDBT) is a vascular dementia recognized with increasing frequency because of new imaging techniques, especially magnetic resonance imaging. SDBT is characterized by an insidious dementia with gait disturbance, urinary incontinence, and neurologic signs early in the course of the illness. Infarctions in the subcortical white matter result in isolation of cerebral cortex from deeper structures. Risk factors for small artery disease (diabetes, hypertension) may predispose to SDBT (Roman 1987).

Dementias associated with movement disorders such as tremors are sometimes referred to as subcortical dementias. Patients with Parkinson's disease, for example, have muscular rigidity, tremor, and abnormalities of posture and gait. The patient's intellectual processes seem to be slowed down as well. Other so-called subcortical dementias are associated with Huntington's disease, progressive supranuclear palsy, and Wilson's disease (Cummings and Benson 1983).

Normal pressure hydrocephalus is characterized by the triad of gait disturbance, urinary incontinence, and dementia. Physical examination reveals spasticity in the legs with hyperreflexia and plantar extension reflexes. Of course the classic triad need not be present, but the cranial CT scan will reveal dilated ventricles. The value of shunt surgery in most cases is controversial.

Testing for apathetic hyperthyroidism or for occult hypothyroidism is part of the complete work-up for dementia. Thiamine deficiency, which is associated with alcohol abuse, may result in Wernicke's encephalopathy or an organic amnestic syndrome that may resemble dementia. Niacin deficiency is associated with dementia as well. Vitamin $B_{12}$ deficiency may result in psychologic changes without concomitant macrocytosis. Evidence of folate deficiency also should be sought in demented patients.

Infections of the central nervous system can result in mental status changes, but the lumbar puncture is probably best reserved for specific circumstances, such as acute deterioration with fever. Infections that cause dementia include neurosyphilis (which can be present even with a negative rapid plasma reagin), Jakob-Creutzfeldt disease (caused by a "slow" virus and characterized by myoclonus in its late stages and a burst-silence pattern on electroencephalography), fungi (and related organisms), and human immunodeficiency virus (AIDS dementia).

Depression should be considered in the differential diagnosis of dementia. The patient with the appearance of cognitive impairment due to depression ("pseudodementia" or the "dementia syndrome of depression") does remain oriented and with coaxing can perform intellectual tasks at one time or another. On close observation, the patient may be able to learn new facts and might give a detailed account of his or her memory problems. The coexistence of depression with dementia may be a more valuable concept. Patients with AD may suffer from depression as well, particularly in the early stages of the illness. In patients in whom the diagnosis of AD appears well founded, the coexistence of depressed mood is commonly cited (Reifler et al. 1982); however, the depression in Alzheimer's patients may be qualitatively different (Merriam et al. 1988).

The only way to "prove" that a concomitant depression exists may be careful empiric therapy with antidepressant medications. Treatment of the depression could conceivably improve cognitive deficits that are mistakenly ascribed to a primary degenerative dementia. Even if there is an underlying dementia, cognitive symptoms due to depression may improve enough with treatment to improve significantly the overall functioning of the patient, particularly when the cognitive decline is mild (Reifler et al. 1982).

Some studies have shown that when certain clinical features of an affective illness were present, the patient with AD did not deteriorate as would be expected from the natural history of the disease (Reynolds et al. 1986; Ron et al. 1979). For example, in a cohort of 51 patients followed for an average of nine years, the diagnosis of dementia was confirmed in 35 patients (69 percent) and rejected in 16 patients (31 percent). Seven patients were found to have a purely psychiatric illness, especially affective disorders. Clinical features portending a "wrong" diagnosis of dementia included a history of affective disorder and a clearly depressed affect when first evaluated (Ron et al. 1979).

Psychiatric disorders other than depression may result in mental status and behavioral abnormalities as well. For example, acute mania may feature incoherence, hallucinations, hyperactivity, inattention, poor judgment, and insomnia, which may cause confusion with a dementia syndrome. There may be a neurologic, systemic, or pharmacologic basis for mania, particularly when onset occurs after age 35 (Larson 1988). Paranoia with accompanying hallucinations resembling dementia may result from vision loss, hearing impairment, or adverse social or environmental circumstances associated with sensory deprivation. Late-onset schizophrenia (paraphrenia) is perhaps a less common cause of paranoid psychosis in the elderly, although the classification of these disorders is in a state of flux. Patients with a long-standing diagnosis of schizophrenia may have more favorable outcomes with age than previously appreciated; specifically, the older patient with schizophrenia may experience diminished paranoia and hallucinations with improved social skills (Miller and Cohen 1987). These patients deserve a trial of withdrawal from psychoactive medications that have extrapyramidal side effects; indeed, some elderly patients with the diagnosis of chronic schizophrenia may have actually had other psychiatric illnesses. Unless symptomatic, the older patient with schizophrenia generally should not cause diagnostic confusion with dementia.

Patients with clouding of consciousness as evidenced by inattention or lethargy have delirium, or "acute confusional state," which is generally marked by acute onset (hours or days), hallucinations, altered diurnal rhythm, and fluctuation in alertness. In contrast, patients with dementia are alert and exhibit global decline in intellect, language, personality, judgment, and memory. Delirium may be the result of a direct insult to the central nervous system, such as drug intoxication or electrolyte imbalance, or may occur from medical illness in other organ systems, such as myocardial infarction, pneumonia, or urinary tract infection. Some medications (such as benzo-diazepines) can precipitate a delirium or seizures when discontinued. The list of entities that can result in delirium is long, with virtually every organ system represented.

It is certainly possible for a patient to have delirium superimposed upon a chronic dementia; therefore, it is important to evaluate mental status changes in the patient with Alzheimer's or other dementia through careful physical examination, including a rectal examination to rule out fecal impaction, and appropriate laboratory studies, rather than ascribing impairment to worsening of the underlying dementia. The cranial CT rarely may find a mass lesion, such as a tumor or hematoma, presenting without focal neurologic signs.

In summary, the differential diagnosis of dementia is extensive and the discussion above is in no way exhaustive. Major causes of altered mental state are presented in Table 14.1. The first column summarizes the major causes of global intellectual decline (dementia). Acute confusional state (delirium) has numerous causes as well, as listed in the second column. Many diagnoses causing delirium are clearly reversible, such as drug toxicity or electrolyte abnormalities. Psychiatric disorders, sensory deprivation, and other etiologies (see Table 14.1) can mimic dementia or delirium. Detailed discussion of these disorders is available from other sources (Cummings and Benson 1983; Reichel and Rabins 1989).

### Assessment of the Patient

A critical task is the proper admission assessment and periodic evaluation of mental state, affect, function in activities of daily living, and health status of patients. The assessment of multiple domains is possible, particularly with a team approach involving the physician, nurse, social worker, and other health care professionals, and is facilitated by the use of instruments devised for the purpose (Gallo et al. 1988; Kane and Kane 1981). Changes in the patient can be recognized with more confidence when assessment is repeated the same way or with the same instruments each time. In other words, the following discussion should be viewed as relevant not only to baseline assessment (on admission or initial evaluation) but, importantly, to periodic reassessment as well.

Multidimensional geriatric assessment has received considerable interest in the medical literature (Gallo et al. 1988; Kane and Kane 1981; Epstein et al. 1987) and can be applied to the demented patient

**Table 14.1.**
**Causes of Dementia and of Delirium (Acute Confusional State)**

| *Causes of Dementia* | *Causes of Delirium* |
|---|---|
| Primary degenerative neurologic disorders<br>  Dementia of the Alzheimer's type<br>  Pick's disease<br>Other neurologic disorders<br>  Parkinson's disease<br>  Huntington's disease<br>  Progressive supranuclear palsy<br>  Wilson's disease (hepatolenticular degeneration<br>  Multiple sclerosis<br>  Seizure disorders<br>Cerebrovascular disorders<br>  Multi-infarct dementia<br>  Dementia of the Binswanger's type<br>Toxic agents<br>  Chronic drug toxicity<br>  Heavy metals (such as mercury)<br>  Alcohol (Korsakoff dementia)<br>Nutritional deficiencies<br>  Vitamin $B_{12}$<br>  Folic acid<br>  Niacin<br>  Thiamine (Wernicke's encephalopathy)<br>Depression<br>Endocrine disorders<br>  Thyroid disease<br>  Parathyroid disease<br>  Adrenal disease<br>  Hypoglycemia<br>Infectious diseases<br>  Human immunodeficiency virus (AIDS dementia)<br>  Neurosyphilis<br>  Jakob-Creutzfeldt disease<br>  Fungi and related organisms<br>Inflammatory disorders<br>  Systemic lupus erythematosus<br>  Sarcoidosis<br>  Temporal arteritis<br>Normal pressure hydrocephalus<br>Space occupying lesions<br>  Tumors (primary CNS and metastatic)<br>  Subdural hematoma<br>  Abscess | Toxic agents<br>  Drug toxicity<br>  Alcohol<br>Metabolic disorders<br>  Renal failure<br>  Dialysis dementia<br>  Disorders of sodium regulation<br>  Disorders of calcium regulation<br>  Hepatic failure<br>  Porphyria<br>Infectious diseases<br>  Herpes encephalitis<br>  Bacterial meningitis, including:<br>    Gram negative bacteria<br>    *Mycobacterium tuberculosis*<br>  Fungi and related organisms, including:<br>    *Cryptococcus neoformans*<br>    *Coccidioides immitis*<br>    *Histoplasma capsulatum*<br>    *Sporothrix schenckii*<br>Psychiatric disorders<br>  Depression<br>  Mania<br>  Schizophrenia<br>  Paraphrenia (late-onset schizophrenia)<br>Disorders causing hypoxia<br>  Heart diseases<br>  Pulmonary diseases<br>  Anemia<br>Sensory deprivation<br>  Vision loss<br>  Hearing loss<br>  Social isolation<br>  Hospitalization and relocation<br>Disorders causing pain<br>  Urinary retention<br>  Fecal impaction<br>  Surgical abdomen<br>  Fractures |

in long-term care. Multidimensional assessment includes evaluation of mental status and affect, functional status, social situation, economic circumstances, values assessment, and preventive medicine strategies.

### The Assessment of Mental State

Numerus studies demonstrate that physicians do not routinely test the mental status of elderly persons in any setting. Physicians should be familiar with the use and characteristics of at least one short mental status examination. Unless in an advanced stage, patients with AD generally have a normal neurologic examination except for intellectual function. A baseline mental status examination should be mandatory at admission to the unit.

Patients in the earlier stages of AD who are meeting the physician for the first time in an unfamiliar setting may be quite anxious. They may be worried that the physician is testing them to see if they are "crazy," or may become agitated by questions they perceive as intrusive. Confusion and poor performance can be the result of anxiety even in a nonthreatening environment. Introductory statements that indicate interest in the elderly patient as a person, such as occupation, children, grandchildren, and hobbies, indicate the patient's current level of mental and social functioning and may help allay anxiety, although confabulation without anxiety is common.

It sometimes puts the patient at ease when one prefaces the examination, particularly when using a standard questionnaire, with an explanation such as the following: "I'm going to ask you some questions. Some are easy. Some may be hard. Please don't be offended, because it's a routine I use for everyone." Give positive reinforcement during the examination with expressions such as "That's OK" or "That's fine." Approached with sensitivity mental status testing does not have to be embarrassing to the patient.

A number of short mental status screening instruments have been devised. The following section describes three selected instruments, one of which should be used routinely on admission and for follow-up: (1) Short Portable Mental Status Questionnaire (SPMSQ); (2) Mini-Mental State Examination (MMSE); and (3) Cognitive Capacity Screening Examination (CCSE).

The SPMSQ was developed by Pfeiffer and colleagues at Duke University (Pfeiffer 1975). This test comprises ten questions dealing with orientation (date, day, place), personal history (phone number, age, birth date), remote memory (current and prior U.S. president, mother's birth name), and calculations (subtract 3 from 20 all the way down). More than three errors on the SPMSQ suggest cognitive impairment is present. The SPMSQ is compact and requires no special materials. It is a mental status examination covering orientation, remote memory, and calculation; however, no questions assess writing or short-term memory. Other aspects of the mental status examination may be tested separately (signature, writing a sentence, drawings, and short-term memory). The SPMSQ yields few false-positive results (scores that indicate impairment in a normal patient) but many false-negative results (scores that fail to indicate impairment in a demented patient). Although 90 percent of normal elderly persons are identified correctly, as few as half of the demented patients may be identified (Fillenbaum 1980; Erkinjuntti et al. 1987; Smyer et al. 1979).

Another short, convenient test of mental functioning is the Folstein MMSE (Folstein et al. 1975). The MMSE has two parts. The first part requires verbal responses only and assesses orientation, memory, and attention. The three words used to test memory are left up to the examiner, leaving the possibility that this question could vary in difficulty. The second part evaluates the ability to write a sentence, name objects, follow oral and written commands, and copy a complex polygon design. The maximal score is 30. The test is not timed. Generally a score of 24 or less is regarded as evidence of cognitive impairment. The ability of the MMSE to detect mental impairment would be expected to be better than that of the SPMSQ, since the MMSE, unlike the SPMSQ, tests recent memory, written and spoken language, and construction ability (drawing), in addition to orientation (Anthony et al. 1982; Roth et al. 1986).

A 30-question CCSE (Jacobs et al. 1977) was used in the detection of "organic brain syndromes" in patients with medical illness. Patients with scores less than 20 (maximal score of 30) were more likely to meet clinical criteria for dementia. Most psychiatric patients tested scored greater than 20 on the test. The scale is a bit more cumbersome than the SPMSQ or the MMSE, but it includes some areas not tested by the others, such as abstracting ability (similarities).

Patients with diffuse brain injury, such as is typical in AD, may be easier to detect and follow with screening instruments than are patients with focal brain lesions such as tumors, since patients with focal lesions may have deficits not evaluated by the test (Webster et al. 1984; Kaufman et al. 1979).

It should be emphasized that poor performance on a mental status questionnaire does not preclude involvement of the patient in discussion of wishes and desires regarding medical treatment, since such instruments do not measure competence. Although an individual may not be competent to perform certain tasks, there may be adequate understanding, at least for a short time, for participation in decisions regarding health care.

Regardless of the specific instrument used to assess mental state, it is difficult to overemphasize the importance of performing some standard mental status testing on all elderly patients, particularly those admitted to dementia care units. Changes in mental state can be more confidently diagnosed when a baseline has been established by periodic testing.

### The Assessment of Function

Patients who perform poorly on a mental status examination are not necessarily unable to care for themselves. The severity of mental impairment does not even necessarily represent the major factor determining caregiver stress (Deimling and Bass 1986), possibly because difficult behaviors are not directly related to mental impairment (Swearer et al. 1988). In addition, the usual list of medical problems does not directly reflect the elderly person's functional capability. The capacity to function is not well described by the constellation of medical diseases alone. Frequently the family of the demented patient notices impairment in performance of the activities of daily living (ADL) or instrumental activities of daily living (IADL) before mental impairment becomes evident. It is important, therefore, to assess functional capacity in its own right.

Items comprising functional assessment are often divided into ADL and IADL. The ADL are the functions needed to live independently. The Katz Index of ADL, for example, includes the following: bathing, dressing, toileting, transfer from bed or chair, continence, and feeding (Katz et al. 1963). The IADL include more complex tasks, such as using the telephone, preparing meals, and managing medication (Lawton and Brody 1969). The Fillenbaum five-item IADL scale concerns the ability to travel alone or with help, to shop for groceries or clothes, to prepare meals, to do housework, and to handle money (Fillenbaum 1985).

Keying on specific tasks to be performed allows assistance to be more focused. For a patient having difficulty dressing, for example, the caregiver might put picture labels on drawers, taking the patient by the hand and starting the desired actions needed to dress as a cue to the patient. Because abilities in AD differ from patient to patient, characterizing specific abilities helps focus on the positive and unique aspects of the patient. Improvements in function (or deterioration) may be more clearly demonstrated by concentrating on functional ability and strengths.

The informant in functional assessment may affect the information obtained. Patients in one study perceived their level of functioning to be at a much higher level than the nursing assessment. If the nurse's evaluation can be assumed to be most accurate, patients highly overrated their functional status, but families underrated it (Rubenstein et al. 1984). Direct observation of the patient in the unit after a period of adjustment may be necessary to confirm information given by caregivers about the patient's functional status.

The severity of dementia may be estimated using an instrument that combines mental status assessment, ADL and IADL items, and questions regarding the presence of difficult behaviors, such as agitation.

The Functional Dementia Scale (Moore et al. 1983), for example, is a 20-item "review of symptoms" of dementia that can be completed by caregivers. Items include questions regarding wandering, hallucinations, threatening and violent behavior, paranoia, memory disturbance, and the ability to perform ADL.

Investigators who developed the scored Functional Rating Scale for the Symptoms of Dementia believe the scale measures severity, shows change, and might be valuable in predicting when nursing home placement is necessary (Hutton et al. 1985). Scores on the scale ranged from 0 (not demented) to 42. Patients were tested over a two-year period every few months. Persons with a score greater than 21 had an average of 7 months until nursing home placement occurred, and those with scores of 21 or less did not require nursing home placement for an average of 18 months. Interestingly, scores at the time of admission to the nursing home were about the same for both groups (about 32) (Hutton et al. 1985). Patients who were incontinent of bowel and bladder, unable to speak coherently, and unable to bathe and groom had a high risk of nursing home placement before the next evaluation period.

The Functional Assessment Staging of Alzheimer's disease (FAST) consists of seven stages of disease progression (Reisberg 1986; Reisberg et al. 1985). Individuals in stage 1 have no impairment. Stage 2 is characterized by subjective memory complaints. Stage 3 is the earliest level of cognitive decline, characterized by mild confusion and objective memory loss. Through stages 4 and 5, the patient loses the ability to perform more and more IADL and then ADL tasks, from shopping and handling personal finances to bathing and dressing. Patients in stage 5 of Alzheimer's dementia are disoriented and unable to recall major life events. Stages 6 and 7 mark further progression until the patient is unable to walk, speak, or relate to the environment in a meaningful way.

Patients who experience difficulty that seems to vary with the expected sequence as delineated for AD by the FAST may have a treatable condition, rather than a progression of AD. For example, since urinary incontinence (stage 6d) occurs at a later stage than inability to dress or bathe (stages 5 and 6b), the onset of urinary incontinence in a patient who is able to dress or bathe suggests an etiology for incontinence other than the simple progression of AD (Reisberg 1986). The stages correlate to results of the MMSE as well. For example, patients in Global Deterioration Scale stage 4, indicating mild AD, tend to score from 16 to 23 on the MMSE, exactly as expected based on a cutoff of 24 on the MMSE to detect dementia. More advanced stages of the disease correspond to lower MMSE scores, with little overlap from stage to stage (Reisberg et al. 1986).

The Clinical Dementia Rating Scale, still another dementia-rating scale, uses a rating form in which the best description of the patient in each of six domains is checked or circled on the rating form (Hughes et al. 1982). The six areas to be evaluated are memory, orientation, judgment and problem solving, community affairs, home and hobbies, and personal care. The pattern of responses determines the severity stage of dementia (Gallo et al. 1988; Hughes et al. 1982).

### The Assessment of Affect

The presence of depression should be sought even in demented patients. As alluded to earlier, depression may coexist with a degenerative dementia; indeed, depression may itself result in cognitive deficits that resemble dementia.

A screening questionnaire to detect depression might be useful but would have to be short and simple to be comprehended by the patient without taking an undue amount of time to administer. A number of instruments have been devised primarily for ambulatory outpatients or for the medically ill and not specifically for demented elderly persons. Examples include the Zung Self-rating Depression Scale (Zung 1965), the scaled version of the General Health Questionnaire (Goldberg and Hillier 1979), and the Beck Depression Inventory (Beck et al. 1961). A short form of the Beck Depression Inventory has been published; however, as with the parent instrument, the several possible responses for each item may be confusing to some patients (Beck and Beck 1972).

The Geriatric Depression Scale (GDS) is a depression screening instrument that consists of 30 questions to be answered with a yes or no. The scale demonstrates excellent sensitivity and specificity, with a score of greater than 11 indicating possible depression (Yesavage and Brink 1983; Norris et al. 1987; Koenig et al. 1988); however, the GDS must be interpreted cautiously when the patient is demented. Questions concern such issues as satisfaction with life, boredom, hopelessness, helplessness, irritability, memory, mood, energy level, and socialization. A short 15-item version of the GDS has been developed as well; patients with scores greater than 5 may be depressed (Yesavage 1986). Such an instrument can be administered with a mental status examination at admission to the unit.

### Physical Assessment

The conduct of the physical examination of an older person must often be modified because of impaired hearing, sight, comprehension, or mobility. It is better to complete the examination over two or more visits rather than to rush, which can be disconcerting to the patient. It is precisely because elderly patients frequently have impaired communication skills as a result of illness or lack of schooling that it is crucial for the examiner to pay special attention to communication issues in history taking and physical examination for such patients. Mental impairment in AD severely limits the ability of patients to express themselves. Nonverbal as well as verbal communication must be carefully considered when dealing with such patients. For example, a calm, firm manner with appropriate use of touch accompanied by a reassuring tone of voice and facial expression may be helpful.

Not only may the Alzheimer's patient have communication difficulties, but also he or she may not cooperate with the examiner. Because of memory impairment, the patient may need repetitive gentle reminders of what is expected. The patient may be extraordinarily restless. Firm, reassuring touch, as in holding the hand or shoulder, using clear and simple one-step requests, and maintaining eye contact forge the necessary links to communication and cooperation. Often a family member or friend can have a calming, orienting effect on the person being examined, but when this is not the case, the patient should be examined alone.

Physical examination of the patient with AD may be useful to identify subgroups with certain features that predict subsequent progression. For example, patients with AD who have extrapyramidal signs such as a rigidity and bradykinesia have more hallucinations and delusions (Mayeux et al. 1985) and may have more rapid decline (Stern et al. 1987). Aphasia in patients who are mildly demented may be associated with more rapid progression of AD as well (Faber-Langendoen et al. 1986).

Although patients with AD seem to have fewer medical problems such as hypertension, diabetes, and seizure disorders, it is important to make a thorough assessment of nutritional status and any concurrent illnesses. The physician must be aware that, in the elderly, medical problems like congestive heart failure, infections, or pulmonary emboli may present only as acute confusion (or, more subtly, as worsening of a preexisting dementia) in a patient in whom the central nervous system is the most vulnerable. Illness in the elderly often presents not as a single, specific symptomatic complaint localizing the organ system in trouble but as nonspecific functional disability. Examples include falling, urinary incontinence, dizziness, confusion, or not eating or drinking ("failure to thrive").

Good medical care of nursing home residents would dictate periodic review of medications and medical problems at a minimum of once every 6 to 12 months. Avoiding polypharmacy through careful review of medications cannot be overemphasized, and it is prudent to discontinue all unnecessary medications in the demented patient. The review of medications must be ongoing, because indications for a particular medication may no longer be present. For example, a phenothiazine prescribed to help the patient with a specific behavioral problem may no longer be necessary once an initial adjustment period following admission has passed, or if a behavior has waned with the progression of dementia.

### Health-related Screening

Screening procedures (i.e., efforts purely directed to detect asymptomatic disease, such as the Pap smear, mammography, or stools for occult blood) depend on the clinician's judgment, after consultation with the patient and family, of the benefit to be derived from the discovery of an asymptomatic condition in a particular nursing home resident. Thus, screening for cancer may make less sense in a functionally debilitated population, while more clearly "geriatric" screening, such as for visual loss and hearing deficits, becomes more important (Stults 1984).

Influenza vaccine is recommended for the elderly, although healthy people over the age of 65 are probably at less risk from influenza than are younger high-risk patients. Elderly patients with concurrent chronic heart, lung, or metabolic diseases are certainly at increased risk compared with the general population during influenza epidemics, especially in nursing homes. Pneumococcal vaccine is recommended at least once for all elderly patients.

## The Assessment of Values

The emphasis on respecting patient wishes with regard to therapies such as cardiopulmonary resuscitation and artificial nutrition has focused on the hospital setting and on patients with terminal illness, rather than on functionally impaired older patients with multiple medical problems, including dementia, who are residents of long-term care facilities.

The nursing home milieu presents therapeutic goals, limitations, and expectations that are quite different from those in the acute care hospital. Ethical issues in the setting of diminished capacity for decision making, functional dependency, loss of personal autonomy, social isolation, extreme age, and chronic disease have only recently been addressed. Planning treatment options in advance of acute need, particularly for the elderly nursing home resident, mitigates the obstacles to patient participation in health care decisions when the patient can no longer make his or her wishes known and fosters respect for the patient's wishes and personal worth even in the face of chronic disease and dependency.

Demented patients with memory impairment should still be consulted regarding medical decisions affecting them. Since cognitive impairment in AD tends to be uneven, it is possible an affected patient would evidence understanding despite imperfect memory. In many cases, however, the patient will be unable to participate in decision making. The family should then be consulted in an attempt to discover what wishes the patient had expressed, if any, when lucid. Advanced directives or proxy instruments show promise, each having advantages and disadvantages, though currently these instruments may be unavailable in many clinical situations. Unless there are severe disagreements about the course of action, possibly requiring adjudication, decision making is best seen as a cooperative effort among patient, family, and physician, avoiding recourse to the courts. A patient care advisory committee or ethics committee may find a role as a forum for such discussions.

Decisions to limit treatment in the event of critical illness should be considered separately from decisions regarding cardiopulmonary resuscitation. Patients or families might wish to pursue some treatments, such as antibiotics, even though cardiopulmonary resuscitation is felt to be overly burdensome. In addition, diagnostic testing can be reserved for situations in which it has been determined that treatment is appropriate.

The management of dementia in the nursing home may take on palliative goals: avoiding isolation, attempting symptomatic relief, providing personal care, and supporting the family (Rango 1985). It is possible that such goals may be facilitated by the dementia care unit, in which comfort, privacy, staff toleration of difficult behaviors, and maximization of patient autonomy are valued.

## Criteria for Admission to and Discharge from Dementia Care Units

Although criteria for admission to and discharge from dementia care units have not been worked out, clinical characteristics that predict appropriate placement would be important for physicians and nurses to delineate. For this reason, careful evaluation at admission of mental status and functional ability through the use of instruments such as the Mini-Mental State Examination (Folstein et al. 1975) and the Functional Assessment Staging of Alzheimer's Disease (Reisberg 1986; Reisberg et al. 1985), discussed above, cannot be overemphasized. In this way, discharge criteria may be more uniform as well, providing guidance for staff and family to identify the point beyond which the patient no longer benefits from the special environment. Since some families may be reluctant to admit disease progression by allowing discharge from a unit, establishing specific admission and discharge criteria makes patients, family, and the staff aware beforehand what will make discharge from the unit necessary. In any case, the few dementia care units available will require guidelines regarding admission, given the large number of Alzheimer's patients.

Benson and colleagues (1987), in a nursing home dementia unit, set forth several admission criteria including diagnosis of dementia for a minimum of six months, inability to perform some or all ADL, and behavioral problems such as incontinence or wandering. Patients who were actively combative or who had severe language impairment were excluded (Benson et al. 1987).

It would seem that mobile patients who are in the middle stages of dementia (FAST stages 4, 5, and 6) with impairment of ADL are good candidates to benefit from a special milieu. Severely unstable patients who are a danger to themselves or others, or who are in terminal stages of dementia, may not be appropriate for such units.

## Behavioral Problems in Alzheimer's Disease

Specific strategies to deal with the behavioral problems of AD, such as wandering, incontinence, paranoia, hallucinations, restlessness, communication difficulties, and catastrophic reactions, may be found in other chapters and texts. Eventually, patients with AD will show progression of the disease while resident in the unit.

Swearer and associates found that behavioral symptoms in dementia fell into three broad categories: aggressiveness (verbal and physical outbursts), disordered ideation (hallucinations, paranoia, phobias), and vegetative dysfunction (incontinence, insomnia, anorexia), and that, for the most part, behaviors were not necessarily more common in the patients with more impaired mental state (Swearer et al. 1988). Rubin and colleagues showed that, over a four-year period, agitated behavior increased in prevalence in 44 patients from 25 percent to 67 percent while self-centered behaviors, including coarsening of affect, increased from 21 percent to 63 percent (Rubin et al. 1987). Thus, despite heterogeneity in behavioral characteristics of AD (Friedland 1988), longitudinal care of such patients demands that the staff and family be prepared for relatively predictable management challenges of the illness.

Although difficult behaviors may arise as dementia progresses, it is important to consider alternative explanations, such as fecal impaction, electrolyte imbalance, occult fracture or dislocation, and so on, when difficulties arise anew. In other words, attempt to exclude a remedial concurrent delirium. Consequently, "reassessment" receives appropriate emphasis as the first of the five Rs of behavioral management outlined by Mace (1985). Next, reconsider if the behavior is serious enough to try to stop. If not, try to rechannel behavior so it may continue in a less disruptive way, or redirect the patient's attention if a catastrophic reaction seems imminent. Paranoia and hallucinations, for example, may not require treatment with antipsychotic medication. Finally, provide reassurance through understanding and empathy with the emotional content of behaviors (Mace 1985).

Excessive use of physical restraints in nursing homes is often a problem. Physical restraints would rarely be indicated in dementia care units because the environment allows more freedom of movement, provides for the use of time, and involves the family in care. Situations in which use of physical restraints are considered should also prompt proper evaluation of the problem behavior.

Until specific pharmacologic agents are available for AD, symptomatic improvement of some behaviors can be obtained with the careful use of antipsychotic drugs such as haloperidol and thioridazine. It is noteworthy that the beta-blocker propranolol has been reported to be effective for the treatment of agitated, disruptive behavior in patients with AD when antipsychotic drugs have failed.

Antipsychotic medication should be used within the context of behavioral approaches, and with specific target symptoms in mind. Antipsychotic medications do not affect judgment, memory, orientation, or the progression of the illness, but combativeness, restlessness, hallucinations, and insomnia may respond to pharmacologic therapy. It is imperative to identify target symptoms before starting these drugs so that ineffective medication can be discontinued. General rules regarding pharmacologic therapy for the aged apply when antipsychotics are used; it is particularly important to understand how very low dosages of such agents may be quite effective (such as 1 mg of haloperidol or 10 mg of thioridazine twice a day).

Physicians and nurses need to be familiar with side effects of antipsychotic medications. Extrapyramidal side effects such as tremors and rigidity are more commonly encountered when more highly potent, though less sedating, agents are used. Involuntary tonic contraction of skeletal muscles (dystonia), resulting in torticolis or scoliosis, occurs early in treatment with these drugs, but may be less likely to pose a problem for the elderly. Akathisia (extreme restlessness and inability to sit still) is quite important to recognize, since this drug-induced agitation may be interpreted as worsening of a behavioral symptom such as wandering, leading to inappropriate increases in medication dosage.

Tardive dyskinesia refers to involuntary repetitive movements that generally occur in patients exposed to the drugs for years. Since tardive dyskinesia is very difficult to extinguish, the key is prevention. Judicious application of these agents means identification of clear indications for use (e.g., specific target symptoms), prescription of the lowest possible effective dosage (start low and gradually increase dosage while monitoring response), and gradual discontinuation when possible (requiring repetitive appraisal of the situation, since the reasons the medication was started may no longer be pertinent). Other potential side effects of antipsychotic drugs include worsening of dementia, precipitation of arrhythmias, postural hypotension, blurry vision, exacerbation of glaucoma, photosensitivity skin reactions, galactorrhea, and elevated hepatic enzymes.

As for medications with direct effect on the disease process, ergoloid mesylates may enhance the function of some patients who are mildly demented; however, there is no consensus that such medications are helpful in the dosages used clinically. A three- to six-month trial of ergoloid mesylages may be reasonable in selected cases. Other medications being investigated for the treatment of AD include the anticholinesterase tetrahydroaminoacridine (THA) and the monoamine oxidase inhibitor L-deprenyl.

## Conclusion

Physicians clearly have a decisive impact on the quality of care rendered to Alzheimer's patients through close working relationships with family members and other health care professionals. In addition, the attending physician coordinates the patient's primary medical care needs, both evaluative and therapeutic, with consultant input when appropriate.

The specific etiologic diagnosis of dementia should be established with as much certainty as possible; however, it is the wise physician who periodically reviews the case to determine that the patient's course is consistent with the diagnosis. Patients who appear to be deteriorating should be evaluated for a superimposed reversible process. Careful attention must be paid to concomitant medical problems. If dementia care units are to succeed, an initial step will be to delineate characteristics and progress of patients in such units. Multidimensional assessment can play an important role in this regard.

The dementia care unit can provide a safe environment in which patients are soothed and accepted, in which the family is involved in care and provided with emotional support, in which difficult behaviors are tolerated, and in which medical decisions are made in the light of functional and ethical factors. Importantly, strategies and skills tested in such units will be applicable in general nursing home wards as well, where, in all likelihood, the majority of institutionalized demented elderly patients will continue to reside in the future. As a focus for educational and therapeutic efforts to treat a dread disease, the unit offering care for Alzheimer's disease and other dementias has the potential to bring to affected individuals and their families an element of hope that has often been lacking.

## References

Anthony, J. C., L. LeResche, U. Niaz, et al. 1982. Limits of the "Mini-Mental State" as a screening test for dementia and delirium among hospital patients. *Psychological Medicine,* 12:397–408.

Beck, A. T., and R. W. Beck. 1972. Screening depressed patients in family practice: A rapid technique. *Postgraduate Medicine*, 52:81–85.

Beck, A. T., C. H. Ward, M. Mendelson, et al. 1961. An inventory for measuring depression. *Archives of General Psychiatry*, 4:53–63.

Benson, D. M., D. Cameron, E. Humbach, et al. 1987. Establishment and impact of a dementia unit within the nursing home. *Journal of the American Geriatrics Society*, 35(4):319–323.

Clarfield, A. M. 1988. The reversible dementias: Do they reverse? *Annals of Internal Medicine*, 109:476–486.

Cummings, J., and D. F. Benson. 1986. Dementia of the Alzheimer type: An inventory of diagnostic clinical features. *Journal of the American Geriatrics Society*, 34:12–19.

Cummings, J. L., and D. F. Benson. 1983. *Dementia: A clinical approach.* Stoneham, Mass.: Butterworths.

Deimling, G. T., and D. M. Bass. 1986. Symptoms of mental impairment among elderly adults and their effects on family caregivers. *Journal of Gerontology*, 41(6):778–784.

Epstein, A. M., J. A. Hall, R. Besdine, et al. 1987. The emergence of geriatric assessment units: The "new technology of geriatrics." *Annals of Internal Medicine*, 106:299–303.

Erkinjuntti, T., R. Sulkava, J. Wikstrom, et al. 1987. Short Portable Mental Status Questionnaire as a screening test for dementia and delirium among the elderly. *Journal of the American Geriatrics Society*, 35(5):412–416.

Faber-Langendoen, K., J. C. Morris, J. W. Knesevich, et al. 1986. Aphasia in senile dementia of the Alzheimer type, abstract. *Annals of Neurology*, 20:125.

Fillenbaum, G. 1980. Comparison of two brief tests of organic brain impairment, the MSQ and the short portable MSQ. *Journal of the American Geriatrics Society*, 28:381–384.

Fillenbaum, G. 1985. Screening the elderly: A brief instrumental activities of daily living measure. *Journal of the American Geriatrics Society*, 33(10):698–706.

Folstein, M. F., S. E. Folstein, and P. R. McHugh. 1975. "Mini-Mental State," a practical method for grading the cognitive state of patients for the clinician. *Journal of Psychiatric Research*, 12:189–198.

Friedland, R. P., moderator. 1988. Alzheimer disease: Clinical and biological heterogeneity. *Annals of Internal Medicine*, 109:298–311.

Gallo, J. J., W. Reichel, and L. A. Andersen. 1988. *Handbook of geriatric assessment.* Rockville, Md.: Aspen Publishers.

Goldberg, D. P., and V. F. Hillier. 1979. A scaled version of the General Health Questionnaire. *Psychological Medicine*, 9:139–145.

Hachinski, V. C., L. D. Iliff, E. Zilhka, et al. 1975. Cerebral blood flow in dementia. *Archives of Neurology*, 32:632–637.

Hughes, C. P., L. Berg, W. L. Danziger, et al. 1982. A new clinical scale for the staging of dementia. *British Journal of Psychiatry*, 140:566–572.

Hutton, J. T., R. L. Dippel, R. B. Loewenson, et al. 1985. Predictors of nursing home placement of patients with Alzheimer's disease. *Texas Medicine*, 81:40–43.

Jacobs, J., M. R. Bernhard, A. Delgado, et al. 1977 Screening for organic mental syndromes in the medically ill. *Annals of Internal Medicine*, 86:40–46.

Kane, R. A., and R. L. Kane. 1981. *Assessing the elderly: A practical guide to measurement*. Lexington, Mass.: Lexington Books.

Katz, S., A. B. Ford, R. W. Moskowitz, et al. 1963. Studies of illness in the aged: The index of ADL. *Journal of the American Medical Association*, 185:914–919.

Kaufman, D. M., M. Weinberger, J. J. Strain, et al. 1979. Detection of cognitive deficits by a brief mental status examination: The Cognitive Capacity Screening Examination. *General Hospital Psychiatry*, 1:247–254.

Koenig, H. G., K. G. Meador, H. J. Cohen, et al. 1988. Self-rated depression scales and screening for major depression in the older hospitalized patient with medical illness. *Journal of the American Geriatrics Society*, 36(8):699–706.

Larson, E. W. 1988. Organic causes of mania. *Mayo Clinic Proceedings*, 63:906–912.

Lawton, M. P., and E. M. Brody. 1969. Assessment of older people: Self-maintaining and instrumental activities of daily living. *Gerontologist*, 9(3):179–186.

Liston, E. H., and A. LaRue. 1983. Clinical differentiation of primary degenerative and multi-infarct dementia: A critical review of the evidence: II. Pathological studies. *Biological Psychiatry*, 18:1467–1484.

Mace, N. L. 1985. Do we need special care units for dementia patients? *Journal of Gerontological Nursing*, 11:37–38.

Mace, N. L., and P. V. Rabins. 1981. *The thirty-six-hour day*. Baltimore: Johns Hopkins University Press.

McKhann, G., D. Drachman, M. Folstein, et al. 1984. Clinical diagnosis of Alzheimer's disease: Report of the NINCDS-ADRDA work group under the auspices of Department of Health and Human Services Task Force on Alzheimer's Disease. *Neurology*, 34:939–944.

Mayeux, R., Y. Stern, and S. Spanton. 1985. Heterogeneity in dementia of Alzheimer type: Evidence of subgroups. *Neurology*, 35:453–461.

Merriam, A. E., M. K. Aronson, P. Gaston, et al. 1988. The psychiatric symptoms of Alzheimer's disease. *Journal of the American Geriatrics Society*, 36(1):7–12.

Meyer, J. S., B. W. Judd, T. Tawakina, et al. 1986. Improved cognition after control of risk factors for multi-infarct dementia. *Journal of the American Medical Association*, 256:2203–2209.

Miller, N. E., and G. D. Cohen, editors. 1987. *Schizophrenia and aging*. New York: Guilford Press.

Moore, J., J. A. Bobula, T. B. Short, et al. 1983. A functional dementia scale. *Journal of Family Practice*, 16:499–503.

Norris, J. T., D. Gallagher, A. Wilson, et al. 1987. Assessment of depression in geriatric medical outpatients: The validity of two screening measures. *Journal of the American Geriatrics Society*, 35(11):989–995.

Pfeiffer, E. 1975. A short portable mental status questionnaire for the assessment of organic brain deficit in elderly patients. *Journal of the American Geriatrics Society*, 23(10):433–441.

Rango, N. 1985. The nursing home patient with dementia: Clinical care, ethics, and policy implications. *Annals of Internal Medicine*, 102:835–841.

Reichel, W., and P. Rabins. 1989. The evaluation and management of the confused, disoriented or demented elderly patient. In *Clinical aspects of aging*, 3rd. ed., edited by W. Reichel, 137–153. Baltimore: Williams and Wilkins.

Reifler, B. V., E. Larson, and R. Hanley. 1982. Coexistence of cognitive impairment and depression in geriatric outpatients. *American Journal of Psychiatry*, 139:623–626.

Reisberg, B. 1986. Dementia: A systematic approach to identifying reversible causes. *Geriatrics*, 41(4):30–46.

Reisberg, B., S. H. Ferris, J. Borenstein, et al. 1986. Assessment of presenting symptoms. In *Clinical memory assessment of older adults*, edited by L. W. Poon. Washington, D.C.: American Psychological Association.

Reisberg, B., S. H. Ferris, and E. Franssen. 1985. An ordinal functional assessment tool for Alzheimer type dementia. *Hospital and Community Psychiatry*, 36:593–595.

Reynolds, C. F., D. J. Kupfer, C. C. Hoch, et al. 1986 Two-year follow-up of elderly patients with mixed depression and dementia: Clinical and electroencephalographic sleep findings. *Journal of the American Geriatrics Society*, 34(11):793–799.

Roman, G. C. 1987. Senile dementia of the Binswanger type: A vascular form of dementia in the elderly. *Journal of the American Medical Association*, 258:1782–1788.

Ron, M. A., B. K. Toone, M. E. Garralda, et al. 1979. Diagnostic accuracy in presenile dementia. *British Journal of Psychiatry*, 134:161–168.

Roth, M., E. Tym, C. Q. Mountjoy, et al. 1986. CAMDEX: A standardized instrument for the diagnosis of mental disorder in the elderly with special reference to the early detection of dementia. *British Journal of Psychiatry*, 149:698–709.

Rubenstein, L. Z., C. Schairer, G. D. Willard, et al. 1984. Systematic biases in functional status assessment of elderly adults: Effects of different data sources. *Journal of Gerontology*, 39(6):686–691.

Rubin, E. H., J. C. Morris, and L. Berg. 1987. The progression of personality changes in senile dementia of the Alzheimer's type. *Journal of the American Geriatrics Society*, 35(8):721–725.

Schwartz, T. B. 1982. How to install a first-rate doctor in a third-rate nursing home. *New England Journal of Medicine*, 306:743–744.

Smyer, M. A., B. F. Hofland, and E. A. Jonas. 1979. Validity study of the Short Portable Mental Status Questionnaire for the elderly. *Journal of the American Geriatrics Society*, 27(6):263–269.

Stern, Y., R. Mayeux, M. Sano, et al. 1987. Predictors of disease course in patients with probable Alzheimer's disease. *Neurology*, 37:1649–1653.

Stults, B. M. 1984. Preventive health care for the elderly. *Western Journal of Medicine*, 141:832–845.

Swearer, J. M., D. A. Drachman, B. F. O'Donnell, et al. 1988. Troublesome and disruptive behaviors in dementia: Relationships to diagnosis and disease severity. *Journal of the American Geriatrics Society*, 36(9):784–790.

Teusink, J. P., and S. Mahler. 1984. Helping families cope with Alzheimer's disease. *Hospital and Community Psychiatry*, 35:152–156.

Webster, J. S., R. R. Scott, B. Nunn, et al. 1984. A brief neuropsychological screening procedure that assesses left and right hemispheric function. *Journal of Clinical Psychology*, 40:237–240.

Yesavage, J. A. 1986. The use of self-rating depression scales in the elderly. In *Clinical memory assessment for older adults*, edited by L. W. Poon. Washington, D.C.: American Psychological Association.

Yesavage, J. A., and T. L. Brink. 1983. Development and validation of a geriatric depression screening scale: A preliminary report. *Journal of Psychiatric Research*, 17:37–49.

Zung, W. W. K. 1965. A self-rating depression scale. *Archives of General Psychiatry*, 12:63–70.

# Index

Activities, 43–44, 48–49, 232–33; age-appropriate, 181; childlike, 18; direct care staff involvement in, 63–64; evening, 48, 161; impact of on behaviors, 161–66; lighthearted, 181–84; and normal social roles, 18–19, 162–63; one-to-one, 166; scheduling, 13–14, 48–49, 172–73; spontaneous, 165; therapeutic qualities of, 64

Activities of daily living (ADL), 48, 64, 235; impairment in performance of, 260; as part of activities program, 44

Acute mania, symptoms of, 255

Administration: support of dementia unit, 60, 64, 146–47; support of direct service staff, 13, 144–45

Admission criteria, 38–40, 266

Affect, assessment of, 262–63

Aggressive behaviors. *See* Behavior

Aides. *See* Direct service staff

AIDS dementia, 254

Akathisia, 268

Alzheimer's Association, guide to assist families, 192

Alzheimer's disease: diagnosis of, 251–53; stages of progression of, 261–62

*Alzheimer's Disease: Subjective Experiences of Families* study, 36–37

Alzheimer's disease units (*see* Dementia care units)

Amentia (mental retardation), 238

Anticholinergic properties of drugs, 12

Anticholinesterase tetrahydroaminoacridine (THA), 269

Antipsychotic drugs, 267–68; beta-blocker propranolol, 268; haloperidol, 268; side effects of, 12, 268; thioridazine, 268

Apathetic hyperthyroidism, 254

Aphasia, 217, 263–64

Apraxia, 217, 227

Architectural design, 83–105; activity areas, 96–99; baths and toilets, 100; dining areas, 98–99; exterior (*see* Outdoor environment); family clusters, 93–94; landmarks, 94; residents' rooms, 96–97, 100; therapeutic goals of, 85–87; visiting areas, 99; walking paths, 94–96

Architectural environment: as complex system, 84–85; components of, 84–85; fostering normal social roles, 100; impact on people with dementia, 84–85; negotiable, 91–92; therapeutic role of, 83–84

Assessment: of affect, 262–63; of cognitive functioning, 216–19; definition of, 205; initial, 251–52; ongoing, 231–32; role in intervention, 238–43; of strengths and needs, 131–33, 138–40; team approach in, 256

Assessment instruments, 256–63. *See also specific instruments*

Assessment team, 247; composition of, 247

Autonomy of residents, 8, 15–16, 67; definition of, 15–16

Barrier-free design, 92

Beck Depression Inventory, 262

Behavior: aggressive, 16; factors influencing, 205–6; possible medical causes of, 167; wandering, 94–96, 206

Behavior modification, 236–38; as "psychological restraint," 237

Behavioral patterns, environmental causes of, 205–9

Behavioral problems, 16, 18, 147–48, 208, 267–69

Benzodiazepines, effects of when discontinued, 256

Body language of stress, 180

Bradykinesia, 263–64

275

Designed by Nighthawk Design
Composed by Maryland Composition Company, Inc.
in Baskerville text and Helvetica display
Printed by the Maple Press Company on 60-lb
Glatfelter Hi-Brite and bound in Holliston Roxite B